VALIDATING PRO
THROUGH LEAN USER RESEARC

Tomer Sharon

Rosenfeld Media
Brooklyn, New York

Validating Product Ideas
Through Lean User Research
By Tomer Sharon

Rosenfeld Media, LLC

457 Third Street

Brooklyn, New York

11215 USA

On the Web: www.rosenfeldmedia.com

Please send errors to: errata@rosenfeldmedia.com

Publisher: Louis Rosenfeld

Managing Editor: Marta Justak

Illustrations: Noam Lamdan

Story Photographer: Stephen Dobeck

Interior Layout Tech: Danielle Foster

Cover Design: The Heads of State

Indexer: Sharon Shock

Proofreader: Sue Boshers

ISBN: 1-933820-29-2

ISBN-13: 978-1-933820-29-3

LCCN: 2015956988

Printed and bound in the United States of America

To Iris, Alma, Sella, and Segev.
You make me brave.

HOW TO USE THIS BOOK

Scan the table of contents to identify a burning question (or questions) you (or your team) currently have about your product users or potential users. Then access the relevant chapter, read its premise, gather your team, roll up your sleeves, and start going through the steps while completing the activities described in them.

Who Should Read This Book?

The book has two groups of very different audiences. The primary audience of the book is product managers and startup founders with no experience in user research. The secondary audience is designers and researchers who are interested in leaner ways of conducting user research.

Product Managers and Startup Founders

Product managers and startup founders have the biggest stake at bringing ideas to life through new products and services. They see the bigger picture; they mostly care about providing value to their users; and they are the ones with the power and authority to make critical product roadmap decisions. Nowadays, many of them understand that one of the most important keys to product success and company growth is great design guided by a solid practice of learning from users.

Designers and Researchers

While not targeting designers and researchers as a primary audience for this book, they also have a keen interest in lean user research. Designers and researchers want to do the following:

1. Make sure their stakeholders define exactly what research is for prior to conducting it to eliminate waste and avoid drifting to irrelevant explorations.

2. Focus first and foremost on learning as much as possible about a problem to solve.

3. Prioritize observed user behavior over attitudes.

4. Implement fast, nimble techniques that are not necessarily perfect, nor robust. Their stakeholders expect them to discuss needed research in the morning, launch a study in the afternoon, and get results before 4 p.m.

5. Use jargon-free communication. For that reason, this book has been scanned for jargon, and it uses plain language to educate non-researchers about research.

6. Facilitate a shared understanding, which is the collective knowledge of the team that builds up over time as the team works together. Shared understanding is the currency of lean user research. Figuring out what humans need, which products meet those needs, and what it means is a team sport. It clarifies what different people in the team learn from research and increases the team's commitment to act on research results.

What's in This Book?

The book is organized into nine chapters titled as questions you, the reader, might have about your audience (or potential audience). Each chapter is a step-by-step how-to guide that answers the question at stake with 1–3 user research techniques:

1. **Understanding the need:** Chapters 1 through 4 guide you through answering questions about needs, users, problems, and workflow. You don't have to have a product to answer these questions. They help you explore the world around you before your product exists and figure out if you have a good idea, who it is for, and provide you with insights about what features it should have.

    • Chapter 1 answers the question "What do people need?" with experience sampling.

    • Chapter 2 answers the question "Who are the users?" with interviewing.

    • Chapter 3 answers the question "How do people currently solve a problem?" with observation.

    • Chapter 4 answers the question "What is the user's work-flow?" with a diary study.

2. **Figuring out the want:** Chapter 5 is unique. It guides you through answering the question "What do people want?" with *Concierge MVP and Fake Doors Experiments*. It is a unique chapter because it will help you with marketing your product rather than designing it, unlike the rest of the chapters in this book.

3. **Evaluating the design:** Chapters 6 through 8 show you how to improve an existing design (either a sketch, mockup, prototype, product structure, or a fully functional product).

    • Chapter 6 answers the question "Can people use the product?" with online usability testing.

    • Chapter 7 answers the question "Which design generates better results?" with A/B testing.

- Chapter 8 answers the question "How do people find stuff?" with tree testing, the first-click test, and the lostness metric.

4. **The last chapter of the book** answers a question about how to find participants for research, which is the biggest bottleneck of research.

What Comes with This Book?

This book's companion website (rosenfeldmedia.com/books/lean-user-research) contains additional content. The book's diagrams and other illustrations are available under a Creative Commons license for you to download and include in your own presentations. You can find these on Flickr at www.flickr.com/photos/rosenfeldmedia/sets/.

The book is also accompanied by the following:

- A dedicated YouTube channel with video content organized by chapter (bit.ly/validating-youtube).

- An author's website with resources and references organized by chapter (leanresearch.co).

- Social media channels such as a Facebook page (Facebook.com/leanresearch), Twitter (Twitter.com/tsharon), and Instagram (Instagram.com/tsharon).

FREQUENTLY ASKED QUESTIONS

What is lean user research?

Lean user research is a discipline that provides insights into users, their perspectives, and their abilities to use products and then gives this information to the right people at the right time so that the research is invaluable for developing products. Lean user research focuses on answering three big questions about people: What do people need? (See Chapter 1.) What do people want? (See Chapter 5.) Can people use the thing? (See Chapter 6.)

How is lean user research different than "regular" user research?

Lean user research is mostly conducted by non-researchers who have burning questions about their audience (or potential audience). They want to answer these questions quickly, effectively, and on their own without hiring a professional. Lean user research is not perfect and can be at times quick and dirty, meaning some corners are cut. For example, since non-researchers might not have very good control of their body language, lean user research calls for more indirect approaches to learning. It values remote techniques over in-person ones (see Chapters 7 and 8).

Does this book include everything I need to know about user research?

No! This is a book for product developers and managers who are not skilled researchers. Therefore, research techniques are described in a relatively prescribed manner, skipping underlying factors, options, and dilemmas. The goal here is to help non-skilled product developers to do their own far-from-being-perfect-yet-effective research. If you want to learn more about research techniques described in this book, there are multiple excellent resources available. These are listed on the companion website at leanresearch.co.

I prefer to spend three free hours on writing more code rather than reading yet another book. If I only have time to read one chapter, which one should I read?

The short answer is Chapter 3 "How Do People Currently Solve a Problem?"

The long answer is read the introduction first and then the table of contents, and see if any of the chapters discusses a burning question you might have right now. If so, read that chapter first. I recommend reading Chapter 3 regardless, because observation, the research technique described there, is a fundamental tool about learning from users.

Should I read this book cover to cover?

No! This is a "doing," not a "reading" book. The best way to digest the content of the book is to first scan it to identify a burning question (or questions) you (or your team) currently have. Then access the relevant chapter, read its premise, roll up your sleeves, and start going through the steps while completing the activities described in them. Reading about these activities won't get you anywhere. As Ric Flair used to say, "To be the man, you have to beat the man." Or if you are not a pro-wrestling fan, "If you want to shoot, shoot. Don't talk!"

UX is about designing interfaces. Does this book include guidance on that?

Heck, *no!* UX is about so many things: user interface, interaction design, user research, information architecture, visual design, content strategy, and more. This book includes tons of advice about user research; however, it will not help you with guidance on how to design screens and wireframes. Some of the chapters will help you get insights about your screen design (for example, Chapter 6) or your product's information architecture (Chapter 8), but there aren't any design guidelines in here.

CONTENTS

CHAPTER 4

What Is the User's Workflow?　111

CHAPTER 7

Which Design Generates Better Results?   205

FOREWORD

I still remember when I started using Twitter in 2009. All this information from all my favorite people was in one place: dedicated feeds on TweetDeck for keywords, and conference hashtags I didn't have the money or clout to attend. It was a rush. Then the cruft trickled in—humble brags, Internet drama, and inevitably, ads.

I started looking at new sources of information warily, like a new piece of exercise equipment in the gym—"Ugh, I should really get on that." Who has time to *practice* design when there isn't even enough time to learn it.

Enter daily briefs. Apple News, Nuzzel, Quibb, Hacker News, Pocket, Quartz, TechCrunch, Medium, Mattermark. Not to mention the office email threads and Slack channels. "Did you see what blah posted about blah blah?"

Eric Schmidt said that every two days we generate as much information as we did between the dawn of time up to 2003—6.7 exabytes to be exact. What to do?

Well, there's a trick. There's a pattern that can help us wade through the information ocean.

There are two kinds of information: entertainment and knowledge. We know entertainment when we see it: Aziz, Jane the Virgin, your kid giggling uncontrollably when you say 'Boo!'

Then there is knowledge. We know that, too.

The tricky stuff is the blurry in between. It's the top 10 lists, the 5 habits of successful people, the "One thing you *really* must know to _____," and it's the link bait that poses as information for a better you, but doesn't deliver on the promise.

Validating Product Ideas by Tomer Sharon is the good stuff. In an industry filled with monster drinks and Soylent, this book is your bitter greens. And in a world abundant with ideas, the infrastructure to produce them, and the capital to fund them, Tomer offers perhaps the single most important tool—the ability to recognize ideas worth pursuing.

Tomer's motivation grew out of his own research. After hundreds of interviews with founders, venture capitalists, and product designers, he found them asking the same questions: How do I know who my users are? What do people need? Can people actually use the product? These are the questions that he guides readers through answering in a book that can be put immediately into practice in product development.

This book is not fodder for cocktail conversation. You will not read it on the subway ride to the office and wow your colleagues with a tweetable headline for the company blog. This book doesn't herald a new fad in design. Rather, it charts a course to master the fundamentals that are all too often overlooked.

If you are new to product research, use this book as a primer. If you are a pro, use it as a gut check and a checklist. Use it to clear your head when you feel like you have too many opinions and not enough sound judgment. Use this book, and you will be practicing the hard and rewarding discipline of fast, high-quality, impactful product research.

—Benjamin Gadbaw
Designer, investor, teacher

INTRODUCTION

Eighty-six percent[1] of product ideas are born from a developer's personal pain. These ideas are for products nobody needs. Developers believe research with users is a waste of time. They perceive their product as a coding exercise. To validate their idea, they ask their sister if she likes it. She says yes.

I live in North New Jersey, East Coast USA. For four years, we leased a house in which we had a detached garage (see Figure I.1). We never parked our cars there because the driveway between the garage and the street was 100 feet (~30 meters) long and shoveling that much snow in the wintertime was not a skill I had acquired (or wished to acquire). We mostly used it to store "outdoorsy" toys for our kids. Every winter, when the weather turned very cold, the keypad to open the garage door froze over and stopped working. Definitely a problem.

To open the door, once a year, I crawled into the garage through a small window (which became smaller and smaller every year, I have no idea why) and turned the garage door system from Automatic to Manual. This way, the kids were able to open and close the garage door while bypassing the frozen keypad. When spring arrived, I switched the door opening system back to Automatic. Same story every year.

FIGURE I.1
My garage door problem. The keypad froze during winter and instead of calling a technician, I crawled through the window and switched the door to manual.

---

1 172 out of 200 (86%) startup founders and enterprise product managers interviewed for this book.

I had a problem and found a bypass for solving it. The problem was that my garage door keypad froze over every winter. The solution was to pick up the phone, talk with my landlord, get a quote from a technician to fix it, argue with my landlord about the cost, get another quote, and so on. Yet, I wasn't doing that for some reason. I didn't care enough about this problem to solve it properly.

Why I Wrote This Book

My story isn't unique. We all have problems that we work around for one reason or another instead of doing the logical thing. In my story, the important problem was my relationship with my landlord, not the frozen keypad. It's the same thing with product development and user research. In far too many cases, people, teams, and organizations develop products that nobody needs, that do not solve any problem, or even worse, solve problems that users don't care enough about.

In this book, you'll learn how to answer your most burning questions about your users (or potential users) with quick-and-dirty research techniques that anyone can apply. You'll learn (among other things) how to identify what users really need, who these users are, and how they currently solve problems they care about.

The Structure of the Book

The structure of this book is simple: it's based on interviews I held with 200 startup founders, enterprise product managers, and venture capitalists from all over the world. During those interviews, I asked what questions they asked themselves about their users (or future users). I gathered hundreds such questions together, which I then, with the help of 50 entrepreneurs, organized into eight groups. Each group of questions was summarized into one question, which became a chapter in this book. Furthermore, each chapter is a step-by-step, how-to guide that answers the question at stake with one to three user research methods (see Figure I.2).

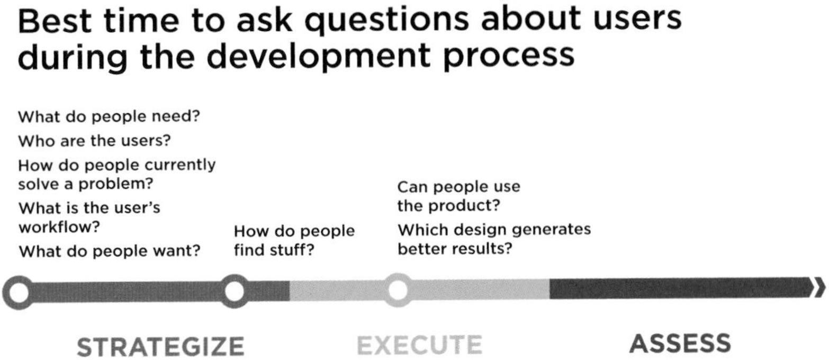

Best time to ask questions about users during the development process

What do people need?

Who are the users?

How do people currently solve a problem?

What is the user's workflow?

What do people want?

How do people find stuff?

Can people use the product?

Which design generates better results?

STRATEGIZE　　　EXECUTE　　　ASSESS

FIGURE I.2

Each question (asked in a different stage of a product's lifecycle) represents a chapter in the book.

Goals of This Book

The clear result of my interviews with 200 product managers and startup founders was that there's a need for lean user research guidance that is specific, approachable, and easy to implement. The following are the goals set for this book.

Change How People Answer Their Most Burning Questions About Users

Probably the most important finding of my research was uncovering the top questions that product managers, startup founders, and venture capitalists ask themselves about their users or potential users (see Figure I.3). The good news is that they ask the right questions. Not only that, but they even know the order of importance of these questions. Sadly, the bad news is that people answer these questions in invalid, unreliable, and sometimes unbelievable ways. Here are some representative examples:

- Who are my customers?
  "We look at analytics data."

- Do people need my product?
  "Doh, of course they do, because we created it."

- Is the product usable?
  "We focus on UX. We use the product ourselves."

- Is our product better than the competition?
  "We have no competition," then (after acknowledging they do),
  "We do things differently."

- Is our product getting better?
  "We improve it all the time, so yes."

- Do people want the product?
  "I asked my sister, and she said yes."

What Questions Did You Ask Yourself?

Percentages of startup founders and enterprise PMs interviewed for this book

FIGURE I.3
The top questions product development practitioners, startup founders, and venture capitalists ask themselves.

Shorten the Road Between Wanting to Do Research and Actually Doing It

This book will show you how to do research, including detailed steps, templates, examples, videos, resources, and practice exercises. You'll have everything you need to start your own research to answer your questions about users. Basically, you'll have everything you need with this book, its companion website (leanresearch.co), and YouTube Channel (bit.ly/validating-youtube).

Change Perceptions About Research

Let's face it—people often have incorrect perceptions and myths associated with user research. This book changes those perceptions and hopefully busts the following myths:

- Research is academic.

- Research is time-consuming.

- Research is very expensive.

- Only an elite squad of PhDs can do research.

- Research isn't actionable.

- Research can't help in making high-risk product design and roadmap decisions.

- Lean user research is all about A/B testing and analyzing analytics data.

Change the Source of Product Ideas

Eighty-six percent of people interviewed for this book testified that their product or startup idea came from pain they had experienced personally. For example, I interviewed a software engineer who lost track of her child at the beach and was frantic until good people helped find him. That engineer started a company that introduced an app to solve this problem. Or a young computer science student who had been coding since he was 9 years old and had an idea for a really smart way of identifying spaghetti code and decided to patent and frame it into a service package.

There's no doubt that personal pain signals there's an opportunity to solve a problem. Many entrepreneurs are sure they have a problem worth solving due to their own personal experience. But, they often fail to recognize that an almost tangible "fact" in their mind is just an assumption that should be tested, validated, or most likely, invalidated. Figure I.4 shows what 200 product managers and startup founders told me about where ideas for products come from. Notice that user research is last with only two percent of my interviewees.

Where Did the Idea Come From?

Percentages of startup founders and enterprise PMs interviewed for this book

Personal Pain	86%
Spinoff	7%
Client Request	3%
Market Research	2%
User Research	2%

FIGURE I.4

The vast majority of ideas for new products and services come from a personal pain the owner of the idea has experienced.

Jump!

In a scene from the film *White Men Can't Jump*, Woody Harrelson and Rosie Perez are in bed together; she is studying for *Jeopardy*, and he is just lying around. She turns to him and says, "Honey, I'm thirsty," so he gets up, walks to the kitchen sink, fills up a glass of water, comes back, lies down in bed, and hands her the glass of water. She takes the glass of water, looks at it, and tosses it in his face. He says, "What the hell, what did I do wrong?" and she says, "Honey, I said I was thirsty. I didn't want a glass of water. I wanted empathy. I wanted you to say I know what it's like to be thirsty."

Brad Feld describes this beautiful, little scene and uses it to explain the essence of the differences between the two—where he went to solve her problem and all she wanted was some empathy.

To understand humans, their needs, and whether products meet those needs, you too need to develop empathy. Empathy is an *intentional* effort of understanding the thoughts of another person while uncovering their reasoning, as Indi Young[2] defines it. It's not just being able to feel what another person feels because you have already experienced a similar situation. When you develop empathy toward another person, a future customer, you want to learn from that person about his or her needs, behavior, and problems.

---

2 Young, Indi. *Practical Empathy: For Collaboration and Creativity in Your Work.* New York: Rosenfeld Media, 2015.

CHAPTER 1

What Do People Need?

Until the moment Steve Jobs went on stage at Moscone Center in San Francisco in January 2007 and introduced the iPhone to the world, nobody knew they needed a smartphone. Nokia had recently sold their one-billionth phone, and it seemed people were generally satisfied with their phones. During the seven months that passed from the time Jobs held the first iPhone in his hands onstage until Apple began shipping iPhones to the masses, there was a bombardment of TV commercials in the U.S. that took a (successful) stab at creating the need.

Today, many people consider their smartphone (whether an iPhone, Android, or other) as an integral extension of their body. They don't leave home without it. If they do, they go back and retrieve it. The reason is because they *need* it. This day and age, smartphones solve problems people have, save time people can never get back, and meet oh-so-many human needs. Yes, smartphones also turn some people into anti-social creatures, but that's for a different book.

Many products are developed based on a hunch, a judgment call, incomplete information, or faith-based hallucinations. Only after they fail miserably do developers ask themselves why. In most cases, the answer is that the product does not meet a real user need or solve a problem people really care about. This chapter walks you through one straightforward technique for uncovering user needs, answering that vital question "What do people need?"

Why Is This Question Important?

"What do people need?" is a critical question to ask when you build products. Wasting your life's savings and your investors' money, risking your reputation, making false promises to employees and potential partners, and trashing months of work you can never get back is a shame. It's also a shame to find out you were completely delusional when you thought that everyone needed the product you were working on.

The question is important because of the risk it entails. Many product development teams tend to ask themselves if they *can* build a product. The answer in most cases is, yes they can. When you realize the importance of first finding out what humans need, then you start asking yourself if you *should* build a product, rather than if you *can*.

When Should You Ask the Question?

"What do people need?" is probably the most important question a product development team will ask itself. Ninety-five percent of founders and product managers interviewed for this book did ask themselves this question. The timing of asking (or rather answering) this question is key because although needs are relatively stable, it's worth being aware that users may not need "it" (whatever "it" may be) in six months' time. The market might also affect needs—for example, legislation changes, entrance of other products to the market, etc.

That said, there are two great times to ask the question: somewhere in the beginning of strategizing your product, and after launching it during the assessment phase (see Figure 1.1).

- When you strategize, you try to figure out a lot of things about the need for your product, who your target audience is, and what your audience wants. Attaining this knowledge and wisdom will serve you well during the execution phase. Discovering user needs will help you figure out *how* the product should be built, because it will generate evidence, validation, and invalidation for various product features.

- During the assessment phase, your users use the product, and you can learn whether or not your product meets their real needs. Beware though. If this is the first time you study your audience's needs, you might find and learn things that will be very hard and costly to fix. The best time to answer the question is prior to execution. However, it is never too late or an inappropriate time to ask the question. The sooner you realize you need an evidence-based answer, the better.

What do people need?

FIGURE 1.1

When is a good time to ask "What do people need?" The big circle represents the best time, while the smaller ones indicate other times recommended for asking the question.

Answering the Question with Experience Sampling

Experience sampling is a strategic research technique that answers a high-level business (or roadmap) question rather than evaluating a design or product that already exists. Experience sampling is good for uncovering unmet needs, which will lead to generating great ideas for new products and for validating (or invalidating) ideas you already have.

In an experience sampling study, research participants are interrupted several times a day or week to note their experience in real time. The idea is based on what was called a *pager study* in the 1950s. The essence of the 1950s version of experience sampling was the use of pagers or other signaling devices to trigger involvement in the research study.

The key to experience sampling is asking the *same* question over and over again at random times during the day or week. This cadence and repetition strengthens your finding's validity and allows you to identify patterns, like participants reporting greater satisfaction right after completing certain tasks. For example, you might ask people what annoyed them recently. Imagine if you ask that question five times a day for a period of five days and 100 people participate in your research. This means you will potentially collect 2,500 data points. That can be turned into a large, useful body of knowledge.

Why Experience Sampling Works

Experience sampling is an effective user research technique that has the following benefits:

- **Offers insights about user needs**: It gives you a glimpse into users' lives and their realities and uncovers their objective needs.

- **Provides evidence-based feature generation**: The results can be transformed easily into product features because they provide a combination of qualitative and quantitative data about very specific needs. This way, you can become confident in your innovation since it is backed by evidence.

- **Highlights current pain points and delights**: When you learn what makes your potential customers happy or angry, you are one step closer to offering a product or service that meets their needs.

- **Gives inspiration for new ideas**: Your viewpoint about your product idea might be narrow, and you wouldn't even know it. It uncovers other viewpoints, or categories, of a topic you might not be aware of. These help you come up with better products or services.

Other Questions Experience Sampling Helps Answer

Other than the "What do people need?" question, experience sampling is a great method for answering the following questions as well. If you ask yourself (not users) any one of these questions, experience sampling is a technique that can help you get an answer.

- Would people be willing to pay to use the product?

- How do we make using this product a habit?

  Clarification: The worst way to know if people would pay to use a product or if they would use it repeatedly is ask them directly. Humans are very bad at predicting their future behavior. In experience sampling, you explore people's current behavior, which is the best predictor of future behavior. You won't know for sure if they'll pay for your product or make a habit of using it. But if you ask the right experience sampling question (see Step 1 later in the chapter), you will know what they currently pay for, how they currently behave, and how painful certain needs are for them. These will give you strong insights and indications of whether they might pay for a product or make a habit of using it. You are not going to be 100% sure because there are many other factors at play here (price point, marketing, timing of product release, and many more), but you will have a greater understanding of a need.

- Is there a need for the product?

  Experience sampling is not a way to evaluate product design. It is, however, helpful in evaluating whether or not there's a need for a specific product you have in mind (or at hand). The key is to explore people's current behavior without your product and evaluate whether or not they indicate a need that matches the value your product is (or will be) adding.

- Why do people sign up and then not use the product?

- What are some use cases we should plan for?

- Would people use the product?

- How do people choose what to use among similar options?

- Does the product solve a problem people care enough about?

- Which customer needs does the product satisfy?

- How do we define the right requirements for the product?

- How will the product solve people's pain points?

- Which features should be included in an MVP?

  Clarification: MVP is an experiment that has a goal of learning as much as you can while making the smallest amount of effort. It's a process, not an end goal. Therefore, although you might be asking yourself which features to include in an MVP, understanding needs and problems real people have through experience sampling (and other methods) puts you in a better position to come up with an experimentation process.

- What are some feature ideas our customers have?

- Which features are most important?

- Should we build [specific feature]?

- How often would people use the product?

- Would people from other cultures use the product?

How to Answer the Question

The following is a how-to guide that takes you step-by-step through the process of using experience sampling to answer the question "What do people need?"

STEP 1: Define the scope and phrase the experience sampling question.

"What do people need?" is a very broad question that probably has an infinite number of answers. To make sure that your study results are effective and useful, first define a very clear scope for your inquiry. You probably have a domain in mind such as grocery shopping, photography, or enterprise sales. This means you will be focusing on this area during the study.

Try to get even more specific. What is it about grocery shopping that you want to learn? What would help you make a decision about your photography-related app? What aspect of enterprise sales are you interested in? Be as specific as possible when you decide how to best use research. For example, maybe your study scope involves challenges in remembering what to buy at the grocery store, or opportunities for saving time spent on uploading photos from a camera to a desktop, or ways in which salespeople prepare for a sales pitch to a potential customer. After you define the scope, it's time to work on the question you will ask your study participants.

The specific question you ask experience sampling study participants must be carefully phrased and tested. As you phrase the question (or come up with a few alternatives), bounce it off other team members early on and run a pre-launch pilot before releasing it to the whole sample group. The most important thing is that the question has to speak to participants' *behavior* that repeats itself. Remember, you are going to ask that question over and over, and you will expect different answers (both across the participant population and from the same individuals at different times) that provide insights into people's needs, pain points, and delights.

Here are some *good* examples of experience sampling questions that target repeated behaviors:

- What was the reason you recently used a piece of paper to write something down?

- What was the reason you recently updated your website?

- What did you want to know recently?

- What was the reason for the last phone call you initiated?

- What were you frustrated about recently when you went grocery shopping?

The experience sampling question must also be specific; otherwise, you are destined to get a lot of irrelevant answers. For example, if you ask, "The last time you went to a shoe store, what did you do?"— that's too general and vague. People will tell you they met a friend and talked about their recent spring break vacation or called their mother. If you are interested in uncovering needs related to buying shoes, be specific about it. For example, ask, "The last time you went to a shoe store, what frustrated you the most about buying shoes?"

The following are some questions to ask about behavior that is probably *not* so repetitive:

- What annoyed you the most the last time you moved to a new house or apartment?
- What was the primary reason for choosing your most recent vacation destination?
- Which laptop computer did you buy recently?

While the above questions are legitimate, good questions to ask, they are not recommended for experience sampling because the frequency of the behavior doesn't make sense for this research format. If you are looking to uncover needs related to behaviors that are not repeated very frequently, consider interviewing (Chapter 2), observation (Chapter 3), or a diary study (Chapter 4).

Make sure that the question you ask helps you figure out what users need. There are several types of questions you should *avoid* in an experience sampling study because they will never help you uncover needs:

1. **Questions about opinions**: Asking for someone's opinion about something several times a day or week is useless. Opinions don't change five times a day or week, and there's no point in asking for them that much. Examples might include:

   - What do you think about hiring a Web developer for updating your website?
   - Should links be blue or black?

2. **Questions that speak to "average" behavior**: A common trap people who phrase questions for experience sampling fall into is asking them in a way that vaguely refers to a time frame about which the question is asked. For example, when you ask, "What frustrates you most about boarding a train?" you are setting yourself up for failure. Let's assume the person who tries to answer this question has boarded trains 300 times during her lifetime, 50 of them in the past year, one last week. This person will probably not remember all of the frustrations about boarding a train and will try to come up with an answer that "averages" the ones she does remember (maybe the last five). She will also try to satisfy you with the answer and give you a real

interesting one with a nice anecdote. The answer will probably not represent many real frustrations very well. The best way to avoid this trap is to ask about the last time the behavior happened. This way, her memory is still fresh, and it is less likely the participant will pick and choose an answer she thinks will satisfy you. Here are some examples for questions that ask people to "average" their behavior:

- What frustrates you the most when you board a plane?

- How do you spend time while you wait in a long line?

3. **Questions that are too general**: While taking a broad approach to learning from people is usually a good thing to do, asking a general question in experience sampling is going to force you to deal with a lot of noise. If you are interested in one aspect of a topic, ask about that aspect rather than asking about the entire topic. For example, if you decided that the scope of your research was uncovering needs related to finding a parking spot, don't ask, "What annoys you about driving in a city?" Instead, ask, "What was the most frustrating thing that happened to you the last time you were looking for a parking space?" Here are some more examples of questions that are too general:

- What frustrated you recently?

- How did you decide which smartphone to purchase?

- What is email good for?

4. **Yes/no questions**: Experience sampling is a research method that integrates qualitative, rich data with quantitative, numerical data. Asking a yes/no question eliminates the qualitative aspect of the study to a point where you'll have nothing actionable to do when you see the results. If you ask, "Did you update your website this morning?" and 78% of the answers are *yes*, then what are you going to do next? What did you learn about user needs? Which pain points did you uncover? Here are some more bad examples:

- Did you buy milk today?

- Was your bus late this morning?

- Do you like your boss?

5. **Quantitative questions**: Similar to yes/no questions, quantitative ones are also not going to be very helpful. A number, an average, or a percentage tells you nothing about unmet needs, missing features, painful problems, or joyful delights. It's just a number. Here are some examples:

- How many emails did you receive in the past hour?

- What time did you wake up this morning?

- How many items did you purchase the last time you went grocery shopping?

As mentioned earlier, phrasing an experience sampling question is a critical factor in the success of your research. Before you launch your experience sampling study, refer to the following imaginary scenario and then read sample questions and explanations about why these questions are right or wrong in Table 1.1.

Scenario: Imagine that Stop & Shop, a grocery shopping retailer in the northeastern U.S., came to you with this challenge: they want to identify ways to improve their customers' in-store grocery shopping experience with technology. In other words, they want to uncover user needs, or answer the infamous question "What do people need?"

To sum it up, after you phrase your question, make sure that it:

- Asks about repeated behavior.

- Does not ask about opinions.

- Does not ask to "average" a behavior.

- Is not too general but very specific.

- Is not a yes/no question.

- Is not a quantitative question in which the answer is a number.

TABLE 1.1 SAMPLE EXPERIENCE SAMPLING QUESTIONS AND EXPLANATIONS

	Question	Good?	Why?	Better Question
1	How did you create your shopping list the last time you went to the grocery store?	Yes	Asks about repeated behavior and is open-ended enough for getting valuable responses.	-
2	What is the reason you use your mobile phone while grocery shopping?	No	Phrased as if it is asked once, not repeatedly. Also, it does not meet a most likely situation where a phone is used multiple times for different purposes during grocery shopping.	The last time you went grocery shopping, what was the reason you used your phone to help you shop?
3	How often did you check the time when you recently went grocery shopping?	No	Asks for a number. Numbers will not help in identifying needs. Also, people would be making a guess because they are not aware of the number of times they use their phone. It might seem to you that asking this type of question is helpful for validating a need (e.g., if it happened zero times, it's not a real need; if it happened many times, it is a need), but you will need to make a big leap from a number to a need. Numbers will never tell you why something is happening.	
4	Would you prefer to do your grocery shopping online to save time?	No	Asks for an opinion rather than a behavior. Also, this is a Yes/No question, which is useless for identifying needs.	What was the reason you recently grocery shopped online?
5	What did you do when you were last in the grocery store?	No	Too vague and general. People do many things while grocery shopping. Pick one thing and ask about it.	What was the biggest challenge for you the last time you went to the grocery store?
6	What part of the shopping experience is most difficult for you?	No	While asking about repeated behavior, this question is asking respondents to average their recent store visits.	What was most difficult for you the last time you went to the grocery store?
7	How do you decide what to buy?	No	Too general, asks respondents to average multiple experiences.	What was the most important consideration for deciding what to buy the last time you went to the grocery store?
8	What did you buy today?	No	Not a question for experience sampling. Can be answered by looking at store purchasing logs and cashier data.	
9	How often do you come to Stop & Shop?	No	Asks for a number. Numbers will not help in identifying needs.	
10	What would make finding items easier?	No	Asks for an opinion and predictions of the future, which are not helpful in identifying human needs.	

Begin looking for research participants immediately. Recruiting participants is *the* greatest bottleneck of user research. Start as soon as you can.

Experience sampling generates huge amounts of data that affect your choice for the number of participants you can include in the study. The number of participants should be a trade-off between having enough participants who contribute enough answers to the question you ask over and over again and having a number that is too much to handle. For example, 5 participants is a very small number that will not get you enough data and verity. If these participants give you 5 answers each day for 5 days, you'll have 125 answers. That's not enough. On the other hand, 1,000 participants are probably too many for you to handle. Imagine if each one of them contributes 5 answers each day for 5 days. That's 25,000 answers that need to be read, classified, and analyzed. Can you handle that?

Depending on how many answers you want, make sure that the number of participants is relatively low and digestible. Almost any number between 25 and 200 participants is something that probably makes sense.

To find the right participants for your experience sampling study that both qualify to participate in your research and are willing and available to do so, craft a screening questionnaire that will screen people into or out of your study:

1. List your assumptions about participant criteria (e.g., business traveler).

2. Transform participant criteria into measurable benchmarks (e.g., travels for business at least three times a year).

3. Transform the benchmark into a screening question or questions (e.g., How often do you go on an airplane?). If a person chooses the "right" answer, she's in. If not, she's out.

4. Craft a screening questionnaire (also called a *screener*) you can send people. (Here is a sample screener— bit.ly/validating-chapter-1-screener.)

5. Pilot-test the screener with a couple of people and make improvements.

6. Utilize social media to find research participants quickly and effectively. Chapter 9 guides you through social media usage for finding research participants, as well as detailed steps and examples for creating greater screeners.

STEP 3: Decide how long it will take participants to answer.

Carefully consider the time it will take study participants to answer the question each time you ask. Keep in mind that you can definitely ask a lead question, as well as some follow-up questions. You can even ask participants to take a picture if it better explains their answer. As a general rule of thumb, try not to take more than one minute of each participant's time. So if you ask the question five times a day, the required effort of participation is five minutes per day. If you increase this time, you increase the likelihood of getting fewer answers from your participants. They'll be overwhelmed and quickly lose interest in the study.

STEP 4: Decide how many data points you need.

You need to make three decisions before you start the study:

- The number of study participants
- The length of the study
- The frequency you ask the question

First, think about how many valuable data points (single responses to the question) you want to have by the end of the study. You have two bad options and one good one:

1. **Too much**: Gathering 20,000 answers is going to be extremely time consuming to analyze. Even 2,000 answers are a lot to handle. As you'll see in a later step, each answer will need to be read, understood, classified, and verified. It can take 1 to 5 minutes to complete this analysis per answer. This translates to 4–20 workdays of analysis for 2,000 answers. That's too much.

2. **Too little**: 20, 50, or even 200 answers is not going to give you enough information to work with. You won't feel very confident in your data, or be sure what to do next.

3. **Just about right**: 500–1,000 answers is a range of answers you can work with, be confident it's comprehensive, and handle alone or with a team of people who support the analysis. This number of data points can take 1–4 days or a couple of hours to a day of teamwork to handle.

As soon as you have a target number of answers to be collected, calculate backward. Take into account that about a third of the answers you want will be lost (see Figure 1.2) due to your participants' inability to answer (they don't give you all the answers they committed to give), the fact that you have duplicates (they submit several identical answers in a matter of seconds), or the number of useless answers you received (they submit answers you don't understand). For example, let's assume that you want 1,000 valuable responses. Assuming one-third will be lost, you need to collect 1,500 responses. If you ask the question 5 times a day for 3 days and 100 people participate in the study, you will potentially get 1,500 responses (5 times a day x 3 days x 100 participants = 1,500 potential answers).

What was the reason you recently used a piece of paper to write something down?

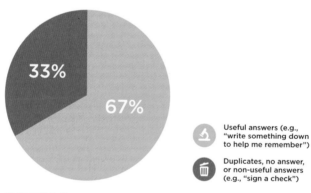

Useful answers (e.g., "write something down to help me remember")

Duplicates, no answer, or non-useful answers (e.g., "sign a check")

FIGURE 1.2

Only about ⅔ of the answers gathered in an experience sampling study are useful. The chart shows useful and not so useful answers to the question "What was the reason you recently used a piece of paper to write something down?"

The number of notifications you send each day is a trade-off between the times you think the behavior you ask about is happening and a number that would annoy or overwhelm your participants to the point where they would choose not to respond. For example, if you think people take notes on a piece of paper 10 times a day, ask them about it 3–5 times a day. Obviously, 10 times is too much. Also, your estimation might be wrong and if you ask 10 times a day about something that happens only 5 times a day, your participants will feel uncomfortable.

Another example is about behaviors that occur relatively rarely. For example, if you estimate your audience updates their websites twice a week, don't ask about them every day. Ask the question once a week for a period of 10 weeks. If you do that with 50 people, you will get 500 reasons that people update their sites. That's a good number of data points to learn from. Table 1.2 provides additional examples for frequency of asking an experience sampling question.

TABLE 1.2   EXAMPLES FOR FREQUENCY OF ASKING AN EXPERIENCE SAMPLING QUESTION

Behavior at Stake	Assumed Behavior Frequency	Question Frequency
Using paper to write something down	10 times a day	3–5 times a day
Updating a website	Twice a week	Once a week
Grocery shopping	2–3 times a week	Once a week
Searching on Google	5 times a day	1–2 times a day
Using a smartphone	150 times a day	5–8 times a day
Boarding a plane	1–2 times a year	Not a good candidate for experience sampling. Better to apply interviewing (Chapter 2), observation (Chapter 3), or diary study (Chapter 4).

STEP 5: ## Choose a medium to send and collect data.

Decide how you are going to send the question to your study participants: text message (SMS), email, an app, or voice message are all good options. Think about how the data will be collected and choose the simplest way for you. For example, use email through which you send a simple Google Form. If you are technically savvy, consider using text messages combined with an automation tool (e.g., an IFTTT[1] recipe) that drops them in a Google spreadsheet. Don't send text messages to participants with the intention of copying and pasting 1,500 text messages into a spreadsheet because this will be extremely tedious and time consuming. Whatever medium you choose, make sure that your data is collected in one spreadsheet, ready to be analyzed the moment you need it, which is about 10 minutes from the time you launch the study.

STEP 6: ## Plan the analysis.

The main activity you will perform during the analysis phase is classifying all of the answers to the question. Classification is no easy task, especially if you are on your own. If you work in a team, have everyone participate. To prepare for group classification, predetermine the categories by which you'll classify the answers. Create this list with your team and invest a little time clarifying what goes under each category. For example, imagine your experience sampling question is "What frustrated you the last time you went grocery shopping?" Categories for answers for this question might be the following:

- **Location**, refers to where the frustration took place, and the options are: home, way to store, in car, at parking lot, at store, and way from store.

- **Close people** are the friends and family who might be involved in grocery shopping frustrations: spouse, parent, sibling, roommate, and child.

- **People at the store** might be other customers, cashier, deli personnel, produce personnel, dairy personnel, and other service people.

- **Issue** could be finding items, understanding costs, long lines, and shopping cart.

---

1 www.ifttt.com

During analysis, you are disassembling each qualitative answer into components that you will later reassemble quantitatively. For example, in the previous example, you might be able to say the frequency at which people were frustrated during grocery shopping was the result of a long line created by other customers in the parking lot. You'll then be more informed when you try to uncover user needs.

STEP 7: **Set participant expectations.**

Study participants will make or break an experience sampling study. When the study is run, you are not there to see what your participants do and correct it if needed. Therefore, take all the necessary steps to make sure that participants understand what is asked of them and that they provide useful answers.

Tell participants in advance what's expected of them. For example, if you expect them to answer five notifications per day for three days, tell them exactly that. Explain that fewer responses do not help you learn from them. Don't give them an example of a good answer to the study question; otherwise, you'll bias them, and you'll just get answers similar to your example. Stay vague. Tell them a good answer is one that you can understand, that is detailed enough, and that does not include one or two words but at least a full sentence.

Always double-check that the participants do not have a holiday or foreign travel planned, unless it's the focus of the research. Let them know that it's okay to miss an answer here and there if they're busy and that they can answer a little bit later.

Tell participants they will get an incentive if they meet your answer quota. If you can't pay participants with money, be creative and think of other ways to provide an incentive for participation. For example, dedicate a wall in your office (or a page on your website if you don't have an office) to study participants. Call it *The Wall of Research Fame* and print their names on it after they participate. Take a picture and share it with each participant. We humans love our names. Take advantage of it!

STEP 8: Launch a pilot, then the study, and monitor responses.

To make sure that participants understand what's required of them and to test your notification mechanism, schedule a practice test where you send one notification to participants and they answer once. Do that a couple of days before the actual study begins. This way, you'll have some time to make changes in case something does not work as expected. It's also a great opportunity to make sure that participants give you the answers you need with enough level of detail. Don't skip this step, because you'll regret it if you do.

After you iterated the study details following the pilot-test and all of the preparations are complete, it is time to start the study. Here are the steps you need to take:

1. **Launch and track**: Launch the study, start sending notifications, and immediately track answers. Evaluate each individual participant's responses and make sure that each person is giving you what you need.

2. **Adjust participant behavior and clarify**: Contact participants who do not give you what you need or do not respond at all. Ask them to allow you to help them. Troubleshoot their issues and refine their participation. For example, if people give you one-word answers, explain that you need to be sure you understand what they meant and ask them to provide longer sentences as answers. Or if participants say they did not receive any notification, figure out the reason.

3. **Pat participants on the back**: Encourage participants who cooperate fully and provide clear, useful answers. Tell them you are very happy with their participation and the level of detail they provided in their answers. Be careful not to say that any specific answers they gave were great. Otherwise, you'll bias them to think this is what you need, and they'll keep giving you the same answers. This way, you'll miss other useful answers.

4. **Thank participants**: Be sure to thank participants, no matter what. Some people will stop participating if they think their effort is underappreciated.

Analyze data.

Begin analysis when you've collected about five percent of the expected number of responses. This will help you fine-tune the rest of the analysis. Look at each of the answers you collected, and one by one, classify them into the categories you have predefined. If you work in a team, do the first chunk together. This way you'll understand better how to classify answers in a consistent manner. For example, here's an answer you might get:

> A slow cashier combined with an elderly person who was in front of me in the line caused me to be late to pick up my son from school.

This answer could be classified as follows:

1. Location: at the store

2. Close people: N/A

3. People at the store: other customers, cashier

4. Issue: long lines

Get the idea? This way, you disassemble each and every answer you collected into components you can count later.

As you make progress with classification, you will realize that some categories need to change, split, merge, or be removed, and that new ones should be added. For example, you might find that under *Location*, it doesn't make sense to have both *in car* and *way to store*, because they are redundant. Or you might find there are many answers that would benefit from creating a separate *Cost* category with values such as *item, expensive, cheap, compare to other store*, and so on.

Eliminate answers that are just incomprehensible or irrelevant. Don't assume you understand what they mean. Only refer to the text in the answer. If there's doubt, there's no doubt. For example, if your question was "What frustrated you the last time you went grocery shopping?" and you get the answer "Dogs," don't guess what the reason was or assume any type of category for classification. This is an incomprehensible answer you should ignore.

If you classify data as a team, work together while you are all in the same room so that you can discuss things as you make progress. If this is not possible, catch up with team members once in a couple of hours (or at least daily) to do the following:

- Spot-test how team members are classifying so that you ensure the whole team is being consistent. (It's a pain to undo later with thousands of data points.)

- Highlight and discuss any data that is hard to classify with existing categories.

- Create new categories and then share them with the whole team as soon as possible. If you don't do this, then team members start to invent their own inconsistent categories or just use existing categories that are inappropriate, which is harder to consolidate later.

Work on one spreadsheet when you classify. This spreadsheet should include all individual answers in one column and categories in columns to the right. This process allows you to filter easily and sort by category later. Sorting by a particular category makes it super easy to eyeball the data for that issue and understand what happened. Set up the spreadsheet to automatically tally up frequency counts as you analyze (see Figure 1.3). The resource page for experience sampling on the book's companion website at leanresearch.co includes a template spreadsheet for you to use during the analysis step.

	B	C	D	E	F	G
1	What was the reason you recently used a piece of paper to write something down?	Category 1	Category 2	Category 3	Category 4	Category 5
2		7	5	5	10	12
3	To make a to-do list for the day.	1				1
4	grocery list					1
5	Making a list	1				
6	Because I'm a visual learner and it helps me to remember				1	1
7	It was better represented with a quick sketch than digitally formatted text.			1		1
8	To take notes on an online class	1				1
9	to address an envelope	1			1	1
10	to take notes			1	1	
11	To keep an idea for later.				1	
12	Taking notes now!	1				
13	convenience				1	1
14	ideas				1	
15	To remember to do it later			1	1	1
16	Notes in class	1				
17	Tasks for the day.			1		1
18	To-dos			1	1	1
19	In a meeting, had an idea, needed to record it quickly	1		1	1	1
20	Write notes on this topic			1		
21	visualize				1	
22	Post it note for immediate todo list					
23	wireframe			1	1	1
24	Only when I take notes				1	
25	its how I write my thoughts				1	

FIGURE 1.3

An experience sampling spreadsheet set for tallying up categories.

STEP 10: **Generate bar charts.**

As soon as you are finished classifying the answers, merge all of the classification data into one long spreadsheet. Create tables in which you calculate the number of times different category values happened and their percentages (see Table 1.3).

TABLE 1.3 SAMPLE EXPERIENCE SAMPLING TABULATED DATA

Location Category	Count	Percentage
Home	274	18%
Way to store	12	1%
In car	46	3%
At parking lot	32	2%
At store	1,058	70%
Way from store	97	6%
Total	**1,519**	**100%**

You can further break down the data by "user type" in columns to the right. For example, you can use men vs. women, younger vs. older, or whatever other user types have been identified/recruited.

You can then easily produce bar charts to indicate what's happening most frequently. These charts show how many times certain values occurred for any particular variable in any given category. For example, you can create a bar chart for the *Location* category (Figure 1.4). You can also create bar charts that look deeper into one variable across a certain category. For instance, what are the grocery shopping issues that occurred at people's homes? (See Figure 1.5.) These bar charts will tell you the story of the data you collected in numbers.

Location Category Value Distribution

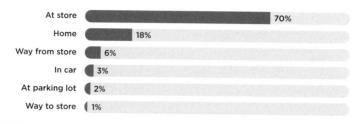

At store	70%
Home	18%
Way from store	6%
In car	3%
At parking lot	2%
Way to store	1%

FIGURE 1.4
A bar chart for the Location category.

Location Category Value Distribution

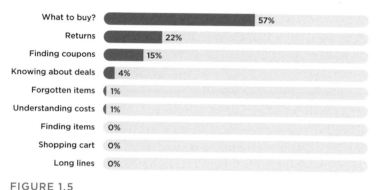

What to buy?	57%
Returns	22%
Finding coupons	15%
Knowing about deals	4%
Forgotten items	1%
Understanding costs	1%
Finding items	0%
Shopping cart	0%
Long lines	0%

FIGURE 1.5
A bar chart that crosses a variable and a category—
grocery shopping issues at home.

STEP 11: Eyeball the data and identify themes.

Another way to get a good grasp of experience sampling data is
eyeballing. *Eyeballing* means you simply read the answers to the
experience sampling question and get a feel for what answers are
like and what categories are out there. Without any analysis, you'll be
able to reach conclusions about what you found.

Glance over the sample list of answers in Figure 1.6. What can you
say about what you see there? You can see several categories bub-
bling up here very quickly (Figure 1.7). Some people are taking notes
for creating lists, some are writing down ideas, and others are sketch-
ing stuff. What you just did was eyeball the data.

What was the reason you recently used a piece of paper to write something down?
To make a to-do list for the day.
grocery list
Making a list
Because I'm a visual learner and it helps me to remember
It was better represented with a quick sketch than digitally formatted text.
To take notes on an online class
to address an envelope
to take notes
To keep an idea for later.
Taking notes now!
convenience
ideas
To remember to do it later
Notes in class
Tasks for the day.
To-dos
In a meeting, had an idea, needed to record it quickly
Write notes on this topic
visualize
Post it note for immediate todo list
wireframe
Only when I take notes
its how I write my thoughts
sketching wireframes
write something down to help me remember
in a meeting without computer available
To take notes
To-do list
jot a note
Note down an idea.

FIGURE 1.6

Sample experience sampling raw data.

What was the reason you recently used a piece of paper to write something down?
To make a to-do list for the day.
grocery list
Making a list
Because I'm a visual learner and it helps me to remember
It was better represented with a quick sketch than digitally formatted text.
To take notes on an online class
to address an envelope
to take notes
To keep an idea for later.
Taking notes now!
convenience
ideas
To remember to do it later
Notes in class
Tasks for the day.
To-dos
In a meeting, had an idea, needed to record it quickly
Write notes on this topic
visualize
Post it note for immediate todo list
wireframe
Only when I take notes
its how I write my thoughts
sketching wireframes
write something down to help me remember
in a meeting without computer available
To take notes
To-do list
jot a note
Note down an idea.

FIGURE 1.7

Categories bubble up quickly when eyeball-ing the data.

After you analyzed the data, it's time to synthesize it into themes and an answer (or answers) to the question you started with, which is "What do people need?" Have a look at the information you gathered about frequency. What questions come to mind when you look at it? Is there a certain category you need to dig into more? Why? List to yourself the big, emerging themes that came out of the data. What insights do they provide about user needs? Are there any features you think might support things you discovered in the data? If you work in a team, it's best to complete this step together. Different team members will reach different conclusions from one another. Have those conversations to understand better what the data tells you.

Once you have reached conclusions and answered your research question ("What do people need?"), consider developing a product concept and have potential users react to it. More on how to do that, in the next chapters.

A theme is an answer to the research question. Each theme has a title, a one- to two-paragraph description, and a design implication. Let's look at the following example.

Men Are Lost in Aisles

Men have trouble finding items at grocery stores. They perceive the time they spend looking for items to be unacceptably long. They have difficulties identifying items they need to purchase and sometimes just wander, completely lost and helpless, in the aisles looking for what they need without asking for help.

Design Implication: Solve the problem either prior to getting to the store or at the store. Bypass the problem by repurposing past grocery lists or purchased items and provide personalized, in-store navigation guidance.

If a pattern starts to emerge during the research, you could follow up with participants to probe deeper. Without knowing the root cause, it could be easy to prescribe the wrong solution.

For example, if the issue is that they don't know what the grocery items look like, then product navigation might also need to show images of items on the shopping list.

Other Methods to Answer the Question

While experience sampling is a fast, effective way for answering the "What do people need?" question, the following are three additional methods for answering it. Ideally, if time is on your side, a combination of two to three methods is the best way for uncovering insights to help you answer this question.

- **Interviewing** is a research activity in which you gather information through direct dialogue. It is a great way to uncover and understand people's feelings, desires, struggles, delights, attitudes, and opinions. Interviewing people whom you know to be your target audience (and those you think are not) lets you get to know your users, segment them, design for them, solve their problems, and provide value. An interview can be held in person or remotely over a phone or some kind of video conference. Chapter 2 guides you through conducting interviews for uncovering needs.

- **Observation** is a research technique for learning from people in their natural context of using products or services. It can take you a long way into learning everything you can about a problem and uncovering people's needs. Observation involves gathering data at the user's environment, so it is the science of contextualization. Chapter 3 takes you step-by-step into conducting effective observations.

- In a **diary study**, participants document their activities, thoughts, and opinions and share them with you over a period of time. A diary might be a record of their experience using a product or a means of gaining understanding about ordinary life situations in which products might be usefully applied. Diary studies are best for learning about more complex processes. Chapter 4 walks you through conducting a useful diary study.

> **NOTE** EXPERIENCE SAMPLING RESOURCES
>
> Access the online resource page for experience sampling on the book's companion website at leanresearch.co. You'll find templates, checklists, videos, slide decks, articles, and book recommendations.

Experience Sampling Checklist

- ☐ Define the scope and phrase an experience sampling question.
- ☐ Find research participants.
- ☐ Decide how long it will take participants to answer.
- ☐ Decide how many data points you need.
- ☐ Choose a medium to send and collect data.
- ☐ Plan the analysis.
- ☐ Set participant expectations.
- ☐ Launch a pilot, then the study, and monitor responses.
- ☐ Analyze data.
- ☐ Generate bar charts.
- ☐ Eyeball the data and identify themes.

Will smiled at the woman coding next to him. "Hey, thanks for the assist. I love hackathons."

The woman grinned back, pulling off an MIT sweatshirt. "I've only done hackathons with BGC—Black Girls Code. I thought it might be time to branch out a bit, though. If women of color are going to take their place in digital space, it means broadening our scope."

"Big plans, huh?"

Her smile was wide, and her expression was determined. "Huge plans."

He felt a sense of kinship. "Me, too. Zuckerberg,

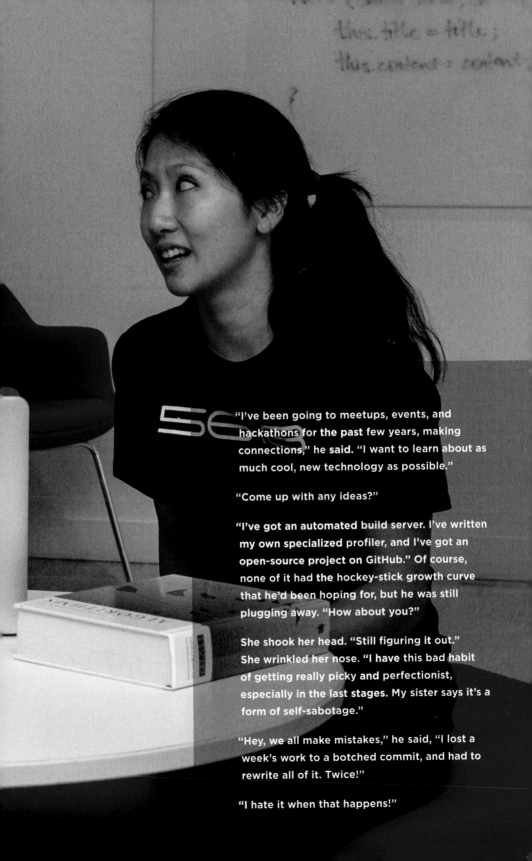

"I've been going to meetups, events, and hackathons for the past few years, making connections," he said. "I want to learn about as much cool, new technology as possible."

"Come up with any ideas?"

"I've got an automated build server. I've written my own specialized profiler, and I've got an open-source project on GitHub." Of course, none of it had the hockey-stick growth curve that he'd been hoping for, but he was still plugging away. "How about you?"

She shook her head. "Still figuring it out." She wrinkled her nose. "I have this bad habit of getting really picky and perfectionist, especially in the last stages. My sister says it's a form of self-sabotage."

"Hey, we all make mistakes," he said, "I lost a week's work to a botched commit, and had to rewrite all of it. Twice!"

"I hate it when that happens!"

"You've got great coding skills," he noticed.
"We work well together. We should totally work
on a project. What do you say?"

"Yeah, sure. Why not?" She shook hands with
him, a firm handshake that meant business.

"I can show you what I'm working on right now,"
he said, opening his laptop.

"Hey, that's really good," she said, after
scanning the lines. Then she frowned. "You put
this on Reddit?"

"Yeah. So?"

She shook her head. "Dude, there's got to be a
better way to share this stuff."

CHAPTER 2

Who Are the Users?

Years ago, New York City decided to redesign all of its street crossing curbs so they were flat. The intended audience was people who used wheelchairs. The assumption was that the flat curbs would help them cross the streets easily and safely. While that was true, city officials were surprised to learn that people who used baby strollers, as well as ones who used skateboards and rollerblades, were also fans of the flat curbs (see Figure 2.1).

FIGURE 2.1
A flat curb in front of a New York City crossing.

Play-Doh, the modeling clay used by young children for arts and crafts projects (see Figure 2.2) was not originally intended for children when it was first introduced to the market in the 1930s. *Kutol Products*, a soap manufacturer in Cincinnati, Ohio, targeted it at people who wanted to remove coal residue from wallpaper. Only after a classroom of children in Cincinnati started using it as a modeling compound (20 years later) did the manufacturer realize its true audience was completely different. Long story short, in 2003 Play-Doh was included in the Toy Industry Association's list of toys of the century.

FIGURE 2.2
Play-Doh.

One of the hardest things to know in product development is who your target audience is. Product developers might come up with a very specific target audience only to find out that a completely different audience is finding value in their product, which is a good thing. Or, even more surprising, they might discover that their actual audience is very different than the intended one.

Why Is This Question Important?

Getting to know your audience, who they are, what makes them tick, what brings them happiness, frustration, and motivation helps you build a better product, feature, or service. It makes you find better product roadmap decisions when no other data is available. It also prevents your team from going into exhausting debates about different aspects of *assumed* customer behavior or what analytics data mean. The alternative is that you get a Frankenstein product that is just a conglomerate of features that has *everything* for *no one*.

There are two types of information about people that you'll need: demographics and behaviors. Marketing practitioners generally use demographics to target product messaging through customer segmentation. Since this book is about product development, it focuses on *behaviors*, largely because they often cut across traditional demographic segmentations. Table 2.1 provides an example that demonstrates this difference. By the end of this chapter, you will have an archetypical profile of several users or customers (or potential users or customers) differentiated by their behaviors.

TABLE 2.1   HUMAN BEHAVIOR VS. DEMOGRAPHIC LABELS

Behavior	Demographics
Owns an iPhone and Android	Alpha male
Online 20–30 hours every week	Above-average user
Uses a product similar to ours	Millennial
Open to trying new things	Average income
Reads five "self-help" books a year	East or West Coast U.S.

When Should You Ask the Question?

Getting an answer to the question "Who are the users?" just as strategizing begins is the most helpful timing. That said, it almost never happens. Because it is not always clear when a new idea for a product, feature, or service is born, it's also not clear when strategizing around it actually begins. Therefore, any time in the early stages of strategizing is great for asking (and answering) the question (see Figure 2.3).

Assuming the question was answered in the early stages of strategizing, there is no reason to answer it again during the execution stage. After your product has been launched, there might be new, additional audiences using it. If you want to learn who these new audiences are, answering the question anytime after launch is going to be helpful. It will also support future developments and changes to the product.

Who are the users?

STRATEGIZE　　　**EXECUTE**　　　**ASSESS**

Best time to ask ◯　　　Good time to ask ◯

FIGURE 2.3
When is a good time to ask "Who are the users?" The big circle represents the best time, while the smaller ones indicate other times recommended for asking the question.

While many people mistake analytics data as a way to answer the "Who are the users?" question, data gathered on visitors is limited to basic demographics of people who choose to identify themselves. It's extremely limited in terms of describing your true audience, their behaviors, and motivations. Therefore, an answer to the question is qualitative in nature, not quantitative.

A hint for you about good timing to answer the question with lean user research is when you find yourself looking at analytics data over and over again, not knowing how to design using it, not learning anything new about customers that inspires design or roadmap decisions, not agreeing on what it means for the product, or just taking wild (or even thoughtful) guesses about what it means. Answering the question through interviewing users will give meaning to analytics data.

Answering the Question with Interviewing and Personas

Converse like a talk show host, think like a writer, understand subtext like a psychiatrist, have an ear like a musician.

—Lawrence Grobel (celebrity interviewer)

Interviewing is a research activity in which you gather information through direct dialogue. It is a great way to uncover and understand people's feelings, desires, struggles, delights, attitudes, and opinions. Interviewing people whom you assume to be your target audience (and those you think are not) is a great way to get to know your users, segment them, design for them, solve their problems, and provide value. An interview can be held in person (highly recommended and preferred, you'll learn so much more) or remotely over a phone or some kind of a video conference (second best, you'll get your answers but won't learn enough).

Meet Anna, a 37-year-old soccer mom who lives in Fairlawn, New Jersey. Anna is a producer at CNBC in Englewood Cliffs, New Jersey. She has two kids (ages 3 and 8), is married to Bob, an analyst in a brokerage firm in New York City, and has an income of $115,000 per year. Anna's biggest challenge related to grocery shopping is that she's struggling to come up with a variety of dishes that are both healthy and desirable for her kids. She also finds herself spending a lot of time at the store dealing with her kids' behavior rather than focusing on getting what she needs quickly. And she always is looking for great deals that will save her money. She would love to get more organized with her grocery shopping and cooking and find someone to occupy her kids and prevent tantrums while at the grocery store.

Makes sense, right? Looks like the beginning of a useful persona, doesn't it? If we had just a few more of these, we could be well on our way to tailoring a kick-ass app for grocery shopping.

Well, everything you just read about Anna is false. I jotted it down in five minutes, and it is all based on my guesses and assumptions gathered through my own grocery shopping experiences (at least ones I can remember) and of my wife's.

A word about personas. A *persona* is a description of an archetypical user of a product. It's a communication tool that helps align development (and other) teams with different types of users. Personas are a great way to create a common language about users and raise empathy toward them within an organization. Unlike what many people think, personas are *not* a research methodology. The biggest problem with personas is that, in many cases, they are not based on research but on assumptions, guesses, and beliefs. It's perfectly fine to start with an assumption and then validate or invalidate it, yet creating a persona based on guesses and then trusting it without any research behind it is just wrong.

These non-research-based personas were given names such as *assumptive* or *ad-hoc personas* (coined by Tamara Adlin), *provisional personas* (coined by Kim Goodwin), or *proto-personas* (coined by Jeff Gothelf). If there's no research behind a persona, I prefer a more direct name for it. I like to call it a *bullshit persona*. You start with a bullshit persona, you do your research, and only then do you have a persona. If you skip research, you're left with just bullshit.

Why Interviewing Works

Interviewing combined with persona development for answering the critical question "Who are the users?" is a priceless lean user research technique with the following benefits:

- **Direct:** Nothing beats primary, face-to-face, in-context research where you ask questions, get answers, and observe human behavior. This direct, in-your-face setup is a priceless benefit of interviewing.

- **Challenges perceptions:** Each person who is involved in product development approaches new ideas for features, products, and services with a set of assumptions and perceptions about users, their needs, and their motivations. An interview is when these assumptions and perceptions are being fundamentally shaken, challenged, and in many cases, changed. All of that is moving toward one goal—uncovering (and caring about) the truth.

- **Increases empathy:** Just by conducting interviews with existing or potential users, taking notes during someone else's interview, or observing live (or recorded) interviews, you become significantly more empathetic toward humans, especially those whom you see as your users. There's probably no better way to attain this empathy.

- **Builds credibility:** Interview findings support product design and roadmap decisions in a way that adds credibility to your decision-making processes. Backing your product decisions with interview data is showing everyone around (investors, senior executives, paying customers) that your work is based on serious science, not on taking huge risks, intuition, or guesstimates.

Other Questions Interviewing Helps Answer

Other than the "Who are the users?" question, interviewing is a great method for answering the following questions. If you ask yourself any one of these questions, interviewing can help you get an answer:

- What are the different lifestyles of potential product users?

- What motivates people to behave in certain ways?

- Which user/s should I focus on?

- What jargon do people use to talk about a domain?

- What is the user's workflow?

- Is there a need for the product/feature?

- What are the right requirements for the product?

How to Answer the Question

The following is a how-to guide that takes you step-by-step through the process of using interviewing and personas to answer the question "Who are the users?"

STEP 1: Create BS personas.

Gather your team, grab a sticky pad, whiteboard, or flip chart and bullshit your way into a couple of personas. A persona is an archetypical user of your product or service. Each product might have several personas. For example, an app for grocery shopping might have the following personas:

- The soccer mom

- The clueless male student

- The bored toddler

- And more...

Developing product personas is great for improving communication between different product development practitioners in your organization by creating a common language to describe groups of product users. Personas can help teams make product roadmap decisions. That said, personas will not help you decide if a button should say "Buy now" or "Pay now" or whether it should be green or blue.

A *bullshit persona* is a persona that is based on guesses (educated or not) and assumptions, rather than actual research and factual data. Sadly, many people stop after creating bullshit personas, thinking that by doing that they "are doing UX" or checking the box for research. To be clear, a persona (real or assumptive) is not a user research methodology. Rather, it's a communication tool.

The power of the bullshit persona is that it helps you and your team focus your research, validate or invalidate your assumptions, and lead you to developing a real, research-based, valid, and reliable (no bullshit) persona.

Together with your team, ask yourselves the following questions and identify which aspects of your audience you are less sure of or familiar with.

1. How would you describe your target users? What are their primary characteristics?

2. Are there different groups of users?

3. How are user groups different?

4. Is there a particular group that is more important than the other ones?

5. Is there a particular group that you want to learn more about? Why?

6. Who are (or would be) the early adopters of your product? What are their characteristics?

The best way to answer these questions is by listing your assumptions about the answers. Recognizing your answers as assumptions, not as facts, is a great early step toward a successful lean user research study. By the end of your research, you will validate or most likely invalidate these assumptions, as well as have a clearer idea of who your users are.

If you feel that some of the questions are similar to one another, it is not a mistake. Asking the same question in different ways will help you exhaust all of your team's assumptions about your users. Some of the things you and your team might have as objectives could be to find out more about the goals, tasks, pain points, behaviors, experiences, and attitudes (including concerns) that are important to each user group.

As you are answering the previous questions with your team, bullshitting your way into a persona or two becomes easy:

1. Draw a large rectangle and divide it into four (see Figure 2.4).

2. Give each part a title: [Persona name], Demographics, Problems, and Solutions (see Figure 2.5).

3. In the first part, sketch the face of the persona. Don't worry about not creating a Da Vinci (see Figure 2.6).

4. In the second part, brainstorm and list a few bullet points to indicate some demographic data about the persona, such as age, occupation, marital status, kids, education, income, etc.

5. In the third part, brainstorm and list a few bullet points to indicate key problems you guess the persona has regarding the domain you are interested in.

6. In the fourth part, list a few ideas for features or products that will hopefully solve the persona's problems you listed earlier (see Figure 2.7).

7. Repeat steps 1–6 for additional bullshit personas. You can potentially have as many as 12 personas, but don't overdo it. A handful of personas is probably enough bullshitting at this point.

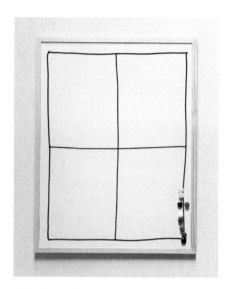

FIGURE 2.4
Rectangle divided into four.

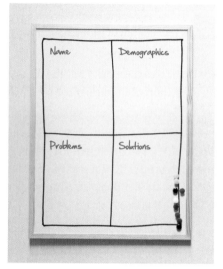

FIGURE 2.5
BS persona template.

FIGURE 2.6
Not a Da Vinci.

FIGURE 2.7
Complete BS persona.

STEP 2: Decide who, how, and where to interview.

When product managers, developers, or designers think of interviewing, in most cases, they think of interviewing users or potential users in a quiet room or online through a video conversation of some sort. While there's nothing wrong with those scenarios, there are some other options and types of interviews that will help you make a decision regarding what you want to do. Whom you invite to the party is going to define what kind of party you have, so choose carefully the people you want for these in-depth interviews.

Who?

These are the different people you can interview to learn about your users:

- **User or potential user:** This is the most common target audience for interviews. Based on assumptive criteria, you select current or potential users of a product or service and interview them. Choose this user to interview as the default or when you are not sure whom to interview.

- **Limiting user:** Someone who is least knowledgeable or able, so the team can consider what trade-offs might be necessary to make sure the limiting users can still use the product. For example, it might be someone who doesn't normally use technology to solve problems, but would really benefit from it. Choose this user to interview when you feel or suspect your plans for the actual product are becoming too sophisticated and advanced.

- **Extreme user:** Someone with exceptional and extraordinary experience and knowledge about the product or domain. He is a user, but there are very few people like him. For example, if your users are business travelers, George Clooney in the movie *Up in the Air* (2009) is an extreme user. Or if your potential users are people who buy a pair of jeans once a year, an extreme user would be someone with 100 pairs of jeans in her closet who visits a jeans store once a week and knows a whole lot about jeans. Choose this user to interview because she exhibits behavior that's shared by your core audience, but is more obviously observable as the extreme case.

- **Expert:** Someone who is extremely knowledgeable about the relevant domain, either because she has studied it, covered it for journalism purposes, or meaningfully invested in it (financially or mentally). For example, if you want to learn about the domain of personal weather stations, a potential user might be someone who is relatively interested in weather, while an extreme user is someone who actually has one or two personal weather stations, and an expert would be a meteorologist. To make the most of expert interviews, get familiar enough with this person's expertise so the questions you ask are ones that you couldn't find easily by educating yourself prior to the interview. Choose this interviewee when your domain expertise is really shallow and you want to ramp up quickly.

How and Where?

Now, let's choose how and where to interview:

- **In-person in a quiet room.** This is the most recommended format for conducting an interview. Being there with a human being who is a user or potential user of your creation (or future creation) is the most humbling experience you'll have during the development process. An even better setup would be to conduct the interview in person at a relevant place for your product or service idea. For example, if you have an idea for an app that helps people with their grocery shopping, try an in-person interview at your participants' homes before and after actual grocery shopping, as well as during the store experience. You'll get more rich input than you would imagine, such as people's rituals, artifacts they own, and other people in the ecosystem that might affect your product (kids, spouse, etc.). The fact that it's their domain and you are the guest will have people be more open to sharing things that they would never share otherwise.

- **Street intercept.** An interview format in which you grab passersby on the street and ask them a few questions. Two primary characteristics of street intercepts are 1) you must get out of your comfort zone and accept the fact that many people will refuse to be interviewed. 2) These interviews are not very deep and will only last 5 to 15 minutes. Many startups consider these "Starbucks" interviews as the primary technique for "Getting out of the building," yet that's not the case. Choose this type of interview when you want to collect specific quantitative data you cannot (or have difficulty) collecting otherwise. For example, if your product idea involves people who have no access to the Internet or smartphones, conduct street intercepts in areas where such people are more likely to walk.

- **Remotely through video (through Skype, GoToMeeting, Hangout, etc.) or phone.** A flavor of an interview in which the interviewer is not in the same location as the interviewee. It's better to be there in person, yet in many cases, it's much better to conduct a remote interview rather than to skip it completely and make product roadmap decisions based on guesswork.

The remaining steps refer to interviewing a product user or potential user (not an extreme user or an expert) in person or remotely (not on the street).

STEP 3: Write a one-page plan.

After you state your assumptions through bullshit personas and understand which ones are more important for you to make progress, discuss the following with your team, come to an agreement, have a shared understanding of what's going to happen during the test, and write a one-page plan (see sidebar on p. 46–47).

1. **Background:** What led us here that we want to do personas and interviews?

2. **Goals:** What is the reason for this study? What is the end result of this research activity?

3. **Research questions:** What do we specifically want to learn? For example, who are our target audiences? What characterizes each group? Which group should we focus on?

4. **Methodology:** Which research technique will be used, how long will it take, and where?

5. **Participants:** What are the characteristics of the people we want to interview?

6. **Schedule:** When do we need results? When can people in the team be available to come to conclusions together?

(Sample One-Page Plan)

by Jane Kay-Smith, Co-founder, Jane@azairways.com

Last updated: 13 October 2015

Background

Since January 2011, when A-Z Airways was introduced to the world, it was known for its high-quality flight experience. That said, in the past year there are repeated complaints and growing call center tickets regarding the company's online flight booking experience. Over the years, several improvements have been made to the system, to no avail.

Goals

Identify the audience for A-Z Airways' online flight booking experience, their behavior, motivations, and attitudes.

Research Questions

1. Who are the most important users of A-Z Airways' online flight booking?

2. What are the top tasks users are trying to complete with our flight booking system? Why?

3. What are the primary breakpoints in the process?

STEP 4: Find 10 interviewees.

To find the right interviewees that both qualify to participate in your research and are willing and available to do so, craft a screening questionnaire that will screen people into or out of your study.

1. Together with your teammates, list a minimum of 5 assumptive attributes of your target audience. Don't limit yourself to just 5 attributes. If you have 10 or 20, that's perfectly fine as a starting point.

    Here's a sample list of participant criteria for an imaginary dancing app.

    -   Resides in the U.S.

    -   Has a smartphone

Methodology

Twelve people will be interviewed in person in a neutral location (rented office) for two hours each. Interviews will be led by flight booking project managers (PMs) and will be conducted in pairs while one PM serves as an interviewer and the other as a note taker. We will have a computer with the A-Z airlines booking system available so interviewees can demonstrate and refer to specific elements of their experience. Interviews will be video recorded and later watched and analyzed by flight booking team members in product management, UX, and software engineering. Personas will be developed based on interview data and will be used to make future roadmap decisions.

Participants

These are the primary characteristics of study participants:

- Booked a flight through AZairways.com at least once in the past 30 days

- Not satisfied with A-Z Airways online flight booking

- Have not complained about the system

- 50% members of the A-Z Airways Elite Traveler Club, 50% non-members

Schedule

Recruiting completed: October 20

Study dates: October 25–26

Results available: October 28

- Wants to learn how to dance

- Uses Facebook

- 20% male, 80% female

2. Transform participant criteria into measurable benchmarks. For example, a criterion such as "business traveler" becomes measurable when you turn it into this benchmark: "Travels for business at least once a month." *Once a month* can be measured; *business traveler* can't.

3. The way from this benchmark to phrasing a screening question is easy. To avoid leading people or revealing the answer you are looking for, phrase the question in a neutral way. Rather than "Do you travel for business at least once a month?" or even "How

often do you travel for business?" ask "How often do you go on an airplane?" and then list a few options (see Table 2.2). If a person chooses the "right" answer, they're in. If not, they're out.

TABLE 2.2   HOW OFTEN DO YOU GO ON AN AIRPLANE?

	Never	Once a Year or Less	Once a Quarter or Less	Once a Month or Less	Once a Week or Less
For Vacation	☐	☐	☐	☐	☐
For Business	☐	☐	☐	☐	☐
For Fun	☐	☐	☐	☐	☐
Other Reason	☐	☐	☐	☐	☐

4. Create a table with three columns. On the first column, list the participant criteria you identified. On the second column, enter the measurable benchmark you created for each criterion. Then, on the last column, translate the benchmark into a screening question (see Table 2.3).

TABLE 2.3   FROM PARTICIPANT CRITERIA TO SCREENING QUESTIONS

Criterion	Measurable Benchmark	Screening Question
Business traveler	Travels for business at least once a month	How often do you go on an airplane?

5. Now that you have a good understanding of who you want and don't want to learn from, it's time to compile a screening questionnaire (also, called a *screener*) you can send people. In addition to screening people into and out of your research, a good screener also collects information about people's availability to participate, as well as their contact information.

6. Google Forms is a great tool you can use for free for creating a screener quickly. Here is a sample screener—bit.ly/validating -chapter-2-screener. Have a look at it and try to match questions with these different screener goals:

    - Screening people into the study

    - Screening people out of the study

    - Collecting contact information

    - Understanding availability (asking about availability in the screener saves you from endless back and forth email/phone coordination)

    Use Google Forms to create a screener based on the questions you already phrased. Try to keep it simple. Create a one-page, straight-forward form without branching and redundant complications.

7. After your screener is ready (and please pilot-test it with a couple of people before you send it to half the world only to find out you have a typo or ask a question nobody understands), it is a great time to send it to as many people as possible and find the ones who qualify and are willing and available to participate. Utilizing social media is a great way to find research participants quickly and effectively. Chapter 9 guides you through social media usage for finding research participants.

Interviews generate huge amounts of rich data, somewhat similar to the amounts you might collect in observation (see Chapter 3) or diary studies (see Chapter 4). These large amounts of collected data directly affect your choice for the number of interviewees you include in the study. As in other qualitative methods, keep this number low and digestible. Ten interviewees is a good number. More than that means this is a large study. You will need more time or hands when it comes to analyzing data and coming up with results. Ten interviewees are good also in terms of study length. If your team splits into two interviewing pairs, each pair can complete five interviews in one day and finish data collection in one day. Alternatively, if you can only conduct interviews in the evening, schedule two interviews per pair per evening for a data collection time of three days.

Prepare the interview.

Begin crafting an interview by first going back to the reason you are conducting it. What made you ask yourself who your users are? What triggered your curiosity about them? Why?

Your primary goal during the interview is to encourage the interviewee to tell you stories about things that happened to them in the recent past. These stories will help you get a deeper understanding of who your users are, what motivates them, and why. This is a key point in interviews—no matter what questions you ask, your goal is extracting those stories about things that happened very recently.

1. **Pick and choose questions.** There are many interview questions that will help you get the stories you are looking for. Here is a list of questions to choose from:

   - **Sequence:** A sequence of actions or an event is sometimes hard to remember. Keep that in mind and try to help your interviewees come up with steps while asking what happened next.

     Example: *Walk me through your day yesterday. And then what did you do next?*

   - **Guided tour:** Have the interviewee be your guide, almost teacher, of a process, series of actions, achieving a certain goal, using certain products, etc.

     Example: *Can we take a look at your email account together?*

   - **Specific example:** Asking about something specific will provide you with the little details that help you understand the interviewee's behavior and choices.

     Example: *Who did you call from your cell phone earlier today? What did you talk about?*

   - **Exhaustive list:** While this question might seem impossible to answer, it can surface behaviors that you never imagined. For example, when you ask "What were all the ways you indulged this week?" you might find that your users have a different opinion about indulgence than your product team.

     Example: *What are all the different places you went online in the past week? Were there any others?*

   - **Peer comparison:** Asking about peer behavior and opinions will help you understand the interviewee's behavior and perspective better, but is not a way to learn about peers. If you are interested in peer behavior and opinions, schedule a research session directly with them.

Example: *Think about the last three times your husband sent you photos. Did he send them the same way or differently each time?*

- **Other viewpoint comparison:** Your goal with this question is to extract a story. Your interviewee is not a good source for predicting other people's behavior.

  Example: *What would your friends think about this?*

- **Projection:** Asking about a hypothetical future situation is a way to understand values, current expectations, and explanation for past behavior.

  Example: *What do you think would happen if...? What makes you say that?*

- **Quantitative/inventory:** Usually, an interview held with a relatively small number of people is not a reliable way to gather valid quantitative data. That said, if you are aware of it, you can use quantitative questions to better understand the type of person you are conversing with (e.g., if the answer is 1 or 1,000, it might indicate two very different audiences).

  Example: *How many of your contacts fall into that category?*

- **Changes over time:** A year back is a long time ago and memory of details is not very accurate. Yet this is still a question that might help you understand your interviewee's behavior and allow him to remember relevant stories.

  Example: *How are things different now than a year ago?*

- **Suggestive opinion:** This type of question is used a lot by journalists who conduct interviews they hold with politicians, for example. It generates a reaction from the interviewee that will help you uncover her opinion and motivation. Bear in mind, though, that this question is very leading and may change responses to later answers. So if you plan to try to find out later if interviewees do anything with their phones while driving, don't ask this question a few minutes beforehand.

  Example: *Some people have very negative feelings about using cell phones in cars while others don't. What are your feelings about it?*

- **Activities:** Activity questions are great for understanding workflows and can be a good way to start an inquiry about various tasks that people complete.

  Example: *What did you do the last time you got ready for a trip?*

- **Reenactment:** Rather than asking for attitude or opinions, this question encourages interviewees to show you how they behave, given a specific task. This is one of the best questions to ask during an interview.

  Example: *Please demonstrate exactly how you did that.*

- **Identification:** Identification questions are great for uncovering and understanding user behavior and opinion. It's not that you really care who they think would use something. It's the reason they think that way that is important here.

  Example: *Whom do you think would use something like that? For whom would this be inappropriate? Why?*

- **Outsider perspective:** Asking your interviewee about explaining things to others is a great way to expose their own perspective about the same things. It also reveals what they have understood about a feature, what resonates with them, and what is most important about it to them. An extra benefit to this question is that it's a great way to catch your interviewees off guard when it comes to rationalization because they now think about others, not themselves. Long story short, this is a highly recommended question for an interview.

  Example: *How would you describe <feature or activity> to someone who hadn't done that before? What advice would you give to somebody who was thinking about trying that?*

- **Activity comparison:** Comparisons are great for understanding your interviewee's perceptions and perspectives about the comparison's objects.

  Example: *What's the difference between tweeting and sending an email?*

- **Successes and failures:** Asking about blue- and dark-sky scenarios helps you understand your interviewee's expectations, pain points, delights, and motivations better.

  Example: *What would be the worst-case scenario? Can you tell me about a time when this didn't work?*

- **Fill in the blank:** This is another technique adapted from journalism, specifically from live TV interviews. You ask the question, cut it off, and stay silent expecting the interviewee to complete it. This is an extremely powerful technique that makes your interviewee want to fill the void created by silence with a good answer.

  Example: *So in that situation, you. . . [pregnant pause]?*

- **Three wishes:** A great question for understanding current pain points. What really matters here are not the wishes but the reasons for expressing them.

  Example: *If you had three wishes to make this better for you, what would they be?*

2. **Have an arsenal of follow-up questions.** Follow-up questions are in many cases ones that give you the answer you are looking for, and therefore, they are the more important. In most cases, you cannot plan to ask a follow-up question, so you will need to use your best judgment and be ready to use any of the following questions:

    - **Point to participant's reactions, contradictions, paradoxes, non sequiturs, unexpected reactions, or laughter.**

      Example: *Why do you roll your eyes when you say that?*

    - **Clarification:** Ask about anything you don't understand.

      Example: *When you say "her," you mean your daughter, right?*

    - **Reflecting back:**

      Example: *So, what I hear you saying is _____. Is that right?*

    - **Native language:**

      Example: *Why do you call your computer "my brain"?*

    - **Silence:** Trust your question and wait for participants to fill in the gaps.

      A non-intimidating or awkward way to pause is by keeping silent while taking notes. You'll notice that sometimes during the pauses interviewees elaborate or even change their answers. It's a great strategy against rationalizing, too. One cause of rationalizing is that the interviewee did not anticipate the question and so gives the best "placeholder/default" answer she can think of on the spot. With a pause (and taking notes is a nice stealthy way), she has time to think and give a far more considered and credible answer.

- **Why?**

    Example: *Tell me about it. Why is this happening? Why do you think so? Why did you reach out to your phone?*

3. **Build an arc.** Build your interview so that it starts slow and relaxed, with easy questions your interviewee knows the answers to. (What was the last thing you used your phone for?) It continues with the most important questions you have for your participants, including follow-up questions. This is the time to ask core questions in a logical order. That's the top of the arc. Then you can calm things down with easier, lighter-weight questions, wrap the interview up, and thank them.

4. **Consider time and priorities.** Except for the light-weight questions in the beginning and end of your interview, organize your questions in order of priority. Ask the most important questions first. These are the questions that are supposed to help you answer your research questions and meet your research goals. Some interviewees will have very short answers for you and will require a lot of probing and encouragement. Others will not stop talking, give you very long answers, and will make it challenging for you to ask all the questions you plan to ask. Be aware of it when you plan your interview. Always have a prioritized list of more questions than you think can be answered in the time you have. This way, you won't get stuck if you're getting short answers, and you also cover yourself for people who talk a lot.

5. **Uncover and fix biased questions.** It is very easy to unintentionally ask leading questions. Identify these questions and either eliminate or edit them so they become neutral. Here are some examples:

- **Leading question:** *Would you rather use the current version or this new, improved one?*

    Words such as *new* and *improved* tell the interviewee you think it is new and improved; therefore, it leads that person to support you and say good things about the product.

- **Leading question:** *What did you think about that?*

    People don't always pay attention to or think about different things. These types of questions lead them to think about something they wouldn't have necessarily thought about before; therefore, it leads them to unnatural, biased answers. However, if the interviewee spontaneously brings up a topic, then this question is fine as a follow-up.

- **Leading question:** *Please show me how you'd respond to that message.*

    Similar to the previous example, this type of question biases the interviewee by indicating how she would have responded, while in real life, she would probably not have done so.

- **Leading question:** *Would you click here to submit?*

    Asking such a question is the same as saying to the interviewee *Click here to submit!*

- **Leading question:** *What's wrong with this?*

    Using the word *wrong* in this question tells the interviewee that you, the interviewer, think this is wrong, so the interviewee should be helpful and say this is wrong.

6. **Eliminate bad questions.** Bad questions are ones that make it hard for an interviewee to give answers or ones that will not generate reliable answers. Scan your list of questions and either remove or fix these questions:

    - **Predictions of the future.** We have already established that humans are very bad at predicting the future. Therefore, it is pointless to ask what they *would* do. Eliminate any question that starts with the words *would* or *will*. For example, "Would you pay for such a feature if we offer it?"

    - **Instead, ask how your interviewee solves a problem today.** Specifically ask about problems you think your future feature will solve (without mentioning it).

    - **Double-barreled.** Asking two (or more) questions in one is confusing to interviewees. They will either not understand the question or will answer only part of it. Split double-barreled questions into single ones. For example, "Tell me how you discovered and responded to this piece of information."

- **Internal jargon.** Terminology that is only being used and understood by people in your company confuses interviewees. Interviewees do not know what such terms mean and feel embarrassed when you use them in questions as if they are supposed to understand them. For example, "What did you do after you accessed your Adv Tiered Interest Chkg account?"

  Instead, learn about your audience's jargon. Several techniques for that are described in Chapter 8.

- **Unknown terminology.** Similar to internal jargon is terminology the interviewee just doesn't understand. Very few interviewees will say they don't understand certain terminology, and using it in a question puts them in an awkward, uncomfortable position.

  Example: *How does Facebook's Ad Manager compare to the way ad campaigns are created on Google Adwords?*

  Instead, ask questions that lead to what you want to learn step-by-step to figure out what your interviewee uses or understands. For example:

  - When was the last time you advertised online?

  - Show me what you used to run your advertising campaign?

  - Did you ever try a different tool for online advertising?

  - How do you compare these tools?

STEP 6: **Prepare for data collection.**

A great way to analyze interview results and get an answer to the question "Who are the users?" is by using the KJ Technique. The KJ Technique (sometimes referred to as an *affinity diagram*) is named after its creator, Jiro Kawakita, and it allows teams to reach a consensus quickly on results of qualitative data that you collect in interviews.

To analyze data using the KJ Technique, follow these three steps:

1. **Organize the team:** Invite people in the team for a one-hour activity scheduled shortly after the last interview. Make an effort to include people from various disciplines (product managers, programmers, designers, marketers, writers, support, bizdev).

2. **Get hundreds of sticky notes:** During the activity, you'll be asking people to put their observations, opinions, questions, and thoughts on sticky notes, one item on each note. Have enough of these at hand.

3. **Have a large wall:** During the activity, team members will put sticky notes on the wall, so find a space that can handle hundreds of notes.

We'll get back to the KJ Technique in Step 10 when we get to the actual analysis.

STEP 7: Establish rapport.

When people agree to participate in "research," they imagine meeting someone who spends all his time in a lab, wearing a white robe with a name tag, holding a writing pad, experimenting with rats all day long, and wearing rectangular glasses on half his nose.

Then you show up.

All the things you say in the first five minutes—every word, each of your voice intonations, the things you do, your gestures and body language—have a tremendous, sometimes underestimated, effect on your participant's behavior throughout the entire interview session.

The following things to say and do will help you create rapport with your participant. Your participants will perceive you and this whole weird situation of interviewing in a more positive way. Not completely positive, but more positive. Most of these things are also true for first dates. There's a good reason for it.

1. **Smile.** It's our most powerful gesture as humans. Research shows that smiling reduces your stress levels, lifts your mood, and lifts the mood of others around you.[1] It will also make you live a longer, happier life, but that's for a different book.

2. **Look 'em in the eye.** When you look someone in the eye, it shows you are interested. When you do it all the time, it's creepy. Try to look your participants in the eye during the first 10 minutes of the session for at least 30% to 60% of the time—more when you are listening and less when you are talking.

---

1 Seaward, B. L. *Managing Stress: Principles and Strategies for Health and Well-Being.* Sudbury, Mass.: Jones and Bartlett, 2009.

What Is "Rationalization" and Why You Do Not Want One

Most people are extremely happy to participate in research. Humans need to feel they are helpful, and want to be perceived as good people, smart, and nice. The problem with this is *rationalization*. When asked a question about something that happened to them, people almost always change their story and answer differently than what actually happened. They rationalize. They are completely unaware they do that.

People tend to think (often unconsciously) about what a good story or answer might be that would satisfy the person who is asking, or alternatively what answer would make them look good, smart, sophisticated, or nice. And then they give an answer or tell a story that sounds very real and believable. The even bigger problem is that you as the person who is asking the question have no idea whether the answer or story you just heard is true or false.

Here are three tricks you can apply to uncover, avoid, and overcome rationalization:

1. **Double-check:** For very critical questions, verify the answer with another question, if possible. For example, let's assume you are interested in people's book reading habits in a specific domain. You present to your interviewees a list of five books and ask them to tell you which ones they read cover to cover. Since people want to be both helpful and perceived as smart, good, and nice, the answer you might get from many interviewees would include at least one book, while in reality, most haven't even read one book on the list. After asking a few more questions, you can ask a verification question that asks them what a certain term means in their opinion. If you ask about a term that was introduced and explained in one or more of the books you have previously asked if they had read, you can verify if they actually read it. This trick is not always possible and highly depends on the nature of questions you are asking, yet it is the only thing you can use to uncover rationalization. When you have identified a conflict among answers, don't confront your interviewees about it. Just note to yourself that their answers on these specific questions are irrelevant and ignore them.

2. **Very recent past:** Ask about something that happened very recently, e.g., yesterday, last week, the last time, etc. This way, things are still fresh in the minds of your interviewees. Don't ask people to "average" their experience, i.e., to think about their collective experiences and make them into one. For example, don't ask what they do "typically" or what they "normally" or "usually" do. It's easy to fall into this trap even without using these words. For example, when you ask "How do you choose a hotel?" it's a question that asks people to average their experience. What if they chose three hotels in the past year? What your interviewees will do is tell you a story that never happened because they now pick and choose details from different times and places and craft an answer that is not helpful for you because it's not real. They'll also add details to make their answer present them as smart, sophisticated travelers. Avoid such questions by asking about the last time they booked a hotel. Some of your interviewees will respond that the last time was atypical or not normal. Life never is. That's okay. Have them tell you something that happened very recently. That's a great way to avoid rationalization. When you ask people to average their experiences, you're inviting them to rationalize.

3. **Specific, then broad:** When you get (or ask for) a specific example in detail, once you have all the details, ask the interviewee, "Is this how you normally do it?" This way you get the best of both worlds. A specific real example and an idea if it's an outlier compared to their normal behavior. Of course, their normal behavior may be a rationalization, but it might also reveal more than just the one atypical example. You can always probe around the "normal behavior." How many times did you do it that way in the last six months? Why is that the way you normally do it? Why did you do it differently the most recent time?

3. **Avoid verbal vs. nonverbal contradictions.** When your participants identify such contradictions, they will be five times more likely to believe the nonverbal signal than the verbal one.[2] For example, if you say to participants you will not use the study's video recording publicly while you wipe sweat from your forehead three times, they are going to think you are lying. When you are sending inconsistent messages, you are confusing participants and making them believe you are insincere.

4. **Listen.** From the moment you first meet your research participants, listen carefully to every word they say. Show them you care about what they have to say.

5. **Say thank you.** Keep in mind they volunteered to help you. Agreeing to have someone follow you, look at you, take notes about everything you say and do, sometimes in your own home is something you should appreciate and be grateful for. Don't forget to thank your participants from the very first moment. They should know you really mean it.

6. **Check out your appearance.** Make sure that you don't have parsley stuck in between your teeth since you ate lunch. That little piece of parsley will make your participants perceive you as unprofessional, which will not help with establishing rapport.

7. **Read the brief for the interview from a piece of paper, phone, tablet, or laptop.** Tell your interviewees that you read it because you can't remember all of it by heart and that the details are important, and you want the explanation to all participants to be identical. Here is a sample brief you can use. Feel free to modify it to meet your needs.

---

2 Argyle, M., Alkema, F., and Gilmour, R. (1971). The communication of friendly and hostile attitudes by verbal and non-verbal signals. *Eur. J. Soc. Psychol.*, 1: 385–402.

Thanks. First of all, I would like to say that we really appreciate it that you agreed to join us today. It's great to be able to talk with you and have the opportunity to learn from you.

Goal. The reason for this interview is that we are trying to learn as much as possible about people who might use a product we are currently working on. We hope that if we learn that, we will be able to come up with a product that meets your needs and the needs of people like you.

Procedure. Let me give you an idea of what's going to happen in the next hour or so. Basically, what I am going to do is ask you a bunch of questions and ask that you answer them to the best of your knowledge.

Confidentiality. This is a good opportunity to say that we treat this conversation as confidential. We will not share the information you choose to share with us with anyone except for relevant team members and only for the purpose of designing the product. When we do share information internally, your name will not be associated with the findings in any way. The information we collect will never be used for any other purpose without your permission.

Do you have any questions for me about how we will use the information we collect today?

Honest. Please be candid about what you say. You can't flatter or offend me with any comment, so please feel free to share what's on your mind.

Not a test of you. Also, very important—this is not a test of you. We are here to learn from you. There are no right or wrong answers to any of our questions. Your opinions are extremely useful for us and are the main reason we are conducting this interview today.

Withdrawal. Your participation in this interview is completely voluntary. You may withdraw at any time without any consequences. If you feel you want to stop the interview, just let me know. We will stop it on the spot, no questions asked.

NDA. You don't need to sign any legal form today. Having said that, we ask that you please not talk to anyone about the content of this interview.

Do you have any questions for me before we begin?

Obtain consent.

Informed consent means that your research participants are aware of their rights during a research session. It is not about whether they sign a form or not. It's about having people truly understand and agree to the following:

1. They agree to participate in the research session.

2. They understand what is going to happen during the research session.

3. They understand how data collected during the research session will be used.

4. They understand they are being recorded.

5. They agree to being recorded.

6. They understand how the recording will be used.

7. They understand that their identity and privacy will be kept.

8. They understand that participation is voluntary.

9. They understand they have the right to stop the session at any point.

10. They agree to raise any concerns immediately that they might have.

11. They have an opportunity to ask questions before the session starts.

STEP 9: **Conduct the interviews.**

When conducting the interviews, do the following:

- **Have a team member sit next to you and take notes.** It will be much easier for you to focus on listening and asking questions this way. You can switch roles from time to time (not during the same interview, though).

- **Walk a mile in your interviewees' shoes.** Back at the ranch, you can debrief and figure out whether their needs match yours. When you interview, your goal is to collect unbiased data.

Why You *Must* Obtain Consent

I can give you my spiel about how applying the scientific method[3] is important and that obtaining consent from research participants is a key part of it. But I'm not going to do that. Instead, I'll just say that obtaining consent is the right, ethical thing to do even if you are "just talking with people." Half-assing your research ethics, means you're half-assing your learning process, means you are half-assing your product development. Although *informed consent* sounds like a term taken from a court of law, it is not. It is the fair thing to do and the best way to treat people who happen to be your research participants.

- **Try to read facial expressions, body language, and tone, not just words.** Watch for non-verbal cues that don't match words your interviewees say. Look for signs of discomfort, withholding, defensiveness, nervousness, and changes in non-verbals during the conversation. Pay attention to emotional cues such as laughter, cringes, eye-rolling, and sighs. These cues and signs will tell you about areas that are worth exploring more during the interview as they might indicate opportunities to uncover pain points, problems, challenges, and frustrations.

- **Explore cultural differences.** Cultural differences can go a long way toward telling you how a product might meet the needs of different audiences. This is where it is going to be hard for you not to be biased since you belong to a certain culture (or cultures). The first step during an interview is to uncover the differences, then explore them (ask more questions), and hopefully understand them and how they help explain who your users are.

- **Use natural body language.** If your interviewee sits, then you sit next to or across from them. Don't sit behind them (if they use a computer during the conversation), don't lean behind their shoulder, and don't stand up when they sit down. All of these gestures intimidate interviewees and make them feel uncomfortable. This discomfort will bias how they answer your questions.

---

3 A method of inquiry based on measurable evidence subject to specific principles of reasoning (Isaac Newton, 1687).

- **Don't pitch your product.** Don't try to sell your product and don't persuade your interviewees that they need it or should pay for it. A user research interview is not a sales call. Your goal is to learn about users. There will be a time (a different time) for selling the product.

STEP 10: Analyze collected data.

The KJ Technique (mentioned in Step 6 earlier in this chapter) allows teams to reach a consensus quickly on results of qualitative data that you collect in interviews. To analyze interview data using this technique, follow these steps:[4]

1. **Put sticky notes on the wall:** Each team member puts his or her sticky notes with observations, opinions, questions, thoughts, or ideas up on the wall, and then reads other people's notes.

2. **Group similar notes:** Once all the notes are up on the wall, team members silently (no discussion allowed at this point since it will always sway the focus to borderline notes) begin grouping related notes in another part of the wall. Let team members know they are free to move notes into and out of groups that others create. This step is complete when all the notes are placed into groups.

3. **Name each group:** Each team member (again, silently) gives each group a name that best represents its sticky notes and sticks the name note above it. This is a good time to split groups that clearly have two subgroups or merge similar groups. This step forces all team members to read everything on the wall and consider it.

4. **Vote for the most important groups** (also completed in complete silence without a discussion):

    a. Each team member lists on a separate piece of paper the names of the three groups that he or she feels are most important. Remind everyone that the goal is answering the question "Who are the users?" and that they should write down the three names of groups that best answer the question.

    b. Team members prioritize their three selected groups from most to least important.

---

4 See bit.ly/validating-chapter-2-kj.

c. Each team member records his or her votes on each group's sticky note by putting an X for least important group, XX for the second, and XXX for the most important group.

5. **Tally the votes:** Count the votes and put the sticky notes in order on a flipchart. The exercise is now finished, and the team has reached consensus quickly and effectively.

Transform BS personas to personas.

After you have conducted a series of interviews and analyzed the data using the KJ Technique, you're in a better position to craft real, no-bullshit personas. Go back to the persona template and create new personas based on what you heard during the interviews and the outcomes of the categorization exercise you went through using the KJ Technique. You can beef up your persona with photos and add more context for demographics, problems, and solution descriptions.

Additional ways to enrich the personas:

1. Add a short paragraph about the person's habits and behaviors to make it easier to relate to.

2. Add a speech bubble coming out of the face with a typical quote (something you heard from one of the interviewees related to the topic of interest) that helps summarize the persona.

3. Add explanations, context, and background for problem and solution descriptions.

4. Identify and describe clear behavioral similarities and differences among personas.

5. List what else the team should explore to provide more validation to each persona.

Adjust and refine these personas as you learn more about your users or potential users through research.

Other Methods to Answer the Question

While interviewing is an effective way for answering the "Who are the users?" question, the following are two additional methods for answering it. Ideally, if time is on your side, a combination of two to three methods is the best way for uncovering insights to help you answer this question.

- **Observation** is a research technique for learning from people in their natural context of using products or services. It can take you a long way toward learning everything you need to know about a problem and uncovering people's needs. Observation involves gathering data in the user's environment, so it is the science of contextualization. Chapter 3 leads you step-by-step into conducting effective observations.

- In a **diary study**, participants document their activities, thoughts, and opinions and share them with you over a period of time. A diary might be a record of their experiences using a product, or a means of gaining understanding of ordinary life situations in which products might be usefully applied. Diary studies are best for learning about more complex processes. Chapter 4 walks you through how to conduct a useful diary study.

NOTE INTERVIEWING AND PERSONAS RESOURCES

Access the online resource page for interviewing and personas on the book's companion website at leanresearch.co. You'll find templates, checklists, videos, slide decks, articles, and book recommendations.

Interviewing Checklist

☐ Create BS personas.

☐ Decide who, how, and where to interview.

☐ Write a one-page plan.

☐ Find 10 interviewees.

☐ Prepare the interview.

☐ Prepare for data collection.

☐ Establish rapport.

☐ Obtain consent.

☐ Conduct the interview.

☐ Analyze collected data.

☐ Transform BS personas to personas.

Seven months later...

"I'm telling you, this is the Facebook of note-taking," Will said.

"They told us not to call it that," said Dana. "At that meetup. Remember?"

After befriending and working with Will, they'd made a good connection, and they'd co-founded note.io, six months ago. They came up with the idea because Will's note-taking was very inefficient. They figured that, on average, they shared 80% of their code-related notes with friends and colleagues. When they'd come up with the app, it seemed like the perfect solution.

"It's great," Will said, steamrolling over the point. "Especially for a minimum viable product. It's more than ready for a launch."

She agreed, feeling some excitement. She was all about Lean principles. "I've got a landing page set up. The analytics are in place, and we'll be collecting emails from people who are interested in learning when the app's ready to roll out."

"Awesome," Will said. "I'll start whiteboarding the app model."

Dana felt a twinge of caution, but figured it was just nerves. The landing page went live, and they were off and running.

THE LEAN STARTUP ERIC RIES

"I think we need to get out of the building," said Will.

"That might not be a bad idea," she muttered. "We've spent the past four days straight trying to decide among native code, a hybrid app, or a really mobile friendly Web app. We're crossing into obsession territory. I swear—I'm even dreaming note.io." Dana rubbed her temples. "I'm not sleeping well."

"Hey, I'm not sleeping well either. But that's not what I meant," said Will. "I heard it at this meetup I went to a few days ago. Get Out of the Building. It means, you know, talking with users. Stuff like that."

"Talk with them about what?"

Will shrugged. "If they'd buy our app. If they'd pay for it. How much. That **kind** of thing."

"That makes sense," she said. "Who'd you have in mind?"

"Just a few people. Maybe my parents? Your sister?"

"I've got a few friends over at BGC we could ask," she added.

"I think about seven would be a representative number," he said, feeling confident. "Then we'll find out what they say."

After a few days, Will reported back. "They all liked it," he said, feeling smug. "Thought it was a great idea. They'd use it, *and* pay for it."

Dana smiled. "We can't lose!"

CHAPTER 3

How Do People Currently Solve a Problem?

If I had an hour to solve a problem I'd spend 55 minutes thinking about the problem and 5 minutes thinking about solutions.

—Albert Einstein

Amazingly, 198 out of the 200 enterprise product managers and startup founders interviewed for this book said they were keeping a list of product ideas they wanted to make a reality some day. While keeping a wish list of solutions is a great thing to have, even more impressive is what only two startup founders were doing. These founders were keeping a list of problems they wanted to solve. They chose to first fall in love with a problem rather than a solution.

Focusing on learning how people solve a problem as IDEO did for Bank of America can lead to innovative solutions, or in this specific case, a successful service offering. IDEO designers and Bank of America employees observed people in Atlanta, Baltimore, and San Francisco. They discovered that many people in both the bank's audience and the general public often rounded up their financial transactions for speed and convenience. They also discovered that moms were not able to save money due to a lack of resources or willpower. The result married these two observations into "Keep the Change," a Bank of America checking account (Figure 3.1). This account "rounds up purchases made with a Bank of America Visa

How Keep the Change works

Enroll in our Keep the Change savings program and when you make everyday purchases with your Bank of America debit card[1], we'll:

- Round up your purchase to the nearest dollar amount
- Transfer the difference from your checking account to your savings account
- Track your savings in Online Banking

Your Purchase	Item Price	Rounded Up To	Transferred to Savings
	$3.50	$4.00	$0.50
	$5.25	$6.00	$0.75
	$35.49	$36.00	$0.51
		Total transferred to savings account = $1.76	

FIGURE 3.1

Bank of America explains on its website how "Keep the Change" works.

debit card to the nearest dollar and transfers the difference from individuals' checking accounts into their savings accounts." In less than a year, the offering attracted 2.5 million customers, generating more than 700,000 new checking accounts and one million new savings accounts for Bank of America.

Why Is This Question Important?

The question is important because it's the biggest blind spot (Figure 3.2) of the Lean Startup approach and its Build-Measure-Learn feedback loop concept. Getting feedback on a product and iterating is generally a convergent process based on what you know, what you experience in the world, what your friends tell you, what you whiteboard with your team, and what analytics tell you about your product. But sometimes the solution is outside.

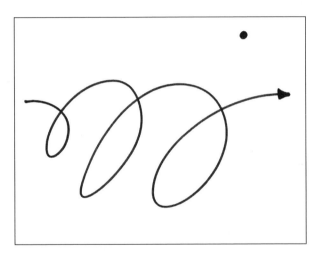

FIGURE 3.2
The value of uncovering observable problems sometimes comes by discovering the blind spot rather than going through the cycles of product iteration (with permission from Benjamin Gadbaw).

The question "How do people currently solve a problem?" is critical, because deeply understanding a problem can go a long way toward solving it with a product, feature, or service. Falling in love with a problem happens through observing it happen in a relevant context, where the problem is occurring to people in your target audience.

The modern GPS network is a great example of how identifying this blind spot resulted in a solution.[1] The GPS network was originally

---

1 Read "Famous products invented for the military" –bit.ly/validating-chapter -3-military.

built in the 1970s for the U.S. Navy and Air Force as a tracking system for planes, boats, and missiles. The Army, however, had always had a problem with mobile ground forces losing their way during a battle. They needed a reliable tracking mechanism for ground navigation. Obviously, the army's need came from real, life-threatening situations where fighting units found themselves in the wrong place at the wrong time or late to arrive to the right place due to mistakes in manual navigation. The personal navigation systems and apps developed for this need are now what we use today as GPS devices on our smartphones.

When Should You Ask the Question?

All. The. Time. Assuming you and your team have fallen in love with a problem to solve, constantly asking (and answering) the, "How do people currently solve a problem?" is critical for achieving Product/Market Fit. Otherwise, after it's too late, you'll find that your audience is already satisfied with a different way of solving the same problem and that your company, startup, or product has become redundant. To be more specific, here are some great times to ask the question (Figure 3.3):

- **When you strategize:** Exploring how people solve a problem today helps you come up with a great idea tomorrow, since the best predictor of future behavior is current behavior. Even if you have a product idea, figuring out the problem it solves might lead you to improve it significantly.

How do people currently solve a problem?

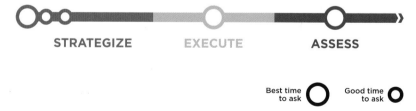

FIGURE 3.3

When is a good time to ask "How do people currently solve a problem?" The big circles represent the best times, while the smaller ones indicate other times recommended for asking the question.

- **When you execute:** Keeping your eyes open even during the development of your product idea can help validate it, fine-tune it, or pivot to a better strategy, if needed. Or perhaps even invalidate it if you find the idea is no longer relevant.

- **When you assess:** Putting your product aside for a moment and bringing fresh eyes to the field to observe how people behave without your product can help prioritize features on your roadmap.

Answering the Question with Observation

One of the most reliable ways to answer the question "How do people currently solve a problem?" is through observation. While not an easy technique to apply, observing people in their natural context of using products or services can take you a long way toward deeper learning about a real problem. Observation involves gathering data in the user's environment, so it is the science of contextualization. *Observation* can be referred to by many names, including:

- Field observation

- Field study, fieldwork, field research

- Contextual inquiry

- Guided tour

- Fly-on-the-wall

- Shadowing

- Ethnography

The different names sometimes indicate how much interaction happens between the participant and the moderator. Fly-on-the-wall and shadowing hint at no interaction, while guided tour and contextual inquiry might indicate there's more of a conversation going on. The only exception to the list of names is ethnography. In classic ethnography, the researcher (that's you) immerses herself among the group she is studying and joins its activities. For example, if family cooking is of interest, the researcher joins a family and cooks *with* them rather than interviewing them, while simultaneously observing what family members do. The truth is that it doesn't *really* matter what you call it. As long as you are observing a person in her natural environment, you are in the observation business.

There are five important pillars for observation:

1. **Observing:** Watching people as they go about their daily lives at home, work, in between, or wherever is relevant to what the product team is interested in. Observing will help you uncover not only *what* happened, but also *why* it happened.

2. **Listening:** Learning the language and jargon people use in their own environments, as well as witnessing conversations they have with others. Listening to people's jargon has an extra benefit of identifying words they use to describe things. For example, when using online banking, many people struggle to find mortgage information because banks use the word *loan* to describe a mortgage. Uncovering user jargon in observation can help you identify language to be used in your product.

3. **Noticing:** Paying attention to a variety of behaviors and occurrences that might have significant implications on user needs. Just standing there watching what people do can be a challenging and overwhelming experience if you don't know what to look for. Looking for and paying attention to behaviors such as routines, annoyances, interferences, habits, etc. turns "just being there" into an effective design tool.

4. **Gathering:** Collecting different things (aka, artifacts) that people use or create to complete certain tasks might signal user needs or missing features or products. For example, an artifact you might find useful if you were conducting an observation in a grocery store would be a person's grocery list.

5. **Interpreting:** Figuring out what the observed behavior means and why the person is doing it that way.

Why Observation Works

Observation is an effective user research technique that carries the following benefits:

- Identifying new features or products
- Validating/invalidating team assumptions about users
- Identifying problems people might have
- Understanding user goals
- Understanding people's workflows

Don't Answer the Question with a Survey

Very few product developers and startup founders ask themselves how people currently solve a problem. Those who ask themselves this question mostly run a survey, or what they call a survey. A survey is probably the easiest, fastest research method you can implement. You can easily field a quick survey about your product within the next 10 minutes. Survey tools nowadays are extremely easy to use and provide instantaneous access to collected data.

That said, a survey is probably the hardest research technique to do right, and I don't encourage you to do it. Running a proper survey is a science that requires expertise. It's very easy to ask very wrong questions in a survey and gather biased, misleading "data." When I need to run a survey, I *always* get advice and work closely with survey experts. You know the statisticians that run exit polls during election season? That's the kind of experts I'm talking about. A survey is a powerful research method that requires skills and knowledge that most product developers don't have.

In summary, the primary problem in bad surveys leads back to the point about attitude and behavior. Bad surveys ask questions about future behavior such as, "Would you use our product?" or "How much would you pay for it?" or "How did you solve this problem?" Good surveys ask questions about facts. Questions such as, "How old are you?" or "Are you male or female?" are good, fact-based survey questions. Yet, life is not black or white. There are, of course, attitude-oriented survey questions that work very well, such as, "On a scale of 1 to 7 where 1 is extremely dissatisfied and 7 is extremely satisfied, how satisfied were you from the check-out process in your last visit to a grocery store?" Running a survey is a good idea if you have the skills to do it right and almost always not right for learning about how people solve problems or uncovering their needs.

Other Questions Observation Helps Answer

Other than the "How do people currently solve a problem?" question, observation is a great method for answering the following questions as well. If you ask yourself any one of these questions, observation can help you get an answer:

- Is there a need for the product?

- Why are people signing up and then not using the product?

- What are some feature ideas our customers have?

- How do people choose what to use among similar options?

- How do we make using this product a habit?

- Does the product solve a problem people care enough about?

- Which customer needs does the product satisfy?

- How do we define the right requirements for the product?

- How will the product solve people's pain points?

- Which features are most important?

- Should we build [specific feature]?

- Who are the product users?

- What are the different lifestyles of potential product users?

- What motivates people?

- What jargon do people use to talk about a specific topic?

How to Answer the Question

The following is a how-to guide that takes you step-by-step through the process of using observation to answer the question "How do people currently solve a problem?"

STEP 1: Find eight research participants.

Finding participants for observation raises a limitation of the method that you should be aware of. Naturally, when you want to observe people, you should be right next to them. This means that you and your participants should be in the same location. However, several situations might happen based on the location of your target audience:

1. Your target audience resides in your location. No problem. Carry on.

2. Your target audience resides in your location *and* in other locations. Try to make an effort to travel to other locations for observation. If traveling is not an option, observe people in your location and apply other research techniques with people in other locations (such as interviewing, experience sampling, or a diary study).

3. Your target audience resides in other locations, some (or all) very far from where you are located. If your most important audience is far away from you, make an effort to travel for observation. If traveling is not an option, you can either be creative with remote observation (ask your participants to broadcast live from their phone as they go about their lives) or apply other research techniques (such as interviewing, experience sampling, or a diary study).

Recruiting participants is *the* greatest bottleneck of user research. Start as soon as you can. Chapter 9 guides you through how to find participants for research through social media. The following are the key steps in this process (previously shown in Chapter 1):

1. List your assumptions about participant criteria (e.g., business traveler).

2. Transform participant criteria into measurable benchmarks (e.g., travels for business at least three times a year).

3. Transform the benchmark into a screening question or questions (e.g., How often do you go on an airplane?). If a person chooses the "right" answer, he's in. If not, he's out.

4. Craft a screening questionnaire (also called a *screener*) that you can send people. (Here is a sample screener— bit.ly/validating-chapter-3-screener.)

5. Pilot-test the screener with a couple of people and make improvements.

6. Identify relevant social media groups, pages, communities, and hashtags where your audience is likely to linger and post calls to take your screener.

Observation generates huge amounts of rich data, somewhat similar to the amounts you might collect in interviewing (see Chapter 2) or diary studies (see Chapter 4). These large amounts of collected data directly affect your choice for the number of participants you observe in the study. As in other qualitative methods, keep this number low and digestible. Eight participants is a good number. More than that requires more time or hands when it comes to analyzing data and coming up with results.

Prepare a field guide.

Before you go to the field to observe people, prepare a field guide that will help you focus on your goals and support your data collection. The first thing on your field guide is a short list of research questions. Research questions are questions that will be answered during the study. Don't confuse them with questions you might ask research participants. They are not the same. Research questions are questions you or the team has. They indicate a knowledge gap you want to fill in with insights. As a ballpark estimate, you should probably have around five research questions. Research questions will help you during observations and will guide you into what parts you need to pay most attention to. For example, here is a list of research questions you might have prior to observing someone during grocery shopping:

- How do people choose which items to buy?

- What are the items people have most difficulty in finding?

- What is the primary challenge people have when grocery shopping?

- In what situations do people use their smartphone to support their grocery shopping? What is the motivation behind it?

The primary goal of a field guide is to help you capture the necessary data during observation sessions. The level of detail in a field guide depends on your level of experience conducting observations and how much structure you need in taking notes. Here are two approaches you can pick from:

- **Less structure:** Create a list of things to pay attention to and look for while keeping an open mind about new, sometimes surprising, things that will reveal themselves to you during observation. If you are a person who trusts her intuition, do just that and allow yourself to add to the list or deviate from it as observation progresses. Here is a sample such list for a grocery shopping observation:

  - Problems we want to observe: Challenges in grocery shopping such as deciding what to purchase, finding items, or wasted time.

  - Problem could occur when: Participant stalls, doesn't know where to go, asks for help, looks repeatedly at grocery list, or calls spouse.

- Details to be recorded: Full description of observable problem, time spent on solving problem, participant's decision tree, participant's motivation to solve the problem, external factors affecting problem or solution (technology, other people), or chosen solution.

- Back-up strategies if the problem/behavior is not happening: Ask for a retrospective demonstration as close to the real thing as possible, ask what was challenging, ask participant if what happened was typical; if not, probe to explore past challenges.

- **More structure:** Structure your note taking and prepare as many placeholders as possible to save time during observations and make sure you pay attention and document everything you need. Structure the field guide so that it begins with simple, specific questions your participant feels comfortable answering. Then go broad and list questions or behaviors to look for that are broader, and finally after setting the context for more targeted questions, finish with deeper probes that will help you with your innovation challenge. Figure 3.4 is a screenshot from a sample field guide for grocery shopping you can use as a reference (find it here: bit.ly/validating-chapter-3-sample-field-guide).

Go broad

5. The perfect grocery shopping is:
- _____
  because _____
- _____
  because _____
- _____
  because _____
- _____
  because _____

6. The worst grocery shopping is:
- _____
  because _____
- _____
  because _____
- _____
  because _____
- _____
  because _____

7. During grocery shopping, I love it when this happens:
- _____
  because _____
- _____
  because _____
- _____
  because _____

Probe deep

8. Grocery shopping artifacts:
- Artifact: _____
  Used for: _____
  Why: _____
- Artifact: _____
  Used for: _____
  Why: _____
- Artifact: _____
  Used for: _____
  Why: _____
- Artifact: _____
  Used for: _____
  Why: _____

FIGURE 3.4

A screenshot from a sample, structured field guide for grocery shopping (bit.ly/validating-chapter-3-sample-field-guide).

What to Communicate to Participants Up Front

Observation is one of the hardest research methods to explain to people whom you want to participate. Naturally, when you ask people to become their shadow for a couple of hours, a full day, and sometimes even longer, most of them resist, especially if you ask people to observe them at their home or workplace. Therefore, it is essential you communicate very clearly what you are asking of them, set the right expectations, get their consent, and have them commit to participate if they understand and agree.

Honesty is your best policy here. If there are likely intrusive situations, be very explicit about it. If they don't agree, then don't waste your time. It can be very frustrating to find out on observation day that there is an issue.

Communicate the following up front:

- The reason for observing them
- Where physically you expect to hold the observation
- Potentially intrusive situations
- What you expect them to do
- How you will record the session (photos, video, audio)
- Time you will show up and leave, expected length of session
- How many team members will attend
- The incentive

The strategy I use for communicating a request for observation is to first put "a foot at the door" through email. Here is a sample script I like to follow. Feel free to use it while customizing it to your needs:

> "Hello,
>
> My name is Tomer Sharon, and I am a user experience researcher at [name of company]. I am following up on a questionnaire we sent you about an upcoming research study I am conducting.
>
> We at [name of company] wish to learn more about [be as general as possible about your topic of interest] how people do their grocery shopping, and hopefully come up with related products or services that meet your needs and the needs of people like you. I would like to join you for an upcoming grocery store visit and interview you as you do your shopping. Let me emphasize that I am not trying to sell you anything, and I do not wish or intend to interfere with your day or waste your time.

If you want to learn more details about participating in this study, I'd be happy to give you a call and explain more.

Thank you for cooperating!

Tomer Sharon

UX Researcher, [name of company]

[Phone number]

[Email address]"

If the participant shows interest, I cover the following on a phone call. Notice how I expose more requests after the participant already showed interest following my email:

1. I would like to spend 3-4 hours with you and observe you doing your grocery shopping. I'd like to start at your home for the first hour, then go with you to the store, and join you for one more hour at home immediately after you finish at the store.

2. I will use the time you allow me to join you mostly in observing how you go about your grocery shopping and ask you questions about it.

3. This research study is very important to us since there are many engineers who develop great products but have never met a customer they develop for. One of the goals of this study is to get engineers to learn more about the people they develop for.

4. To make sure I report the right information back to the team, I am collecting all sorts of data in this study. For example, would you mind if I take a few pictures during this session? Photos help me capture key things I learn from you.

5. Would you mind if I video record my visit? (If not, would it be possible to record only audio?)

6. As I said, this is a great opportunity for people at [company] to really learn about your needs. There are a few people who really want to join me when I visit you. Would it be possible to have one or two more people from the team join me?

7. Do you have any questions for me about this research study?

During the phone conversation, I make sure the participant agrees to the following deal breakers: time commitment, taking pictures, a team of three observers, and giving consent.

Brief observers.

Assign people in your team who join observation sessions with roles such as note-taker, photographer, and videographer. Conduct a brief meeting during which you give observers a short background about the participant and about what's going to happen. Dedicate enough time to discuss expected participant actions and your reactions. An observation might present uncomfortable situations for participants, moderators, and observers.

In a typical observation, a small team, consisting of a moderator and two to three observers, visits a participant in her natural environment such as home or work. The challenge of the team is to overcome situations that might cause participants or other stakeholders (e.g., a participant's spouse or manager) not to cooperate or to put a complete halt to the session. The observer brief is a great opportunity to discuss potential participant reactions during observations and ways to overcome them with appropriate reactions by the team. The more prepared the team is for these situations, the higher the chances are to defuse them.

Following are several situations that might come up during observation sessions and how you should react. The purpose here is not to intimidate you, but to have you be aware of and prepared for unexpected situations that might happen.

How to Decide on How Many Observers?

Sometimes the "lone wolf" approach is required: if the observation needs to be very subtle or covert, if it's critical that the impact on natural behavior is minimal, if it's imperative to blend in quickly, or if the intended behavior happens in a very small space or the topic is very personal.

Sometimes the team approach is better: when more detailed documentation is required, when the participant is completely comfortable, when all the locations that will be visited are likely to or have already given permission, or when the participant is scheduled with and briefed (as opposed to observing people in the wild without them knowing).

However, the bigger the team, the less natural everything will be, and the harder it will be to ensure that it is natural.

1. **The participant is reluctant to share what's on his computer/ phone.** ("Let me go to my bedroom where the computer is, find the answer to your question, and quickly get back here.")

   - Prevention: Ask more personal questions or requests when you are getting on well with the participant. Feel the energy. Spend time building rapport and try to make these requests later in the session.

   - Explain why you are so interested. Have a story prepared for how you are trying to help people, how important your research is, and how many people could benefit.

   - Don't take photos of the participant's screen.

   - In your notes, indicate "return to topic" next to what happened throughout the early parts of the session and try again later if you feel it is right.

2. **The participant refuses to hold the session at the most relevant location.** ("My office is really small so I don't think we can all fit.")

   - Ask if you can pass by his desk or study room or bedroom (wherever the relevant location is) on the way out just to get a feeling of his home or workplace ("That's totally fine. We don't mind sitting on the floor." Or you could ask "Can we pass by on our way out just to get a feel?").

   - If appropriate, ask if you can take a picture of the relevant room or area.

   - Don't push too hard on this.

3. **The participant thinks too many people showed up.** ("Wow, a whole crew!")

   - Apologize if it wasn't communicated clearly enough in advance.

   - Make the participant feel like a superstar: "You have been specially selected because you are so interesting and important. The team wants to model its product on you because you represent the ideal customer so much, but, of course, it will only be worthwhile if you are really honest and act completely naturally."

   - Explain that it is important for team members to attend since they want to learn from her knowledge and experience.

   - Explain that observers will not be very active during the session.

- Worst comes to worst, ask one to two observers to leave. Best thing to do is to completely avoid this situation altogether. Have a maximum of three people show up for observation. If more people want to observe, create an observation shift schedule.

4. **The participant refuses to be photographed or recorded.** This refers to a situation when the participant initially agreed, but when you actually take the camera out or even after you take a few pictures, he is clearly uncomfortable with it or directly asks you to stop.

   - Prevention: Mute the camera's "click" sound and use a smart-phone, which is less intimidating than a huge SLR camera.

   - Prevention: Let the participant know you will ask permission every time you want to take a photo, and he can say no at any time. You will respect his privacy and understand that certain situations should not be recorded.

   - Explain that photos are extremely important for this study since they show important decision-makers in your company that there are real people behind your recommendations.

   - Offer to show him all the photos you took when the session is over and allow him to delete ones he is not comfortable with.

5. **The participant does not answer the questions.**

   - Prevention: Ask the question and stay silent. Your participant will feel an urge to fill in the vacuum with an answer.

   - Try to find out if there is anything that makes her uncomfortable. If you are in a team, you could take the participant aside for a one-to-one meeting. This could be to find out if she feels uncomfortable or to get more detailed data on your own.

   - Tell a story. It can either be about you (something relevant) or about another participant (anonymous, of course) who had similar opinions or experiences. It can show that there is nothing embarrassing about the situation, because you come across it all the time and you can relate to it personally. It also helps to make you more human, likeable, and friendly.

   - If the participant insists, move on.

6. **The participant invites others to join.**

   - Find out who the others are and why they want to join. It might become an advantage by having additional perspectives and seeing how the person behaves in front of friends.

   - Explain this is an individual session and that you cannot have others join it.

   - Explain it is important for you to get his personal perspective.

   - Give up if he insists. Sometimes, it's even the right thing to do.

7. **The participant says she doesn't use X.**

   - Explain that the products she is using are not the focus of the session.

   - Say, "Interesting. What do you use to solve for _____?"

8. **The participant's manager/spouse is not aware of what's happening.**

   - Repeat the introduction sections dealing with goals, procedure, confidentiality, and documentation to the manager or spouse.

   - Apologize that the other person wasn't informed of this in advance.

   - Ask for permission to continue.

   - If you are kicked out, leave quietly. Make no fuss about it.

9. **The participant is nervous, stressed, or physically uncomfortable.**

   - Telling a story can help break the ice. Sometimes pointing out that he seems nervous can make it more awkward, but changing the energy with a story can be a stealthy way to deal with it. Talking to the participant like a friend will help make it seem less like research. The story could be about another participant and how she helped to develop a great solution that solved real-life problems others had.

   - Offer to take a short break.

   - Answer questions the participant has about the session.

   - Sneak in another mention of your confidentiality commitment.

   - If you feel he is at a distress level that is too much, stop the session, politely apologize, and leave.

10. **The participant wants to finish earlier.**

   - Try to figure out why and answer her questions.

   - If she mistakenly scheduled a conflicting event, ask how much time you have, promise to finish on time, and keep your promise.

   - Reschedule for another day. Split the session, but still get all of your data.

11. **You want to finish a few minutes later.**

   - As soon as you realize you need more time, ask the participant if that's okay. Don't do it when time is up.

   - Tell the participant how much more time you will need. Keep your promise. Don't ask for more.

   - If the participant doesn't agree, thank her and finish on time even if you didn't get to ask everything you wanted to.

STEP 4: Practice!

It's a short yet critical step. Gather the observer team, recruit a fake participant (a colleague perhaps), and practice observation for 15–20 minutes. This will help with setting expectations, getting used to paying attention to important things, note-taking, taking photos, recording video, invading personal space, not bumping into one another, and other small logistics stuff that would prevent you from wasting precious time or looking stupid and unprofessional.

STEP 5: Gather equipment.

Whatever equipment you decide to take with you, keep the following in mind:

   - **Small cameras:** Large video cameras with tripods intimidate participants and make them change their behavior. It's enough that three people are there to look at them and document their every move. Don't add to that feeling. Consider using a GoPro (or a similar small size) camera. The size of the camera creates a better feeling than showing up with a four-foot tripod and a high-quality, full-size video camera. There's no rule you have to video record observation sessions. Consider video recording if there are team members who cannot attend sessions yet are interested in watching them, or if you feel you will need to come back to your team with stronger evidence.

- **Smartphones as cameras:** Instead of large or dedicated video cameras, consider using your smartphone as a video and a still photo-recording device. Most people are more or less used to seeing a phone held in front of their face.

- **Quiet cameras:** Silence your camera. Clicks and beeps intimidate participants and remind them they are being recorded, which will cause them to deviate from their natural behavior.

- **A shot list:** This is a list of photos you hope to take—the person's portrait, an artifact, a contextual shot of their space, etc.

- **Extra batteries:** Batteries drain. Take a lot of spare ones for everything that requires charging.

- **Chargers:** Take charging equipment in case you will have an opportunity to charge while in the field. Cables, plugs, dongles, and power splitters can become extremely handy. When you get to an observation location, immediately survey the area to identify power sockets. If there are any, ask for permission to use them. Do that after you establish rapport (see next step). If you don't expect to have a power outlet in your observation area, consider taking with you a charging device or even a fully charged laptop from which you'll charge your other devices.

- **Memory cards:** Make sure that you have spare memory cards for phones, cameras, and videos. Remember to check them and take previous data off so that you have maximum space. Try to calculate how much you will need—for example, if one hour of video recording takes up 4GB, then take enough memory cards or change the recording quality. Don't run out halfway. If you are recording in HD, then consider the implications of how you will store and transfer files. How much space do you have on your laptop if you're in the field and need to transfer every day?

- **NDA:** This is a non-disclosure agreement that describes the confidential aspects of your study as well as why and how you use the recordings and data you collect. There might not be a need to ask participants to sign an NDA if you are not showing them anything confidential. However, sometimes, you might want them to sign one to protect the method you are using and the questions you are asking, which might indicate a confidential aspect of your business.

- **Incentive:** If you promised the participant money or a gift, make sure you take these with you.

- **Audio recorder and lavalier microphone:** While a big bulky camera is intimidating, a recorder and lav is quickly forgotten and ignored by participants.

- **Save juice:** Make sure that you limit your device usage during observation days to observation needs. No Twitter, Facebook, or texting with friends. Watch those cat videos when you're back at home.

- **Office equipment:** Take notebooks, pens, and pencils in case all hell breaks loose. I know it's hard, but I guarantee you will quickly learn what to do with them in case all of your device batteries are drained.

- **Post-it notes:** Taking notes during observation sessions on Post-it notes can save you precious analysis time later on. Get a pack of colored Post-it notes, one color per participant. Make sure that you have enough of them so that every observer can use a pack in each observation session. So, for example, if you plan to observe 6 people and you have a small team of 3 observers, you will need a minimum of 3 blocks of red Post-it notes, 3 blue blocks, 3 yellow, 3 green, 3 purple, and 3 orange blocks.

- **Mints** and **Water.**

STEP 6: Establish rapport.[2]

When people agree to participate in "research," they imagine meeting someone who spends all his time in a lab, wearing a white robe with a name tag, holding a writing pad, experimenting with rats all day long, and wearing rectangular glasses on half his nose.

Then you show up.

All the things you say in the first five minutes—every word, each of your voice intonations, the things you do, your gestures and body language—have a tremendous, sometimes underestimated, effect on your participant's behavior throughout the entire interview session.

The following things to say and do will help you create rapport with your participant. Your participants will perceive you and this whole weird situation of interviewing in a more positive way. Not completely positive, but more positive. Most of these things are also true for first dates. There's a good reason for it.

---

2 Similar to Step 7 in Chapter 2.

1. **Smile.** It's our most powerful gesture as humans. Research shows that smiling reduces your stress levels, lifts your mood, and lifts the mood of others around you.[3] It will also make you live a longer, happier life, but that's for a different book.

2. **Look 'em in the eye.** When you look someone in the eye, it shows you are interested. When you do it all the time, it's creepy. Try to look your participants in the eye during the first 10 minutes of the session for at least 30% to 60% of the time—more when you are listening and less when you are talking.

3. **Avoid verbal vs. nonverbal contradictions.** When your participants identify such contradictions, they will be five times more likely to believe the nonverbal signal than the verbal one.[4] For example, if you say to participants you will not use the study's video recording publicly while you wipe sweat from your forehead three times, they are going to think you are lying. When you are sending inconsistent messages, you are confusing participants and making them believe you are insincere.

4. **Listen.** From the moment you first meet your research participants, listen carefully to every word they say. Show them you care about what they have to say.

5. **Say thank you.** Keep in mind they volunteered to help you. Agreeing to have someone follow you, look at you, take notes about everything you say and do, sometimes in your own home is something you should appreciate and be grateful for. Don't forget to thank your participants from the very first moment. They should know you really mean it.

6. **Dress to match:** If you normally wear a suit and you're meeting a customer in her home who may be wearing sweats and a t-shirt, you might come off intimidating. Likewise, if you are a hoodie and sneakers type meeting someone in a professional setting, then dress to match that setting. You don't want to be disrespectful. Always ask the participant if he would like you to take off your shoes in his home. You are his guest.

---

3 Seaward, B. L. *Managing Stress: Principles and Strategies for Health and Well-Being.* Sudbury, Mass.: Jones and Bartlett, 2009.

4 Argyle, M., Alkema, F., and Gilmour, R. (1971). The communication of friendly and hostile attitudes by verbal and non-verbal signals. *Eur. J. Soc. Psychol.*, 1: 385–402.

7. **Check your appearance:** Make sure that you don't have something stuck in your teeth. That piece of gunk will make you look unprofessional, which will not help with establishing rapport, as stated in Chapter 2.

STEP 7: Obtain consent.

As stated in Chapter 2 and bears repeating, informed consent means that your research participants are aware of their rights during a research session. It is not about whether they sign a form or not. It's about having people truly understand and agree to the following:

1. They agree to participate in the research session.

2. They understand what is going to happen during the research session.

3. They understand how data collected during the research session will be used.

4. They understand they are being recorded.

5. They agree to being recorded.

6. They understand how the recording will be used.

7. They understand that their identity and privacy will be kept.

8. They understand that participation is voluntary.

Why You *Must* Obtain Consent

As I said in the last chapter, I can give you my spiel about how applying the Scientific Method[4] is important and that obtaining consent from research participants is a key part of it. But I'm not going to do that. Instead, I'll just say that obtaining consent is the right, ethical thing to do even if you are "just talking with people." Half-assing your research ethics, means you're half-assing your learning process, means you are half-assing your product development. Although *informed consent* sounds like a term taken from a court of law, it is not. It is the fair thing to do and the best way to treat people who happen to be your research participants.

---

5 A method of inquiry based on measurable evidence subject to specific principles of reasoning (Isaac Newton, 1687).

9. They understand they have the right to stop the session at any point.

10. They agree to raise any concerns they might have immediately.

11. They have an opportunity to ask questions before the session starts.

STEP 8: **Collect data and pay attention.**

The hardest thing to do during field observation is to pay attention to everything that is going on in front of your eyes. You might not realize it, but observing how humans behave generates tons of rich data. It is sometimes challenging to notice when something important happens. Your guide as to what to look for is to stay focused on the reason that you are running this research in the first place and the goals you have set for user research. Focus on things related to your goals. When you are observing a study participant, look for the following occurrences:

- **Routines:** Routines are things that seem to be regular actions the participant is following. For example, each time a new work-related task comes up, the participant logs it on a spreadsheet that he has created. This routine can later turn into a feature in your product.

- **Interactions:** Follow her interactions when a study participant uses a certain product, tool, or service, or when she converses with another person. For example, when a study participant doesn't understand a certain word, she might use an online dictionary to figure it out.

- **Interruptions:** An interruption might occur when a study participant stops a task or breaks its continuity either because he has decided to do so or because another person caused it. For example, when a phone call comes in and diverts the study participant from what he is doing. Note that it is intuitive for the researcher to ignore these interruptions, yet in many cases they can teach you a lot. Life is not always "clean" of interruptions so we must understand them.

- **Shortcuts/workarounds:** When a study participant chooses a shorter alternative, it is sometimes an indication of a small problem to pay attention to. For example, when instead of writing something down, a participant takes a pen and marks an X on the back of her hand. What that means for your product or people's needs is not clear when you observe it. Yet this behavior might relate to a different one you observe that might make sense later on.

- **Contexts:** *Context* occurs when a certain action or behavior is demonstrated in a different manner because of the environment in which it happens. For example, when a participant does not take a note on his smartphone because of direct sunlight that makes it hard for him to see anything he types.

- **Habits:** These are behaviors participants demonstrate that are almost automatic. For example, scribbling something with a pen to make sure it works, even though it is brand new.

- **Rituals:** A ritual is an established sequence of behaviors in a particular context that cannot be explained purely in terms of being functionally necessary. It's almost optional or voluntary; for example, buying a drink if it's someone's birthday and singing happy birthday to them.

- **Jargon:** Paying attention to the language and jargon people use in their own environments, as well as witnessing conversations they have with others, is extremely helpful in empathizing with them and uncovering their needs. Using the unique language people use when they talk about different things will prevent you from using language your audience doesn't understand in your product or service. For example, if a person you observe keeps referring to a *mortgage*, that's a good signal for you to use this label in your online banking app rather than calling it a *loan*. You might learn that people interpret the term *loan* very differently than how you or your team does. It's also a good cue to mimic their language in the observation session in order to appear less different and to build rapport.

- **Annoyances:** Annoyances are obstacles that keep people from completing their tasks or achieving their goals. An annoyance would not necessarily prevent them from reaching their goals, but it would make them angry, frustrated, overwhelmed, or disappointed along the way. For example, a person might get annoyed while filling out an online form while dealing with noise from a nearby room.

- **Delights:** The things people enjoy can teach you a lot about what they need. Many people perceive research as an activity that uncovers problems and frustrations. That's partially true. Uncovering things that delight and work well for users can go a long way toward developing great products. For example, you might notice people who are satisfied by in-field form validation instead of validation done after submitting the form.

- **Transitions:** When people move from place to place, it's a great time for them to share things that might become invaluable—especially when they think the research session is over or on a temporary pause. For example, if you observe someone taking notes in a certain classroom, pay extra attention to what happens when the class is over and until you part ways with the participant.

- **Artifacts:** Artifacts are tools, services, products, any other thing that people use to complete tasks, or seemingly useless yet meaningful objects (such as rubber duckies for developers). Your job is to pay attention to the usage of artifacts, and if possible, collect or document them. For example, if a person is taking notes while using a LiveScribe pen and notebook, that's an important artifact to take note of, no pun intended.

Here are some additional pointers to note in order to get the most out of observation:

- Approach each observation session with an open mind. You'll find that in many cases, you invalidate your initial assumptions about people and their problems and reach insights you never realized.

- Have a conversation with the person, not an interview. Don't just go through the motions of what you planned. If you feel there's something to talk about that's worth the time, make the time for it. Don't feel you must stick to the script.

- Let your participants be. Don't interrupt or talk over them. If you do, they'll avoid sharing additional things with you, and you might be missing key insights.

- Pitch your level of knowledge to match the participants. Try not to make them feel like you're more knowledgeable than they are.

As you observe, that's a lot to track and digest. You need a lot of practice to get it right. Don't worry, though. Even if you miss a few things, you'll still get to learn many valuable lessons and you'll get better in time.

As I mentioned earlier in the chapter, there are multiple names and flavors for field observations. What you'll do next is practice data collection in two very different flavors.

Imagine that Stop & Shop, a northeastern U.S. grocery shopping retailer, came to you with this question "How can we improve the in-store grocery shopping experience with technology?" You decided to observe people do their grocery shopping to better understand their needs.

Watch two videos of field observations held at a Stop & Shop grocery store in New Jersey and write down your observations. Do that with the list of things to look for that I introduced earlier.

In the first video, I asked the study participant to think aloud and describe what she was doing and why. When she talked about things she would do, I asked her to show me how she did them. When I had a question, I asked her. Watch the video and identify as many things worth paying attention to as possible. Don't overanalyze things and don't think of how what you see can be translated into features and products. Focus on gathering insights.

Observation video 1: bit.ly/validating-chapter-3-observation-video-1

In the second video, I asked the participant to completely ignore me. I didn't ask her to think aloud, nor did I ask her any questions during the session. Watch this session and try to look for routines, interactions, interruptions, shortcuts, contexts, habits, rituals, jargon, annoyances, delights, transitions, and artifacts.

Observation video 2: bit.ly/validating-chapter-3-observation-video-2

STEP 9: **Debrief.**

A common mistake is to assume that every observer interpreted the same things you did or placed similar value on certain observations. Debriefs and syntheses are a process of creating a shared understanding so that the team can move forward in a unified direction. Debriefs will help you capture your insights while they are still fresh in your mind and will decrease the load of analysis and synthesis that awaits you after all of the observations are completed. There are two types of debriefs, the quick debrief and the daily debrief.

After watching these two very different approaches to field observation, figure out what works for you. The big advantage of the approach demonstrated in the first video is that you know exactly what the participant is doing and why. The disadvantage is that asking the participant to talk creates a bias. They hear themselves, process it, and then self-monitor what they do and say. They think too much. It's probably not representing reality very well. On the other hand, there's the more silent approach. The big advantage is that you watch reality. This is what truly happens. The big limitation is that you don't always understand what is going on and why.

I can't say that either of these approaches is good or bad, but you should definitely always use one of them. Sometimes thinking aloud makes more sense; sometimes silence is more helpful. And sometimes a combination of the two approaches is what's needed. There's no prescription for what works when. You would need to make a judgment call and see what works for you and your participants. In time, the more experience you gain, the better you get at understanding what to do when.

To complete your practice exercise, here are the two videos including annotations with observations:

Annotated observation video 1: bit.ly/validating-chapter-3-annotated-video-1

Annotated observation video 2: bit.ly/validating-chapter-3-annotated-video-2

Quick Debrief

Shortly after you are done with each field observation session, conduct a quick debrief with observers. Do it in the lobby of the building, in the train, cab, or bus, in a park, on a bench, wherever. The most important thing is to conduct the debriefing shortly after the session ends so that things are still fresh in your mind. This will also prevent you from getting confused if you run several sessions in one day. In addition, take five quiet minutes to yourself and write a short paragraph that summarizes the session.

During the quick debrief, ask yourself and the observers the following four questions (inspired by IDEO's human centered design kit[6]):

1. What did the participant say or do that surprised you? Were there any memorable quotes?

2. What mattered most to the participant?

3. What stood out during this session? What are the big lessons?

4. What should we do differently in future sessions?

If you'd like to try this debriefing technique, run a quick debrief for the second field observation video you watched in the sidebar after Step 8.

Daily Debrief

When you conduct several observations per day for several days (e.g., two half-day observations every day for three consecutive days), gather the team at the end of each day in front of a large wall and run the following exercise (aka, affinity diagramming):

1. Put all of your Post-it observations on the wall.

2. Organize them into temporary, logical groups. The groups can change from daily brief to daily brief.

3. If you used unique Post-it colors per participant, you'll notice very quickly which groups of observations were popular among different participants and which ones were only observed with one or two participants (see Figure 3.5).

FIGURE 3.5
Affinity diagramming wall during a daily brief.

---

6 bit.ly/validating-chapter-3-ideo-design-kit

4. Take photos of the wall (these Post-it notes tend to fly off).

5. Log groups and items into a spreadsheet.

6. Continue working on affinity diagramming until data collection is completed.

What to Do with Photos

Photos you took during observation sessions provide inspiration, visual context, and sometimes, supporting evidence for your findings. The idea is to fill your design space with inspiration from the field. Here are some ideas:

- Organize photos based on groups of observations you identified during debriefs.

- Curate topical photo galleries.

- Print a photo of each participant to remember that person.

- Cover a wall or board in photos from the field and tag them with observations.

STEP 10: Analyze and synthesize.

There is no one way to make sense out of observation data you collect. That said, affinity diagramming combined with storytelling is a straightforward approach that seems to work for teams. Here are the steps to complete an affinity diagramming and storytelling exercise:

1. Complete the affinity diagramming exercise you started in the daily debriefs. Sort all of the observations into groups and give each group a name. Alternatively, you can do that by implementing the KJ Technique.[7]

2. As a team, select the most important and meaningful groups.

3. Per group of observations, write a short story that describes a future scenario of a person using a product or feature that doesn't exist yet. The story can be very short—about 150–200 words. Base the story on a problem or need you identified during observation.

4. Share the stories with the team, gather feedback, and get agreement and shared understanding.

---

7 See Chapter 2, Steps 6 and 10.

Imagine one of the most meaningful observations was a problem that parents had while keeping up with their kids' activities around the house. Here is a story that might come up from such an observed problem.

Jen and Bob were still in bed on a Sunday morning at 10:15 a.m. Their two boys woke up at 6:30 a.m. and went downstairs. "What are they doing?" Jen asked Knowly. Knowly turned on the video feeds from the den that showed Owen playing the Xbox and the basement feed showing Andy watching a live English Premier League game on TV. The kids knew they should tell Knowly what they were doing each time they started a new activity. They had been relatively good at this. "What did Andy do since he woke up?" asked Bob. Knowly projected Andy's reported activities along with pictures on the bedroom's ceiling. Downstairs, Knowly reminded Owen that he needed to read 95 minutes today if he wanted to meet his monthly goal of 2,000 minutes. Knowly reminded him that morning was the time he most enjoyed his reading. "Knowly, I am now reading *Harry Potter and the Philosopher's Stone*," Owen responded, and an update appeared on his schedule, which was projected on the ceiling of his parents' bedroom. Knowly tracked how long Owen read and added the data to his reading log.

Other Methods to Answer the Question

While observation is a great, immersive way for answering the "How do people currently solve a problem?" question, the following are two additional methods for answering it. Ideally, if time is on your side, a combination of two to three methods is the best way for uncovering insights to help you answer this question.

- **Interviewing** is a research activity in which you gather information through direct dialogue. It is a great way to uncover and understand people's feelings, desires, struggles, delights, attitudes, and opinions. Interviewing people whom you know to be your target audience (and those you think are not) is a great way to get to know your users, segment them, design for them, solve their problems, and provide value. An interview can be held in person or remotely over a phone or some kind of a video conference. Chapter 2 guides you through conducting interviews for uncovering needs.

- In a **diary study**, participants document their activities, thoughts, and opinions and share them with you over a period of time. A diary might be a record of their experience using a product or a means to gain understanding of ordinary life situations in which products might be usefully applied. Diary studies are best for learning about more complex processes. Chapter 4 walks you through conducting a useful diary study.

NOTE OBSERVATION RESOURCES

Access the online resource page for observation on the book's companion website at leanresearch.co. You'll find templates, checklists, videos, slide decks, articles, and book recommendations.

Observation Checklist

☐ Find eight research participants.

☐ Prepare a field guide.

☐ Brief observers.

☐ Practice!

☐ Gather equipment.

☐ Establish rapport.

☐ Obtain consent.

☐ Collect data and pay attention.

☐ Debrief.

☐ Analyze and synthesize.

Dana scanned the screen. "We're all over Techcrunch!"

Will was practically doing a victory dance. "We are *killing* it!"

She threw her hands up. "Boom!"

"We have no competition!" Will crowed.

She scrolled through the mentions. "We're going viral for this category. I don't think anything else like this exists."

"All we need is one-percent market share," said Will, and he got that look in his eyes—the one that said he was already envisioning how he was going to spend the IPO money. "We're social, mobile, local, international, *and* Lean!"

She started to shift from the mentions to the
actual analytics, and felt her buoyant attitude
begin to sink. Will didn't notice.

"We are *Zuckerberging* it! All those investors
who turned us down just don't get it."
He grinned. "One billion dollar company, baby!
Nothing's gonna stop us!"

"Well, there is one thing," Dana said, her
voice low.

"First to market! Double-*boom*!"

"Will!"

He stopped, mid cheer. "What?"

"Why do people sign up for note.io and then...
not use it?"

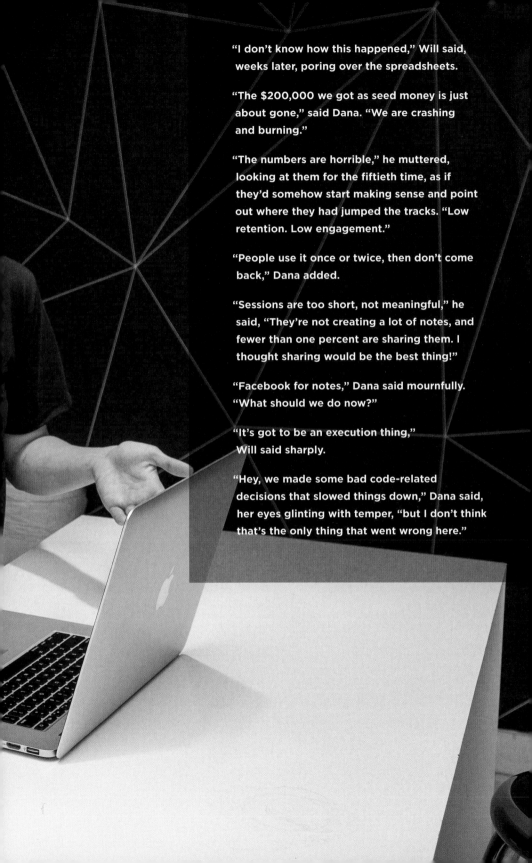

"I don't know how this happened," Will said, weeks later, poring over the spreadsheets.

"The $200,000 we got as seed money is just about gone," said Dana. "We are crashing and burning."

"The numbers are horrible," he muttered, looking at them for the fiftieth time, as if they'd somehow start making sense and point out where they had jumped the tracks. "Low retention. Low engagement."

"People use it once or twice, then don't come back," Dana added.

"Sessions are too short, not meaningful," he said, "They're not creating a lot of notes, and fewer than one percent are sharing them. I thought sharing would be the best thing!"

"Facebook for notes," Dana said mournfully. "What should we do now?"

"It's got to be an execution thing," Will said sharply.

"Hey, we made some bad code-related decisions that slowed things down," Dana said, her eyes glinting with temper, "but I don't think that's the only thing that went wrong here."

Will sighed. "Maybe we just walk away. Try something new."

"Just because it didn't work right away doesn't mean we just quit," she said. "We don't just run away. We can start over."

He didn't want to start over if it wasn't going to be a guaranteed winner. But the part about running away stung. He'd stepped away from plenty of projects, sure. But *running away* sounded bad.

"Maybe we just can't work together," he snapped, then immediately felt badly.

"Okay, now I'm going to get out of the building," she shot back, "and when I come back, you'll either be here and ready to work, or you'll be running. Right now, I don't care which!" And she slammed the door behind her.

CHAPTER 4

What Is the User's Workflow?

A user workflow is a process where a person takes sequential steps toward achieving a goal. A workflow has an entry point and a final goal. Your ultimate goal as a product developer is to uncover your users' workflow to complete tasks you want to support with your product. Uncovering this workflow will guide you into designing a product that matches real-life workflows and improves them. This chapter will walk you through a lean user research technique called a *diary study*, which will help you understand user workflows, needs, and motivations.

Why Is This Question Important?

When people have a certain, specific way of completing a task, yet the digital product that is supposed to help them complete it forces them to change their ways, friction occurs.

Your users' workflow is key to understanding how they function, especially for complex tasks such as planning a vacation, learning how to play a new musical instrument, learning about a health-related situation, buying a new car, etc. There are certain steps in a person's workflow that are necessarily sequential and would never happen before other steps. For example, if a businesswoman is planning a trip to another city for a few days, her workflow might look something like this:

1. Schedule meetings.

2. Book flights.

3. If needed, reschedule meetings based on flight schedule.

4. Book a hotel.

5. Reserve a rental car for the destination city.

6. Reserve a car service for pickup at the home airport.

Let's assume that this businesswoman wants to use a new app she heard about that is supposed to help with all of her trip's reservations while offering good prices. If the app is going to force the businesswoman to first reserve a car and then book flights and a hotel, this workflow creates friction. It does not make sense for the businesswoman to reserve a rental car first before she knows her final flight schedule. What is happening here is a workflow mismatch. If many of this app's users are like our businesswoman, that workflow mismatch is going to be a huge barrier for its success.

Asking and answering the question "What is the user's workflow?" is critical for understanding and learning about complex, relatively long processes, people's habits, and tasks where a specific sequence of actions is involved.

When Should You Ask the Question?

"What is the user's workflow?" is a question far too few product developers answer at the right time. However, there are two great times to ask the question: somewhere in the middle of strategizing your product and after launching it during the assessment phase (see Figure 4.1).

- When you strategize, you figure out a lot of things about the need for your product, your target audience, and what it wants. After you attain this knowledge, it is a good time to start learning about your potential users' workflow. This workflow wisdom will serve you well during the execution phase, when you design the product iteratively.

- During the assessment phase, your users use the product, and you can learn whether or not your product matches their real-life workflow. Beware, though. If this is the first time you study your audience's workflow, you might find and learn things that will be very hard to fix. Implementing workflow changes in a product might get very costly. The best time to answer the question is prior to execution.

What is the user's workflow?

STRATEGIZE   EXECUTE   ASSESS

Best time to ask ○   Good time to ask ○

FIGURE 4.1

When is a good time to ask "What is the user's workflow?" The big circle represents the best time, while the smaller ones indicate other times recommended for asking the question.

Answering the Question with a Diary Study

One of the best ways to learn about your users' workflow is through a diary study. In a diary study, participants document their activities, thoughts, and opinions and share them with you over a period of time. A diary might be a record of their experience using a product or a means to gain understanding of ordinary life situations in which products might be usefully applied. You then analyze the diary data and conclude information about their workflow, habits, and needs.

Data collection takes relatively longer than your typical usability test or interview, and might last days, weeks, and sometimes (depending on the topic, product, and industry) months and years. Diary studies are best for learning about more complex processes such as implementing a new nutrition plan, solving more challenging problems such as planning a sprinkler system for your house, or learning about how physical mail (mail that arrives with an actual postal worker) travels around the house.

In a diary study, participants are given instructions, expectations, and a kit or a tool to use for posting diary entries. They then document their activities, interactions, and attitudes. Depending on the tool used, participants either share their diary entries with you immediately or send a paper diary after data collection is completed. Typically, a diary study ends up with an interview during which participants are debriefed about their experience after you have read all of their diary entries. The outcome of a diary study can be communicated in many ways such as a workflow visualization, a journey map, personas, etc.

Why a Diary Study Works

A diary study is excellent for getting a glimpse into people's lives in a very detailed way. It is great for learning about any type of workflow for the following reasons:

- Uncover what participants actually do.

- Reveal behavior that would be hard to remember in interviews or surveys.

- Generate high-level detail and specificity about different workflow activities.

- Explore participant activities for workflows that last long periods of time or occur at times that are not reasonable for observation (e.g., late night or early morning).

- Neutralize the bias of having someone observe what participants do.

- Understand how products factor into regular habits.

- Assess a novelty effect (quickly getting better at using something new) or learnability (how much a product supports users in learning how to use it).

Other Questions a Diary Study Helps Answer

Other than the "What is the user's workflow?" question, a diary study is a great research method for answering the following questions as well.

- How often would people use the product?

- How do people from other cultures use the product?

- How do people currently solve a certain problem?

- Does the product solve a problem people care enough about?

- Which user needs does the product satisfy?

- What are the different lifestyles of potential product users?

- What motivates people?

- What jargon do people use to talk about a domain?

- Do people enjoy using the product?

- How does the product fit into people's lives?

- What are people's specific habits?

- Do people want the product?

- Where do people use the product?

- When do people use a product?

- How easy or hard is it to learn how to use the product?

How to Answer the Question

The following is a how-to guide that takes you step-by-step through the process of using a diary study to answer the question "What is the user's workflow?"

STEP 1: Choose diary type and structure.

One of the first decisions you need to make is about the structure of the diary study. There are two alternatives: structured or unstructured.

A structured diary is one where you are very specific about what participants share, when they share it, and how they share it. Structuring a diary study can be done in several ways that can be combined:

- **Structure by event:** When it is important for you to learn about specific occurrences in a workflow, ask participants to add posts to their diary when certain things happen. For example, if you run a diary study to learn about participants' workflow in the first week of trying out a new product, you can ask them to add the following diary posts:

  - Unboxing the product (if relevant)

  - First impressions

  - First interaction

  - First problem or challenge with the product

  - Questions about the product

  - Requests or complaints

- **Structure by time interval:** When it's critical to capture participants' behaviors or attitudes in specific times or days, ask them to contribute diary posts by time intervals. For example, if you are interested in people's morning sequence, ask for diary entries every morning.

- **Structure by post format:** Sometimes, it is important that participants communicate their diary contribution in formats different than text. For example, a video diary might be useful when you want to overcome the bias that comes with a diary as a self-reported research technique. You might ask participants to record a video during their morning commute. Or you might ask participants to take still photos of how they cook a certain dish, or of the process of installing a new sprinkler system in their backyard. You might also ask participants to communicate certain actions in a sketch, which they update as the study progresses.

- **A combination:** There are no limitations on choosing a specific structure, and you can always mix and match structure types to tailor the best way to learn from people during a diary study. For example, you might combine a time interval with an event-triggering structure, such as asking participants to document their behavior before, during, and after watching the Super Bowl game.

An unstructured diary is one where you leave it to your participants to decide what to share, when, and how. You may give them options and direct them in terms of focus topics (e.g., only post about things related to using your newly bought drone), but generally speaking, your participants are in control of their diary contributions. A good reason for choosing this alternative is when you are not sure about what specifically you are after or what to expect from participants. When you want to learn about a process you have almost no knowledge about, you might ask participants to just post to their diary anything related to that process. A more open-ended approach to a diary study structure has a big advantage of not limiting your participants to any type of contribution, which might lead you to more meaningful, unexpected insights.

STEP 2: **Set up a data collection tool.**

A traditional approach to collecting diary study data involves sending participants a physical kit. Depending on your study goals and the type of information you want to collect, a kit might include a diary booklet, a camera, high-quality office equipment, graph paper, and anything that might help participants record their diary entries. Study participants then use the contents of the kit throughout the study and mail it back when they are done. Kit materials are then reviewed and analyzed.

Nowadays, diary study data collection is more digital in nature. Diary study tools might be as simple as sending an email, leaving a voice message, using SMS or MMS, or filling in a form. Diary study data can also be collected through private blog posts, shared documents (such as a Google doc or spreadsheet), or dedicated diary study web apps. A third group of digital diary study tools include the usage of instant messaging apps such as WhatsApp, Facebook

Messenger, Google Hangouts, Viber, and more. Lastly, several apps offer dedicated diary study capabilities that allow participants to post rich diary entries that include text, photos, video, audio, current location, current weather, a time stamp, and even motion activity (see Figure 4.2). Some of these apps make the data easily shareable or exported. The resource section in the book's accompanying website (leanresearch.co) includes a list of currently available diary study apps.

FIGURE 4.2
Diary app: Day One offers motion activity capturing.

This chapter references Facebook Messenger as its diary study data collection tool, yet any previously mentioned alternative is recommended (at least for experimenting). Choose a tool that will be the easiest for your participants to use and won't force them to learn how to use yet another poorly designed digital product. Be open to using multiple tools in one study. For example, if you intended to use WhatsApp, yet some of your participants don't use Instant Messaging at all, feel free to have some participants use different tools than others. You'll be merging all the input after they are all done into one place, so it's not extremely important to have all the participants use the same tool. The exception is if you want to collect a certain piece of data that only one tool allows you to gather (for example, current location on a map).

STEP 3: Carefully recruit eight research participants.

Finding people who both qualify and are willing and available to participate in a diary study is harder to do, compared to other research techniques described in this book. The reason is the amount of effort and self-discipline required for keeping a diary.

To find participants for a diary study, follow the steps described in Chapter 9. These steps guide you through identifying the characteristics of whom to invite, preparing a screening questionnaire, and using social media to call for relevant people to fill in the questionnaire to see if they qualify to participate.

As you compile your screening questionnaire, put extra attention on the following:

- The success of a diary study (i.e., whether or not it provides valid and reliable results) is highly dependent on the expressive ability of participants since most of what they'd be required to do during the study is to answer open-ended questions (even in a structured format) in a way that would help you understand what they mean. Therefore, make sure that your screening questions ask people to express themselves a little bit to give you a sense of their writing ability. If you feel it is needed, speak with them over the phone to get a sense of whether they are suitable for the study.

- A diary study might take some time. Make sure that your participants don't have prior commitments such as a long vacation during the planned study duration that would prevent them from completing their ongoing diary assignments (that is, of course, assuming that you are not interested in a diary study related to vacations).

- It is hard to find people who will meet all of your diary study requests. Therefore, make sure that participants understand and accept the level of effort required. Provide clear numbers to demonstrate the effort and include a mandatory screening question that verifies they understand this commitment. For example, ask "Are you aware and willing to spend up to 10 minutes *every day* of the 14 study days, from Monday, March 10, to Sunday, March 23, on writing diary posts?"

- The best way to capture complete data in a diary study is to end it with an interview once the diary part of the study is over. Inform your participants (and make sure they are available) that you'll be conducting an in-person or remote interview shortly after they complete their diary.

Here is a sample screening questionnaire I have prepared for a video game diary study I conducted for this book. Read it and feel free to borrow questions for your upcoming diary study: bit.ly/validating-chapter-4-screener.

Diary studies generate huge amounts of rich data, somewhat similar to the amounts you might collect in observation (see Chapter 3) or interviewing (see Chapter 2). These large amounts of collected data directly affect your choice for the number of participants you include in the study. As in other qualitative methods, keep this number low and digestible. Eight participants is a good number, yet any number between 6 and 12 participants makes sense. More than that means this is a large study. If that is the case, you will need more time or hands when it comes to analyzing data and coming up with results.

STEP 4: Prepare instructions and brief participants.

After you have lined up participants for your diary study, send them written instructions in which you set expectations, provide guidance, and specify diary assignments (in case it is a structured diary format). Your written instructions should include the following (see the sidebar for sample diary study instructions):

- Diary study goals
- Study dates

- Incentive

- Diary tool to be used

- General instructions

- Daily plan (mostly needed for a structured diary format)

- Point of contact person and details for questions

Figure 4.3 demonstrates how one diary study participant followed the instructions in the sidebar.

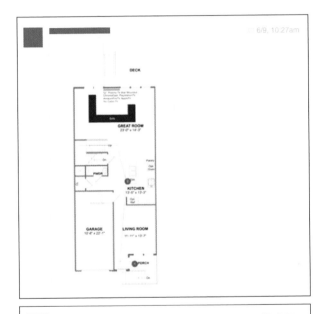

FIGURE 4.3
First posts to a diary study following instructions.

Video Game Diary Study Instructions

Thank you for participating in this study!

Goal

The goal of this diary study is to learn about your thoughts, habits, and behaviors in the first few days of trying out a new video game.

Dates

The study duration is 7 days, and I ask that you invest up to 10 minutes in the study every day. The study will last from Day 1: Monday, June 8 until Day 7, Sunday, June 14.

On Wednesday, June 17, at 2 p.m., you will be interviewed over Skype for an hour about your diary experience.

Thank You

As a token of our appreciation for your time and willingness to participate in this study, we have sent you a video game with a cost value of $60, which you can keep for yourself after the study is completed.

Diary Study Tool

During the diary study, you will use Facebook Messenger to share diary entries with me through short text messages, photos, and short videos. Unlike other times you use Facebook Messenger, during the study I will not respond to most of the material that you post. However, I might remind you of your diary assignments or ask some questions.

Instructions

I have purchased and shipped a video game to you. Starting when the package arrives, document your thoughts, activities, and experience of trying the game out.

- The study duration is 7 days, and I ask that you invest up to 10 minutes in the study every day. You can, of course, play the video game for more than 10 minutes a day.

- Each day, post as many times as you desire. Make sure that you at least meet your daily task with one or more diary entries.

- During the study, I may ask you to answer different questions about the video game.

Daily Plan—Please Read All of It Now!

- **Day 0:** Grab a piece of paper and draw a pencil sketch of your house. It doesn't have to be perfect or accurate. Focus on what the different rooms are, where the TV is, and where you play the game. We will use it to indicate where the video game is located physically. Take a photo of your sketch and send it to me through Facebook Messenger.

- **Day 1** (the day the game arrives):

  Describe in detail everything that happened today related to the game from the moment it arrived at your home. Should be something like that: "1. It's here!" "2. Unboxed it just now." and so on.

  Tasks for the entire duration of the study:

  From now on, send me a Facebook message each time you start and finish playing the game. Facebook will log the time.

  Use your sketch from Day 0 to indicate daily where the game is physically using a red number in a circle. So a red circle with the number 1 in it will be the game's first physical location in your house, the number 2 would indicate the second location, and so on. Draw red lines between the numbers to indicate the route through which the game got to all of its locations. After each time you add a number to the sketch, take a photo of the sketch and send it to me through Facebook Messenger. Let me know if there are no changes in the location.

- **Day 2:** Describe your first impression of the game. What's it about? How did you know? What's the goal?

- **Day 3:** Describe the first interesting interaction you've had with someone related to the game.

- **Day 4:** Describe with photos the first problem or challenge you've had with the game.

- **Day 5:** List three complaints you have about the game.

- **Day 6:** List three things you like about the game.

- **Day 7:** Evaluate your progress playing the game. How are you doing? What have you learned?

- **Any time:** Feel free to share any text, video, or photos to indicate your actions and thoughts about the game throughout the study duration.

Contact Details

If you have any questions for me, please do not hesitate to contact me by sending me a message through Facebook Messenger with your question at any time before, during, or after the study.

STEP 5: **Launch the pilot and then the full study.**

A day, few days, or a week prior to the launch of the diary study is a great time for a pilot. A pilot tests the diary study by asking participants to share one diary entry with you. This one entry from each participant is valuable on oh-so-many levels since it makes sure that participants did the following:

- Installed the diary study tool.

- Understood how to use it.

- Troubleshooted any problem they might have had with the tool.

- Understood and internalized what is expected of them.

- Provided enough details in their entries.

- Responded in a timely manner.

- Were reassured the study is really happening. (Some people agree to participate, although they are skeptical.

Once you have launched a pilot, you'll probably find that you need to adjust a lot of things. Instructions will become clearer, structured diary assignments will be changed and improved, participants will be debriefed, and diary tools will be installed and explained. Everything will become smoother for you and your participants. It's time well spent that will make sure that you hit the ground running during day one of the study. In fact, you'll never regret running a pilot test. Once you have finished learning and implementing the lessons learned during the pilot, launch your diary study and immediately start tracking and monitoring your participants' behavior to make sure that you get the data that you need.

STEP 6: **Prompt participants for the right data.**

As soon as the diary study starts and participants begin posting the entries, make an intentional effort to read each entry and evaluate its usefulness to you. If you don't understand certain words, sentences, or actions, or if you don't think the participant is providing enough details, ask immediately for clarifications. The same goes for any other entry that participants post to their diary throughout the study. There's no need to ask follow-up questions and conduct full interviews through instant messaging, but make sure that you are getting what you need compared to what you asked for from the participants (see Figure 4.4).

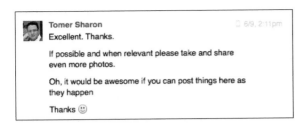

FIGURE 4.4

During Day 1 of the study, one of the participants shared fewer photos than I expected and chose to post at the end of the day while providing time stamps for everything that happened during the day related to the video game. I gently asked him to share more photos and post when things happened, not at the end of the day.

If participants don't understand what you mean and ask for examples, try not to give them. If you give a specific example for a "good" diary entry, you'll find that most of the diary entries from that participant will be very similar to the example you provided. Refrain from biasing participants this way by responding to the example request by saying that entries should be detailed enough so that you can understand what they mean. Ask for photos if they help, support, or even explain better what the entry is about. Provide feedback for the photos that participants submit. (What a great photo! Or too close, too far, too dark, or out of focus.)

STEP 7: **End with interviews.**

The goal of holding an interview with each diary study participant at the end of the diary part of the study is to fill in gaps in the participant's diary, ask follow-up questions, ask for clarifications, understand reasons, causes, and the context for various behaviors, actions, and reactions.

See Chapter 2 for a step-by-step guide into conducting effective interviews (Steps 5 to 10 are extremely helpful for planning and conducting interviews).

STEP 8: **Reframe diary data.**

As you might expect, a diary study produces enormous quantities of raw data. Turning it into a meaningful, insightful body of knowledge requires a systematic and rigorous approach. One of the most effective ways of synthesizing and analyzing a diary study data is to find and understand hidden relationships between diary study entries across participants. These relationships can help create new meaning, ideas, and solutions related to users' workflows. To achieve all of that, reframe your collected diary data by tagging each entry using a tool that allows you to tag text entries and then explore them based on the tags you created. There are many such available tools and services. For demonstration purposes, Reframer by Optimal Workshop is used here for such an analysis.

Reframer allows you to tag data (see Figure 4.5) and generate a comprehensive view of the most meaningful findings of the study by exploring it based on those tags to uncover themes and critical findings (see Figures 4.6 and 4.7).

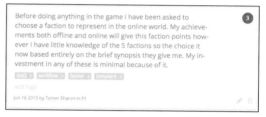

FIGURE 4.5

Tagging a diary study entry in Reframer.

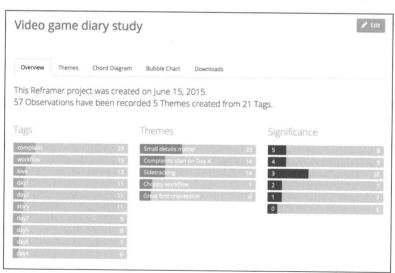

FIGURE 4.6
Uncovering diary data themes with Reframer.

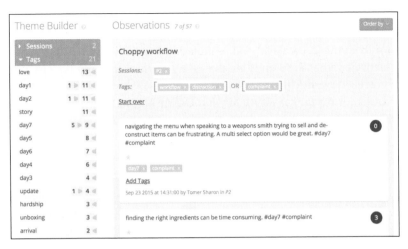

FIGURE 4.7
Exploring diary study entries with Reframer.

STEP 9: **Construct workflow.**

After you have reframed your diary study and interview data and identified commonalities, themes, and interesting relationships related to the participants' workflow, it's time to answer the question you started with, which is "What is the user's workflow?"

A Sample Workflow Constructed from Diary Entries

User Workflow: New Video Game

1. Game arrives at home via mail.

2. Unbox game.

   a. Check receipt.

   b. Enjoy cover art.

   c. Check out giveaways (photos, stickers).

3. Insert game in console.

4. Update game with patches.

5. Pick a faction.

6. Figure out story.

7. Play through the story.

8. Talk with friends about the game.

9. Understand game pros and cons.

10. Read online about game tips.

11. Finish story.

The answer is a numbered list of steps in the user's workflow that includes a name for each step, a short verbal description, a quote or two from the diary itself, and a photo if it helps communicate the essence of what the step is about (see a sample steps workflow in the preceding sidebar). If you asked participants to sketch where a product or thing was physically located throughout the study, such sketches could also support the workflow (see Figure 4.8).

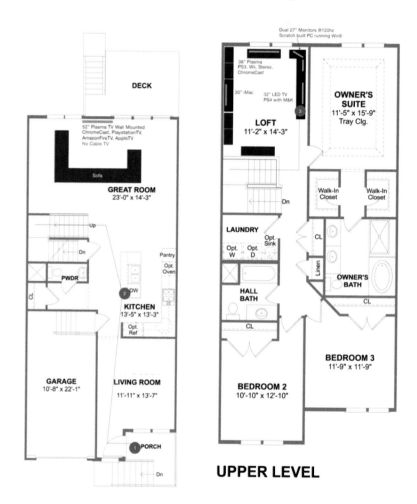

FIGURE 4.8

Asking participants to indicate where a certain item of interest is placed around their home to better understand their workflow.

Other Methods to Answer the Question

While a diary study is a rich, reliable way for answering the "What is the user's workflow?" question, the following are two additional methods for answering it. Ideally, a combination of methods is the best way for uncovering insights to help you answer this question.

- **Observation** is a research technique for learning from people in their natural context of using products or services. It can take you a long way into learning everything you can about a problem and uncovering people's needs. Observation involves gathering data at the user's environment, so it is the science of contextualization.

- **Interviewing** is a research activity in which you gather information through direct dialogue. It's a great way to uncover and understand people's feelings, desires, struggles, delights, attitudes, and opinions. Interviewing people whom you believe to be your target audience (and those you think are not) lets you get to know your users, segment them, design for them, solve their problems, and provide value.

> **NOTE** **DIARY STUDY RESOURCES**
>
> Access the online resource page for a diary study on the book's companion website at leanresearch.co. You'll find templates, checklists, videos, slide decks, articles, and book recommendations.

Diary Study Checklist

- ☐ Choose a diary type and structure.
- ☐ Set up a data collection tool.
- ☐ Carefully recruit eight research participants.
- ☐ Prepare instructions and brief the participants.
- ☐ Launch the pilot and then the full study.
- ☐ Prompt the participants for the right data.
- ☐ End with interviews.
- ☐ Reframe diary data.
- ☐ Construct workflow.

"Low engagement. Low retention. That can only mean one thing," Clark, a startup weekend mentor, said to Will and Dana over lunch.

"What's that?" Dana asked.

"Your product sucks."

Will coughed on his iced tea. Dana pulled her lips into a tight line. She and Will had sworn to stick with note.io, but look for outside guidance to help them identify what the real problem was.

Still, this wasn't what she'd expected.

"Our product is great," Will countered. "All we need is more users. So..."

Clark held up a hand. "I love how passionate you guys are, and I know this is the last thing you want to hear. But you're wrong. Your product is fundamentally broken."

Will's expression was mutinous.

A blonde woman with a stylish purple shirt stepped up to their table. "Guys, this is Jennifer," Clark said, motioning for the woman to join them. "She's an experienced user researcher with 15 years of experience in high-profile companies, and she's helped a lot of startups. I want you to talk to her."

"What problem does note.io solve for people?" Jennifer asked.

Dana could tell Will was growing more and more irritated, so she answered. "Note.io *creates* a need. It's not about solving an existing problem, necessarily. We provide our users with a note taking experience that leaves them speechless. In a good way," she added, with a smile.

Jennifer smiled back. "Still, bottom line: you're not solving a problem."

"I don't understand," said Will. "What's the problem? A lot of people told us they loved the idea and that they would be willing to pay $5 for our app. It's an execution flaw. Aren't we supposed to talk about how to make the UI better?"

"We *are* going to make the design better," said Jennifer. "But first, a few questions."

Dana could practically hear Will grinding his teeth. She glared at him, and he fell silent.

"When you first came up with the idea for note.io," Jennifer continued, "how did you know people really needed it?"

"I'm not sure we really knew the answer back then," said Dana.

"*I* definitely knew the answer," Will snapped. "I knew I would be a customer, so others like me must be interested, too. 100% of the people we talked to said that they liked the idea. For me, the needs were validated."

Dana looked at Jennifer, hoping the woman wasn't getting offended. Jennifer seemed to simply be listening patiently.

"Besides, we found very efficient ways for saving and serving user content across social platforms," Will continued. "I still believe this is a better way to process data in apps."

"Smart people invested in you," said Jennifer, and Dana was relieved when Will calmed down somewhat. "There's probably something there, but you two have to find it. I'm here to help you do that, but you've got to work with me and follow my lead. Now, are you in for the ride?"

Dana nodded. Will, she noticed, was still grimacing, his arms crossed in front of his chest.

CHAPTER 5

Do People Want the Product?

Mmm..." I thought to myself as I was reading Nate Bolt's Facebook post about the Automatic app (see Figure 5.1). "A smart driving assistant? One that hooks up to my car's computer and sends data to an iPhone app that will help me save energy and money? *I want that!*" (See Figure 5.2.)

I ordered an Automatic two minutes after I saw that post. It cost me $70. At the time, the product wasn't shipping yet, and I was paying to participate in a beta that was going to start in a few months. Usually, I'm extremely skeptical about such things. But this was different. I really wanted that thing. I thought the idea was brilliant, and I was 100% positive that I would use and love it. The beautiful, smooth Automatic website and purchasing workflow reassured me that I could trust my instincts. When the Automatic package arrived at my doorstep a few months later, I was happy. Unboxing it was very "Apple-like," and onboarding was great. I hooked the Automatic car adapter to my car (somewhere under the steering wheel where I was able to find the data port quickly), installed the app, and made sure it worked when I drove the car.

FIGURE 5.1

Nate's Facebook post and my comment to it.

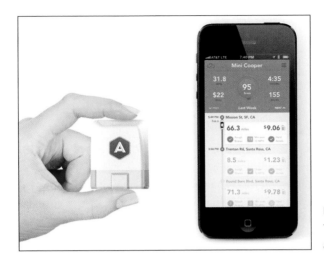

FIGURE 5.2
The Automatic Link
and app.

I didn't really understand what the app was for and what information it presented. "Give it some time," I thought to myself. "Maybe it's learning the car and my driving and will soon present useful information." The app was very well designed. It was beautiful. However, at some point I wasn't sure I was doing everything right, or perhaps I just needed to invest a little more time in trying to figure out what was going on. I didn't get it.

A few days after I installed it, my wife went with the kids to one of their baseball league games 45 minutes away from our home on a weekday evening. It was a cold fall night and when the game was over she found herself in the car with three kids, including a four-month-old screaming, tired baby and a car that wouldn't start. The car was relatively new, without any history of issues, and no mechanical failures at all. "Take it out," I suggested. Immediately after my wife pulled the Automatic car adapter out of its data port, the ignition started. That ended up being our Automatic's swan song. I didn't want it anymore.

Maybe that's a big coincidence, maybe it's me, or maybe the car breaking down had nothing to do with the Automatic. I have no idea. And I'm not mad at Automatic. I'm sure they have a great product. The point is that when I bought it, I wanted it without any clue whether I needed it or not.

One of the most interesting questions that product development practitioners, entrepreneurs, and investors ask themselves is "Do people want the product?" In other words, once people read, hear, or talk about or interact with the product, would they want to buy and use it? This question is interesting, since it can be perceived as a critical question to get an answer to; however, it is not really a question about design and user experience of products, but rather one that concerns marketing them.

User researchers are sometimes uncomfortable answering this question with different methods such as focus groups, opinion polls, and Net Promoter Scores (NPS) because these methods focus on what people think rather than what they actually do. However, the *Lean Startup* management approach has brought to life several lightweight, nimble, and non-wasteful research techniques. These techniques force research participants to demonstrate a behavior that indicates what they want. By that, they help generate useful results to answer the *wants* question.

This chapter will walk you through two fun, effective research methods that provide an answer to the question "Do people want the product?" without writing one line of code. Actually, with one of the methods you will need to write two to three lines of code, but no more than that, I promise.

Why Is This Question Important?

The question "Do people want the product?" is important for understanding and learning about the state of mind of your target audience after it is exposed to the product or some kind of communication about it. Answering this question is key in making *you* more aware of current pain points of your audience. When people express a wish by demonstrating a certain behavior, they imply there's something wrong in the world and that they care about it. This is exactly what you look for when you are on a quest to validate your key product and user assumptions.

Why the *Want* Question Is Different

What people want is a question that can be asked and answered before a specific product or service even exists. It is a question that affects product marketing and communication more than its design and features. Yes, when you ask people what they want, their answer includes products, features, and services. Yet they have no idea what they are talking about. They sound believable, but they're not. They're not bad people, and they are not liars. Basically, they have no clue, but they think they do and want to be helpful. That's human nature. In order for people to want a product or perceive it as something they need, three things must happen:

- **They must know about the product.** Your marketing and public relations channels must meet your audience.

- **They must understand the product's value.** Words, images, demos, and videos must communicate the value of the product and make potential customers feel it solves a problem or meets a need they have. The exception is that sometime, when non-important purchasing decisions are made, people tend to fudge the understanding of the value.

- **They must agree to the product's cost.** Potential customers must accept the price point and be willing to pay what you ask for the product.

Note that all of the above has nothing to do with product design, unlike the rest of the questions discussed in this book.

When Should You Ask It?

You should ask yourself the question "Do people want my product?" all the time—right when you have an idea, when you make a lot of progress with building and developing the product, and definitely after you launch it. Keep doing that. By asking the question *before* you actually build the product, feature, or service, you are reducing waste—time, resources, and energy (Figure 5.3). The more you learn about what people want before you build anything, the less time and effort you will spend on redundant code, hundreds of hours of irrelevant meetings, and negative emotions of team members when they realize they wasted their blood, sweat, and tears on something nobody wanted.

What do people want?

STRATEGIZE   EXECUTE   ASSESS

Best time ⭕ to ask   Good time ⭕ to ask

FIGURE 5.3

The big circle represents the best time to ask what people want, while the smaller ones indicate other times recommended for asking the question.

Research techniques covered in this chapter involve some manner of pretending you have a product or service, and therefore require you to create a manual, prototype, or page that is a key component used during research. It is a great time to ask the "wants" question when you have such a manual, prototype, or page.

Answering the Question with a Concierge MVP and Fake Doors Experiment

To answer the question "Do people want the product?" you must first understand what an MVP is and what it is not. An MVP (minimum viable product) is the process of creating "a version of a new product that allows the team to collect the maximum amount of validated learning about customers with the least amount of effort."[1] In other words, an MVP is a way to quickly validate, or most likely invalidate, an assumption.

An MVP is not version 1 of the product. As a matter of fact, some MVPs are not even products. For example, it could be a contract you try to persuade potential customers to sign and learn if they show enough interest. Or it could be a prototype with minimum functionality that allows its creators to test it with a subset of potential users to avoid building something people do not want. An MVP is not a cheaper product, nor it is a minimal version of a product with the

---

1 Ries, E. *The Lean Startup: How Today's Entrepreneurs Use Continuous Innovation to Create Radically Successful Businesses*. New York: Crown Business, 2011.

smallest possible feature set. Think of an MVP as a series of experiments and research activities with the sole goal of helping you learn. Table 5.1 summarizes what an MVP is and is not.

TABLE 5.1 DEFINING AN MVP

An MVP Is	An MVP Is Not
A process that allows its creators to validate or invalidate assumptions quickly with a subset of potential users	A cheaper product
A prototype with minimum functionality that facilitates learning	A minimal version of a product with the smallest possible feature set.
An experiment to learn about potential users	Designed to scale across the entire customer base
	Version 1 of a product

Concierge MVP

Both Concierge MVP and Fake Doors are minimum viable products. The Concierge MVP is an MVP where you manually provide the functionality of the product to the customer. You guide your user through the solution to a problem. For example, Open Snow is a startup from Boulder, Colorado. It's a team of meteorologists who specialize in (and are passionate about) weather forecasts for skiing resorts and destinations. They solve the problem of the non-existent, specific, and detailed snow sports weather forecast. Skiers invest a lot of time, money, and effort in planning ski trips. These trips might be canceled due to wrong (or too general) weather reports for the area, or even worse, skiers can go ahead with a trip only to find out that the actual weather does not permit any sports activity. Open Snow solves all of that.

One way of going about providing this service to skiers is developing an app or a website that can gather a person's skiing plans and push snow sports weather reports in a timely and effective manner. The Concierge MVP approach is much simpler, less wasteful, and more effective for learning what skiers want. Rather than investing their time and money into building even a primitive version of an app or website, Open Snow can visit ski resorts, approach potential customers in person, and offer them the service they envision the app or website will eventually deliver. When they find someone interested in the service (for free at first), they will continue to provide value to the customer via email. They might ask interested customers to shoot them an email when they need a weather forecast for a ski resort and then respond with a full forecast to the customer's inbox. Eventually, they should ask customers to pay for the service. The act of a customer who chooses to pay for a service serves as validation to Open Snow's assumption about what people want.

Another great example for an MVP is how the founders of Get Maid chose to validate their idea. Get Maid is an app for booking a home cleaning service. The founders first created a front-end app that would send them a text message. They would call their network of maids and see who was available and then text the customer that the appointment was confirmed once they found a maid. This is an example of a more high-fidelity approach to an MVP, yet still one that does not involve fully developing the product.

Fake Doors

A Fake Doors experiment is a minimum viable product where you *pretend* to provide a product, feature, or service to a Web page or app visitors. Without developing anything just yet, you communicate to visitors that the thing exists and ask them to act on it. If they do, you know they want it, and it's time for you to start working on developing it. For example, imagine a grocery store website. If the store is thinking about developing a grocery shopping app and wants to know whether customers are interested or not, a call-to-action button could be added to the website. The button might be labeled as "Download our shopping app." The store would have a powerful decision-making tool at hand if it saw a large ratio of people who clicked the button and divided that by those who were exposed to it.

Why Concierge MVP and Fake Doors Experiments Work

Concierge MVP and Fake Doors are effective and efficient lean research techniques with the following benefits:

- They are great methods for finding how potential customers perceive the value of an offering.

- They are good for evaluating single, very small features through very specific services to entire product suites.

- These techniques will reduce the risk of wasting time on expensive product development.

- They'll keep you from delivering features, products, and services your customers don't really want.

- They will force you to start speaking the language that resonates with customers, and practice and perfect it.

Other Questions Concierge MVP and Fake Doors Experiments Help Answer

Other than the "Do people want the product?" question, Concierge MVP and Fake Doors experiments are great methods for answering the following questions as well.

- Which words should I use to describe my idea to people?

- What will persuade people to try my product?

- What are people's responses when they first hear about my product?

- Would people pay for my product or service?

- How much would people pay for my product or service?

- Do people perceive my product as something that solves a problem they care about?

- Who is the audience of my product?

How to Answer the Question

The following is a how-to guide that takes you step-by-step through the process of using a Concierge MVP and Fake Doors experiment to answer the question "Do people want the product?"

STEP 1: Choose an experiment type.

Technology is awesome. It really is. It helps humans communicate, find old friends, work more effectively, have fun, find places, and oh-so-many other great things. In many cases, technology is also hard, time-consuming, and expensive to develop. In this step, you will find a way to solve a problem you want to solve with or without technology. Manual ways of solving problems are, without a doubt, inefficient, yet they will teach you a lot about what people want without actually developing any technology.

Choose between a Concierge MVP and a Fake Doors experiment:

- Choose a Concierge MVP when you are in exploration mode, when you don't have a product yet, when development hasn't even started, when you don't know a lot about how to solve the problem, or when you are very unsure about your idea.

- Choose a Fake Doors experiment when you want to learn about people's honest reactions to an idea of a product or feature and collect data about their interest level.

Steps 2 to 4 will guide you through Concierge MVP research. If you chose a Fake Doors experiment, jump to Steps 5-6.

The Contract MVP

Another type of an MVP experiment is the Contract MVP. A Contract MVP is when you learn if potential customers want your product (that doesn't exist yet) by asking them to sign a contract for using it. In no way are you pretending that the product does exist. Actually, you are very open about the fact that you don't have it yet. You ask potential customers to sign a contract confirming that they will pay you for your service once it is available. If it will not be available or if they are not interested anymore, you (and they) can take it all back without any consequences.

Ordr.in is a platform for online food ordering. Among other features, Ordr.in's APIs allow businesses to add a widget to their intranets and have employees order lunch for their office from nearby restaurants. To validate that businesses wanted this type of service, Ordr.in's founders crafted a contract MVP and walked into various businesses pitching their idea and asking them to sign the contract, while making potential clients fully aware that the product did not exist yet. The founders decided in advance that if 500 businesses signed their contract, they would start developing a product. The rest is history. Ordr.in was developed, launched, and is now a great success among businesses, restaurants, and developers. Ordr.in revolutionized the restaurant industry.

MVPs are not always successful and don't always validate ideas. Many things can go wrong. Here are some examples:

- Measuring the wrong metric
- Low budget that prevents good distribution
- Customer disbelief
- Difficulties in crafting a good prototype or execution issues
- Wrong customers
- Using surveys or using poorly designed surveys

STEP 2: **Design a Concierge MVP.**

A Concierge MVP manually provides the functionality of the product to the customer. Without developing any expensive technology and without writing one line of code, a concierge MVP helps you figure out if people are interested in your idea. If they are, it means they perceive it as valuable. It means they want it.

The two real strengths of a Concierge MVP are discovering other ideas that might be better perceived by your audience and discovering new audiences. While you are going through the process of creating a Concierge MVP and improving it, pay extra attention to new insights that will introduce themselves to you about other product or service ideas or completely different audiences. These might just become the most important learning opportunities of your Concierge MVP.

To design a Concierge MVP experiment, first think of the value your idea offers to your audience. Ask yourself what the core benefit your product, feature, or service brings to its users. Why would they use it? Why would they need it? A great way of coming up with a Concierge MVP is stating your hypothesis. For example, "We believe that a tablet app that offers recipes for dishes based on what people currently have in their fridge will engage people with limited cooking creativity and skills to come up with tasty dishes that impress their family and friends. We will know this is true when we see our customers use the app at least twice a week for a period of four weeks."

A manual way to create the same value for customers would be asking people to send a photo of the inside of their fridge and have an expert chef quickly send back matching recipes via email. The chef is acting as a human concierge who delivers a personal service. At the core of designing a successful Concierge MVP experiment is the human expertise, which allows you to provide the service combined with existing technology that will replace a digital way of providing it.

Beware though. The quality of the personalized product you will come up with in the end of the process must match the manual curation in your Concierge MVP. It must approximate the real thing or the results of the Concierge MVP could be skewed and misleading. It's a danger that product developers who believe passionately in their product often overestimate the quality in the experiment. It's much easier to be precise when a human is thinking about everything manually.

To help you plan a Concierge MVP study and track its results, use the Concierge MVP board (see Figure 5.4) available for you to use here.

- **Template:** bit.ly/validating-chapter-5-concierge-template

- **Sample board:** bit.ly/validating-chapter-5-concierge-sample

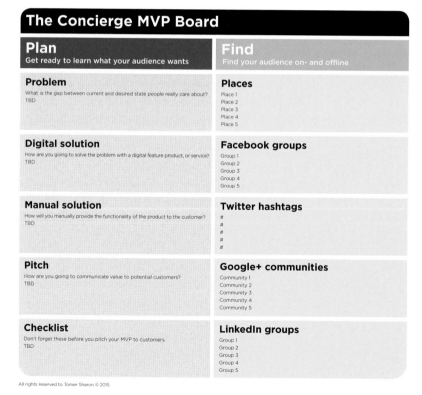

FIGURE 5.4
The Concierge MVP board.

The following are additional examples of Concierge MVP experiments:

1. **Assisting lost shoppers:**

   - Problem: Men find it hard to find their way around a grocery store when they shop for groceries. They waste a lot of time trying to find certain items, while not willing to admit they can't find them and get help from grocery personnel.

   - The big idea: An iPad mounted on a grocery shopping cart with an app that allows shoppers to take a photo of their shopping list. The app then provides the shortest, most effective route to shop for groceries on the list.

   - Manual solution (the Concierge MVP): A personal assistant (not wearing a store uniform so that others don't know the customer is getting help) walks with the customer in the store and shows him where groceries are located. The assistant guides the male shopper through a preferred route, which saves the customer time. Notice that this specific Concierge MVP might be misleading for you since customers might appreciate the fact they have the company of a person while shopping, which you cannot replicate in a digital solution later on. Be sure to pay attention to needs and wants while excluding the noise involved of having a person there with the customer.

2. **Matching colors:**

   - Problem: People who want to paint a room have no idea which wall color goes well with existing room furniture and floor color. They want to be creative and cool, but don't know how.

   - The big idea: A website allows people to upload room photos. As users select walls they want to paint, they are presented with suggestions for matching colors based on the color palette of the furniture in the room.

   - Manual solution (the Concierge MVP): An interior designer who specializes in color theory and practice sends color suggestions accompanied by rationale to customers who sent room photos via email. The designer also offers a 15-minute phone consultation to answer customers' questions. This consultation must also be replicated in the final product; otherwise, the experiment results will be misleading.

3. **Finding customers:**

- Problem: Independent hardware producers find it extremely challenging to find and reach out to potential customers.

- The big idea: A website that features (and sells) five weekly hardware items by independent hardware creators.

- Manual solution (the Concierge MVP): The people behind the website curate a collection of indie-produced hardware items and send a weekly newsletter to interested customers. The email includes contact details of indie creators in case customers want to purchase any of the items directly.

4. **Managing enterprise mobile security:**

- Problem: Enterprises need to deal with multiple unusable applications for managing mobile security and privacy, specifically for mobile messaging and biometrics.

- The big idea: A software product that hooks into various mobile security and networking services while providing a dashboard for evaluating security threats, as well as actionable recommendations for dealing with them.

- Manual solution (the Concierge MVP): An enterprise network security expert who is well informed and experienced provides an in-house review and consultation to enterprise data security departments. The expert's output is a detailed report about potential security breaches and action remedies. Make sure that it's not the concierge that people want, but rather the provided service. Otherwise, again, the experiment results will mislead you.

STEP 3: Find customers and pitch Concierge MVP.

An important aspect of a Concierge MVP experiment is the pitch to potential customers. It's important because this is when you first meet potential customers and understand their perception about your product's value. As soon as you have completed Step 2 and you are ready to provide your service manually, tailor your pitch to prospects and get out of the building to find new customers. Write down your pitch on the Concierge MVP Board (see Figure 5.4).

If you are located close to your audience, identify places where they linger and pitch your product. For example, if your idea solves a problem for teachers, approach them when they leave school or at teacher conferences. If you target people who love to cook, find them at specialty cooking equipment stores. If your audience is music lovers, find them at concerts. People who love to go to New York City for vacation? Go to Times Square. Grocery shoppers? Go to store parking lots. Enterprise security officers? There are dozens of annual conferences on that topic. Use the Concierge MVP Board to write down places where you assume your audience lingers and then physically go there.

If you are located far away from your audience, pitch your product over social media. (Learn more about finding your audience on social media in Chapter 9.)

- Post on Facebook groups and pages relevant to your product domain.

- Tweet a short pitch over Twitter and use hashtags.

- Post on Google Plus communities and pages relevant to your product domain.

- Post on LinkedIn groups relevant to your product domain.

- Post on any other relevant social media. For example, if your audience is primarily German-speaking business people, post your pitch on Xing (the local version of LinkedIn).

Use the Concierge MVP Board to collect links to social media groups, communities, pages, and hashtags your audience spends time with.

As soon as people agree to participate, ask for their email or phone number (whatever makes more sense) and contact them with the next steps. Make sure that you recruit enough customers you can learn from, as well as a number that you can handle. If you plan on recommending dishes to people based on their preferences, 500 people is probably too many to put on your plate, literally. As a rule of thumb, five people should be enough for exploring a concierge MVP. As soon as people agree to participate, set expectations and let them know exactly what is going to happen.

If not enough people agree, change your pitch. If that doesn't help, have someone else pitch it. If that doesn't help, try more locations (both physical and virtual). If that doesn't help and people are just not interested no matter what you say, who says it, or where, maybe you should consider changing your idea.

STEP 4: **Serve the Concierge MVP to customers.**

Without writing one line of code, serve your MVP to customers over phone, email, SMS, IM, or in person. Among these options, put extra consideration on using SMS, because it is the lowest fidelity way of prototyping since it strips away all user interface and interaction design, and it's almost universally accessible across ages and geographies. As you serve your MVP, make sure you do the following:

1. **Keep interaction with customers to a minimum.** Don't communicate more than what you set expectations for. You want customers to react to your product's added value, not the noise you might create around it.

2. **Track key "events."** Several key events will take place as your first customers experience your service. These might be understanding the instructions you sent, the first impression of your service, the first interaction, the first problem your customers have, requests they make and complaints they submit, as well as their reaction to your request for payment. Note down every such event per participant in the Concierge MVP board.

3. **Proactively seek feedback.** In addition to understanding *what* happens when your first customers consume your service, try to understand *why*. Ask them to share their feedback, perspectives, and thoughts each time something meaningful is happening (e.g., the first time their expectations are not met) or once every day or week. Again, don't nag too much. Otherwise, you'll lose them for the wrong reason. Pay extra attention and put more weight on how customers behave rather than what they think and say. Always keep in mind that rationalization might occur in these feedback-requesting situations (read more about rationalization in Chapter 2, Step 5).

4. **Make changes.** Once you realize something is not working well for your customers, take action and change it. There are no rules in terms of how many people need to report or experience the same thing for you to decide to change something. This is a qualitative evaluation, not a quantitative one. You will need to make a judgment call and decide to change something only after you are sure it's creating a challenge for your participants. Alternatively, you might find yourself in front of a "head-banger." A "head-banger" is a problem you obviously need to solve yet you

never realized it before someone experienced it. It is so obvious that you bang your head against a wall, not understanding how you could have missed it. A head-banging issue is one that happens once, and that one time is enough for you to realize you should change something.

5. **Ask for payment.** At a certain point in time, when you feel things are running smoothly, you should pop the question. Ask your customers to pay for the manual service. Give them notice in advance that the service will become a premium one starting at an upcoming date. Offer them a good deal since they were kind enough to help you learn. That said, the price point should be one that shows their commitment. If customers are willing to pay, excellent! It signals they perceive the service as something they need. That's a very good sign you struck a chord with your first customers. If they are not willing to pay, it's a learning opportunity for you. Try to get down to the root cause of their resistance. After you understand *why*, make the necessary changes. A word of warning: do not confuse asking for payment as described above with just asking "Would you pay for this?" Asking this question is not a substitute or shortcut for asking for payment. In fact, it has nothing to do with this technique at all. If you ask for payment, you gather behavioral data, while if you ask the "would you" question, you are collecting attitudinal data that will mislead you since people have no idea what they would do in the future. Also, people in these situations will want to be nice and helpful and will tell you they would pay for it. *Don't fall into this trap.*

Track your customers' behavior, reaction, and feedback, as well as lessons you learned in the Concierge MVP board (see Figure 5.5). Concierge MVP exploration is an iterative process. There are no time limitations to running it and no rules in terms of how many times you can or should use it. If it makes sense for you to run three rounds of Concierge MVP experiments, go for it. Just make sure that you document lessons you learned and make necessary changes between each round. The Concierge MVP board can support such an iterative process. Just add a sheet per MVP iteration, and track and monitor from round to round if specific issues disappear once addressed, if new issues come up, overall satisfaction increases, and propensity to pay goes up as you iterate.

Round 1						
Event Add, remove, or edit events as you see fit	**P1** [name]	**P2** [name] [email], [phone]	**P3** [name] [email], [phone]	**P4** [name] [email], [phone]	**P5** [name] [email], [phone]	**Lessons Learned**
Introductions						
1st impression						
1st interaction						
1st problem						
Requests/ complaints						
Payment ask						

FIGURE 5.5

Track customer behavior and feedback using the Concierge MVP Board.

STEP 5: **Design a Fake Doors experiment.**

Many people with new product ideas have two ways of finding out if potential customers want it:

- Launch a landing page with key benefits and a screenshot and collect email addresses of people who are interested. If conversion rates of people giving their email address divided by landing page impressions are high enough, a decision is made to develop the product.

- Ask potential customers if they want it. What's considered as a healthy process in many organizations is sending a team with a new product idea to the organization's top customers. The team then passionately describes the idea and asks for feedback. Would you use it? Would you pay for it? How much? What features do you want? If 10–15 customers show they are interested, the organization goes ahead and develops the product.

These two activities are seductive to startups and huge corporations alike. They feel science-y and data-ish. An entrepreneur having a customer tell her he wants her product is inherently validating during a time when the entrepreneur is probably vastly insecure about what she's building and is desperate for someone to compliment the product. It's innately human. Don't be tricked. This kind of research will mislead you and waste your time, as it's profoundly wrong, unreliable, and invalid. For example, startups tend to launch a landing page, thinking it's the right way to learn if people need their product. The problem is that the only question landing pages answer is "Are people interested enough to give us their email address?" They learn nothing about what people want or need. Humans have no idea what they need and will almost always be nice to people who ask them. It doesn't cost them much to be nice and say it's a great idea.

That said, not everything is black and white when you ask "Will you use this?" Some people do actually know—for example, specialists (like doctors) in fields with atrocious user experiences where there are obvious design opportunities.

The Fake Doors technique is a powerful, quick, waste-reducing way to find out if people want a product, feature, or service. There are three ways to design a Fake Doors experiment:

- **Landing or crowdfunding page:** Launch a landing page that attempts to prove some kind of commitment on behalf of its visitors. This commitment could be asking them to pay for a product that doesn't exist yet. Starting an IndieGoGo or Kickstarter project is a variation of evaluating such a commitment. Be aware, though, that crowdfunding attracts very specific types of audiences that might not overlap with yours.

- **The button to nowhere:** When you want to evaluate if people need a certain feature within an existing product, add a button or link or tap target to your product indicating that a certain capability or feature exists behind it. When users press, click, or tap it, show an indication that the feature doesn't exist yet—a "coming soon" note or an "in progress" banner. Obviously, this technique requires you to have a product and enough visitor traffic.

- **404 testing:** Launch an advertising campaign, for example, with Google Adwords or Facebook Ads. (A word of warning: advertising involves brand, imagery, tone of the messaging, targeting, and more. If you are a beginner in online advertising, be aware that if done poorly, it can be a huge barrier to attracting people that would really benefit from the experience.)

Ads included in the campaign lead to a 404 error page. You don't need to develop anything. Your only goal is evaluating if people are interested in the product based on the ads. Personally, I wouldn't recommend using a 404 page. I think it's too nasty. You can decide for yourself.

To prevent visitors from getting angry with you and feeling tricked, be completely honest with them. In your "coming soon" message, be sure to thank them for helping you learn about their needs. If you have the budget for it, apologize and consider compensating them with a small token of appreciation, such as a $5 gift certificate on Amazon.

Would Google Do That?

I get asked a lot about whether or not Google does any of those Fake Doors, button to nowhere, or 404 testing. To the best of my knowledge, the answer is no. For a good reason, in my opinion. In a world where thousands of news articles and social media posts burst into the air worldwide after Google moves one letter in its logo one pixel to the right, you can only imagine what would happen if Google implemented a 404 test.

My point is simple: if you work for or founded an organization that is willing to experiment and does not have half the world watching every step you make, go for it and use Fake Doors studies. Just do yourself a favor and don't be nasty. Never intentionally lead to a 404 page only because you want to learn. Have the courtesy to admit it and apologize for not having the product available. Be open about it. Thank the people who help you learn, and if you can, give them a small gift as a gesture.

STEP 6: Determine a Fake Doors threshold.

There is one piece of data coming out of a Fake Doors experiment that helps you get an answer to the "Do people want my product?" question: the ratio between how many people showed interest in the product/feature and the number of people who got exposed to the message about it. "Showed interest" means they either paid to buy the product, funded it, clicked the button to nowhere, or clicked through an ad.

When you decide in advance what the ratio (or dollar value) is that will make you want to develop the product or feature, you have a powerful research tool that drives decisions at hand.

STEP 7: Make a decision and move on.

Jeff Bezos, Amazon's founder and CEO, says, "Experiments are by their very nature prone to failure."[2]

After you have collected data through either a Concierge MVP or a Fake Doors experiment, it's time to evaluate, make an informed decision, iterate, and move on. When the threshold you've set in advance is crossed, or if participants are so enthusiastic about your offering that they're willing to pay for it even in its manual version, these are all great signals that potential customers recognize the value of your product, feature, or service and that they want it. This serves as validation, and you can go ahead to make progress with developing a product prototype.

In most cases, though, you will find that your assumptions are invalidated. You learn that your idea has failed. Potential customers don't provide any clear signal they want your product. This is where a lot of entrepreneurs, product managers, and startup founders make bad decisions. In my research for this book, I discovered that many of them decide to ignore what they learned and still chase their passion for making a product out of their idea.

Don't get me wrong. I am not suggesting that after you learn people don't want your product you should stop chasing your dream and vision. Not at all. I am calling you to pivot, to make informed decisions that will help you change your idea a little bit so that it appeals to your intended audience. Research is to help inform your intuition. Sometimes, it's the *audience* that you need to pivot, not the *product*. In any case, be sure to make a decision based on data you collect, then implement it, and experiment again. A lot of people use terms such as *UX, design thinking,* and *innovation* without truly understanding what they mean. Iteration, pivot, and evaluation is exactly that. When you get frustrated that people don't want your product, then change and test it—that's innovation, design thinking, and user experience.

---

2 bit.ly/validating-chapter-5-bezos

Other Methods to Answer the Question

While a Concierge MVP and a Fake Doors experiment are fast, effective ways for answering the "What do people want?" question, here are some additional MVP techniques for answering it.

- Interview (in-person or phone call)
- Paper prototype
- Pre-order page
- Blog
- Online ad campaign
- Crowdfunding campaign
- Mechanical Turk
- Contract
- Video
- Software or hardware prototype
- Wizard of OZ
- Single-feature product
- The product itself

> **NOTE** CONCIERGE MVP AND FAKE DOORS EXPERIMENT RESOURCES
>
> Access the online resource page for Concierge MVP and Fake Doors experiments on the book's companion website at leanresearch.co. You'll find templates, checklists, videos, slide decks, articles, and book recommendations.

Concierge MVP and Fake Doors Experiments Checklist

☐ Choose an experiment type.

☐ Design a Concierge MVP.

☐ Find customers and pitch Concierge MVP.

☐ Serve the Concierge MVP to customers.

☐ Design a Fake Doors experiment.

☐ Determine a Fake Doors threshold.

☐ Make a decision and move on.

"After you guys gave me the go-ahead, we launched a UserTesting study with six participants," said Jennifer, queuing up videos on a laptop in their conference room. "They were asked to complete three basic tasks with note.io: sign up, create a list, and share a list with a friend. There were a few other things they could do, but those three were the most important."

Dana sat at the table next to Will, who was still irritated, she noticed.

"Now, I want you to write down three big things you learn as you watch the videos," said Jennifer.

Dana paid attention and hoped Will was as well. She also hoped it wouldn't take too long. Fortunately, most of the videos were short— only about three minutes; the longest maybe fifteen. Still, she could feel Will getting more and more angry as the videos went on. Finally, it was over, and Jennifer looked over at them.

"So, Will. What did you think?" Jennifer asked, her expression curious but otherwise neutral.

"I can't believe we didn't do anything like this before," he said, in a low voice.

"It was kind of painful to watch," admitted Dana. Why had they thought friends and family would be good enough for this kind of research?

"It felt like a slap in the face," Will continued. "Most of the time, I felt like either holding my head or banging it on the table!"

Dana felt some tension ease in her chest. She was afraid Will would just flat out refuse to work with Jennifer, but based on his comments, at least it sounded like he was seeing just how badly they needed what she offered.

"Still," said Will, "it was just six people. Can we really make a big deal about this data?"

"You'd be surprised," replied Jennifer. "What did you learn?"

Will looked down at the notes he'd scrawled hastily. "The onboarding funnel is buggy. It doesn't explain what note.io is in terms people understand, and it's too long, which makes people doubt they'd use it."

"Those are easy to fix," Jennifer assured him. "Anything else?"

Dana cleared her throat. "This is probably stupid, but did you notice that four of the women mentioned they created grocery shopping lists for their husbands, so they knew what to buy?"

Will snorted with contempt, and Dana shrank back a bit, embarrassed.

"I noticed that, too," Jennifer mused. "Maybe we should look into it."

CHAPTER 6

Can People Use the Product?

> When I hear "launching in two weeks" and "usability testing" in one sentence, I start to get that old fireman-headed-into-the-burning-chemical-factory feeling, because I have a pretty good idea of what's going on.
>
> If it's two weeks, then it's almost certainly a request for a disaster check. The launch is fast approaching and everyone's getting nervous, and someone finally says, "Maybe we better do some usability testing.
>
> —Steve Krug[1]

I recently traveled to San Francisco and as usual, I rented a car for the week. I immediately noticed the car was equipped with a weird-looking device (Figure 6.1). The device had a screen and one button, but it didn't seem to work, no matter what I tried. So I let it be. My curiosity throughout the week caused me to ask a few people about it and make some phone calls.

Apparently, this was a failed experiment. The rental company had installed these devices for drivers who had questions about their car. The company built this device to create a shortcut to the company's service center. Drivers with questions were to click the button, have a representative immediately respond, and have their questions answered. For example, when a driver was getting a new rental car and couldn't find the switch to turn the lights on, he would contact the service center using this device.

FIGURE 6.1
The failed device in my rental car.

---

1 Krug, Steve. *Don't Make Me Think*, 2nd Ed. New Riders, 2005.

However, it turned out that nobody used the device. There was no communication from the rental company about it, so drivers did not know what that thing was. People didn't want to try it out since they thought it would break the car. The experiment failed. Thousands of devices were deployed, yet not used, even though they were very easy to use.

Finding out if your audience can use the product is the easiest question to answer in this book. It is also one of the most important ones. Usability of a product, or whether its audience can use it effectively and efficiently with high satisfaction is a critical quality attribute. That said, far too many startup founders and product managers choose not to answer this question with user research. They consider themselves to be the representative users, and consequently, feel they can intuitively identify and fix usability issues. Others answer the question just before a product is launched to make sure it doesn't have any staggering issues, as beautifully described above by Steve Krug.

This chapter will walk you through a process for evaluating websites, Web applications, and mobile products (apps and mobile websites), and help you answer the question "Can people use the product?" That said, this question can and should be answered for all types of products and platforms such as hardware products, wearables, physical objects, machinery, VR products, video games, devices, instructions (e.g., a recipe), and more. Identifying usability strengths and weaknesses of a product in any shape or form, from a sketch on a piece of paper through mockups, prototypes, half-baked products, to launched products (yours and others') will inform your design and product roadmap decisions in ways you've never imagined to be possible.

Why Is This Question Important?

Simply put, if people can't use your product, they won't. If they don't have a choice but to use it (e.g., when it's their job), then they'll be extremely frustrated and dissatisfied, and blame you for it not being easy to use. Getting a valid and reliable answer to the question "Can people use the product?" is not a luxury. It's something you or your team should be busy doing on an ongoing basis. There's no such thing as a perfect design. Great design is hard to create, and no design is great at first attempt. Answering this question during the design and development process is the only way to perfect it.

To clarify, there's a big difference between a usable product and a beautiful product. A usable product could be ugly, and a beautiful product could be unusable. That said, studies have shown that beautiful products are perceived as more usable than ugly ones.[2] So if you don't have the time or budget for visual design, at the minimum, make sure your product is usable.

When Should You Ask the Question?

The question "Can people use the product?" is best answered as early as possible—preferably when you have an initial design, and definitely each time you iterate on it in a meaningful way (Figure 6.2). Early, because finding issues early in the process saves you time and money later when it's hard or impossible to fix them. Often, because each new or added design element or component potentially poses new challenges for people who use it. If you are testing a concept or in the process of evaluating an MVP, which is a prototype of a product, answering the question will help you identify and fix big usability issues. In other words, if usability is really bad, it might influence your concept evaluation because people are fast in coming to conclusions that a product idea is bad when they can't use it or understand what is going on.

Can people use the product?

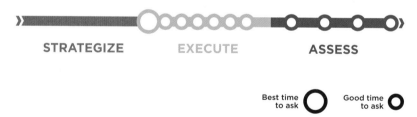

STRATEGIZE   EXECUTE   ASSESS

Best time ⬤   Good time ⬤
to ask   to ask

FIGURE 6.2
When is a good time to ask "Can people use the product?" The big circle represents the best time, while the smaller ones indicate other times recommended to ask the question.

---

2 What is beautiful is usable: bit.ly/validating-chapter-6-beautiful-usable.

A myth among product development practitioners is that the question should be asked only when the product is almost ready, in good shape, visually designed, and when it's "appropriate" to show it to users. The complete opposite is true. Finding out if people can use the product is most useful when it's not ready, when it's in bad shape, when it's still ugly, and when you are going to be ashamed to show it to people. That's exactly the time you have an opportunity to not only learn about important issues people have with it but also enough time and resources to fix them. Be aware of running a usability test closer to launch time for the first time in the product development life cycle because this timing will have the team identify huge problems they can't fix. The team will be challenged with a long list of usability problems at a time when the last thing it needs is, well, a long list of problems.

When you design an MPV, usability doesn't have to be a critical aspect of it. That said, when you want to validate a concept, thinking you'll work on making it more usable later, things might get tricky. If your MVP is a product that people might use or interact with, it's best to answer the question "Can they use it?" earlier, since concept validation data will be biased by bad usability. Try to answer the question quickly while fixing low-hanging fruit and taking care of the rest after the concept has been validated.

There are two ways to get an answer to the question "Can people use the product?"—qualitative and quantitative. If your goal is to gather insights (e.g., How can we improve the onboarding process?), choose a qualitative approach. When you need a clearer answer (e.g., How successful are people trying to buy a dress using a suggested, new product page?), a quantitative approach will do a better job. In a qualitative approach, you'll have a few participants, and you will see with your own eyes what they do with your product. You'll notice that patterns will start to emerge with about four to five participants. In a quantitative approach, you'll have hundreds or more participants and rather than seeing what they do with your own eyes, you'll get the numbers that will tell you what happened (hence quantitative). In summary, a quantitative approach usually explains *what* happened while a qualitative approach tells you *why* it happened. So the best you can do is to combine these approaches to get the full picture.

Answering the Question with Online Usability Testing

Usability testing helps you figure out which elements of the design are worth keeping because they work well, and which to improve (or get rid of) because they either prevent people from completing their tasks, make it hard for them to use the product, or really annoy them. In a traditional usability test, participants complete tasks with a product while a moderator guides them through the tasks, asks them questions, and makes sure they answer research questions and provide useful feedback. The moderator also makes sure they feel comfortable, don't stress out, and are okay if they can't complete a task or don't understand what to do.

Usability testing is a perfect way for shaking a product real hard in a way that things that are not tightly held together expose themselves and fall off. (These are the usability problems you find during such a test.) The testing also helps make sure that the things that are well connected and thought of remain a strong part of it. (These are the things you find that work well during a usability test.) Usability testing is excellent for evaluating a few screens sketched on a piece of paper, an early stage prototype, a half-baked product, a working demo, a product just after release, or somebody else's product.

Usability testing is great for answering the question "Can they use it?" for Web products and mobile apps, but it's also good for environmental design, non-digital products, and general physical experience design. The scope of this book focuses on the first group (Web, apps). If you work on a product that belongs to the second group, it's best to answer the question with a traditional, in-person usability test. To learn how to run an in-person usability test quickly and effectively, read and follow guidance given by Steve Krug in his great, short book, *Rocket Surgery Made Easy*.[3]

There are two approaches to (or categories of) usability testing: qualitative and quantitative (see Table 6.1). Generally speaking, a qualitative approach is an effective way for learning *why* things happen and how they can improve, while a quantitative approach gives you a clear idea of *what* is happening and what the numbers are to support it.

---

3 New Riders, 2009.

TABLE 6.1 CHARACTERISTICS OF THE TWO APPROACHES FOR USABILITY TESTING

	Qualitative Usability Testing	Quantitative Usability Testing
Focus	Improving the evaluated product, feature, or service	Quantifying product usage, comparing products, identifying problematic aspects
Explains	Why things happen	What happens
Example for research question	How can we improve the onboarding process?	How successful are people trying to buy a dress using a product page?
Results	Insights	Answers
Tools	UserTesting, Validately	UserZoom, Loop11
What is being captured?	Videos of people completing tasks and thinking aloud	UX metrics (e.g., task success, time-on-task, satisfaction, etc.)
Number of research participants	5	500

Online usability testing (for Web products and mobile apps) is a quick, reliable way of answering the question "Can people use the product?" This chapter guides you on running online usability testing rather than the more traditional in-person usability testing for several reasons:

- **You won't need to moderate.** Moderating usability tests is a skill that requires a lot of knowledge, practice, and experience. In online usability testing, you'll prepare tasks and questions, click a button, and then participants will get everything you've prepared for them, do it, click a button, and then you'll get all the data.

- **Significantly reduced hassle of finding participants.** Finding people who qualify and are willing and available to participate in a usability test is a tedious, time-consuming, and expensive task. Online usability testing can save you a lot of these efforts and sometimes even do all of it for you.

- **Access to broader audiences.** While in-person usability testing limits you to invite research participants from the area where the test is being held, online usability testing does not have that limitation. Participants can come from anywhere. In many cases, this flexibility will be a huge advantage for you because participants will represent your true target audience better.

Why Online Usability Testing Works

Online usability testing is an effective user research technique that carries the following benefits:

- **Quick, cheap, and easy:** A qualitative online usability test can be completed in 24 hours or less. A quantitative study will last a couple of days.

- **Involves real people:** It allows the team to observe real people use the product. No more, "We use the product, so we know how usable it is."

- **Provides immediate product usability feedback:** Input from participants is clear and immediate. Team members who watch videos get a pat on their backs or a hammer on their fingers within seconds or minutes.

- **Eliminates redundant arguments:** The clear feedback coming from real people, external to the organization that develops the product resolves many team dilemmas, arguments, and slow decision-making processes.

- **Eye-opening experience:** It instantly tells the team about people's motivations, perceptions, and behavior.

Other Questions Online Usability Testing Helps Answer

Other than the "Can people use the product?" question, online usability testing is a great method for answering the following questions as well. If you ask yourself any one of these questions, online usability testing can help you get an answer. The questions are organized in a way to help you pick an approach (qualitative or quantitative) and data type to be collected, as shown in Table 6.2.

TABLE 6.2 WHICH APPROACH IS BEST FOR ANSWERING WHAT QUESTION?

Question	Approach	Data Type
What are people's overall experiences with the product?	Qualitative & quantitative	Observation, numeric task performance data, and follow-up question
When do people use a product?	Quantitative	Numeric task performance data
How lost are people when they use the product?	Quantitative	Numeric task performance data
Does the product overload users' minds more than necessary?	Qualitative	Observation and follow-up question
What are the product's design strengths?	Qualitative	Observation and follow-up question
What are the things that should be improved in the product?	Qualitative	Observation and follow-up question
How easy or hard is it to learn how to use the product?	Quantitative	Numeric task performance data
Why does a product work well?	Qualitative	Observation and follow-up question
Why does a product fail?	Qualitative	Observation and follow-up question
Do people notice a certain screen element?	Qualitative	Observation and follow-up question
What signals the product's success or failure?	Quantitative	Numeric task performance data
What pain points do people have that are related to the product?	Qualitative	Observation and follow-up question
Where are people getting stuck on the product?	Quantitative	Numeric task performance data
How do we know when to kill a feature or pivot?	Qualitative	Observation and follow-up question

(Sample One-Page Plan)

by Jane Kay-Smith, co-founder, Jane@azairways.com

Last updated: 13 August 2015

Background

Since January, 2009, when the A-Z Airways was introduced to the world, it was known for its high-quality flight experience. That said, there were repeat complaints and growing call center tickets regarding the company's online flight booking experience. Over the years, several improvements had been made to the system, to no avail.

Goals

Identify the strengths and weaknesses of the A-Z Airways online flight booking process, and provide opportunities for improvement.

Research Questions

1. Can people use the online flight booking system effectively and efficiently?
2. What is the satisfaction level from our online flight booking?
3. What are the breakpoints in the process?

Methodology

250 people will complete the study by clicking a URL. When participants click the study link, they will be taken to the study environment, shown participation instructions, and answer an opening questionnaire. Participants will then complete tasks with the online flight booking system such as find a destination, compare prices, select a flight, and book a trip. Participants' actions and responses to task-related questions will be recorded and analyzed. The study will last about 15 minute. Study results will include the following metrics:

How to Answer the Question

The following is a how-to guide that takes you step-by-step through the process of using online usability testing to answer the question "Can people use the product?"

STEP 1: Write a one-page plan.

As stated previously in Chapter 2, discuss the following with your team, come to an agreement, and have a shared understanding of what's going to happen during the test. Ask team members individually about what

1. For each task:

   - Task success

   - Time to complete task

   - Task ease-of-use rating

   - Task success confidence

2. Generally:

   - Visual appeal

   - Challenging or frustrating aspects

   - Effective or intuitive aspects

   - Satisfaction score

Participants

These are the primary characteristics of study participants:

- Business or leisure travelers

- Ages 22 to 75

- 50% booked online with A-Z Airways before, 50% who didn't

Schedule

Study dates: August 25–26

Results available: August 28

they want to learn and find patterns. Often, different team members will have the same questions worded differently. For inconsistencies, gather the group for a discussion of priorities. After the team comes to an agreement, write a one-page plan. Make sure that you answer the following questions with your plan:

1. **Background:** What led us here so that we want a usability test?

2. **Goals:** What is the reason for this study? What is the end result of this research activity? For example, identify strengths and weaknesses of the design, and improve it before the next version is released.

3. **Research questions:** What do we specifically want to learn? For example, are there too many options in the navigation bar? Do people find out how to sign up for the service quickly enough?

4. **Methodology:** Which research technique will be used, how long will it take, and where?

5. **Participants:** What are the characteristics of the people we want to invite to participate in this study?

6. **Schedule:** When do we need results? When can people in the team be available to come to conclusions together?

STEP 2: Find 5 or 500 participants.

For a qualitative online usability testing study, five participants will serve you well. A quantitative study requires you to find 500 participants to be confident with numerical results. Consider the number of participants based on the following information:

- How many participants can you afford: finding people takes time, effort, and sometimes costs money.

- What is a credible number: 5 or 500 are good and credible for qualitative and quantitative usability tests, respectively. That said, the standards for your team might be different.

- For qualitative studies, how many do you have time to watch: consider the analysis effort attached to launching a study that generates too much video and more than you and your team can handle.

- For quantitative studies, avoid tie situations: if you recruit too few participants, your confidence interval might be too wide, and results might not be statistically significant. In other words, you will have no way of knowing if your numbers are pointing in one direction or not. More on that in Chapter 7.

To find the right participants for your usability test that both qualify to participate and are willing and available to do so, craft a screening questionnaire[4] that will screen people into or out of your study:

1. List your assumptions about participant criteria (e.g., business traveler).

2. Transform participant criteria into measurable benchmarks (e.g., travels for business at least three times a year).

---

4 This is the same list that was highlighted in other chapters.

3. Transform the benchmark into a screening question or questions (e.g., How often do you go on an airplane?). If a person chooses the "right" answer, she's in. If not, she's out.

4. Craft a screening questionnaire (also called a *screener*) that you can send people. (Here is a sample screener— bit.ly/validating-chapter-6-screener).

5. Pilot-test the screener with a couple of people and make improvements.

6. Utilize social media to find research participants quickly and effectively. Chapter 9 will guide you through social media usage for finding research participants, as well as detailed steps and examples for creating a great screener.

STEP 3: Phrase instructions, tasks, and questions.

When it comes to what study participants get from you and what you need to prepare for them, there are three things you need to craft: instructions, tasks, and questions.

Instructions are what participants see first when they click the link to participate in the study (after the specific service makes sure they meet the qualifications that you have expressed through the screening questionnaire). The role of the instructions is to explain briefly to participants what is going to happen, why, and what is expected of them. Instructions must take into account that there are two types of participants—ones that are new to using the online usability service and those who are already experienced with it. Figures 6.3 and 6.4 provide examples for instructions given to participants of UserTesting and Loop11.

Starting Instructions
What participants need to know before they begin

URL (where users start the test) *

www.kayak.com

Test this link

Introduction: The Mindset Users Should Have *

Imagine your spouse's boss surprisingly gave him or her next week off. You both decided you want to go on a short-notice vacation in the Caribbean, although you are on a tight budget these days.

Characters left: 556

FIGURE 6.3
Instructions in UserTesting.

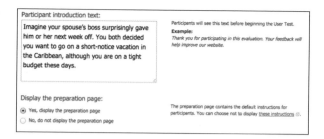

FIGURE 6.4

Instructions in Loop11.

Before you craft the tasks and questions, figure out which ones will help you get answers to your research questions. For example, if you had the research question "Are there too many options in the navigation bar?" here are a few ways you could deduce that there are, in fact, too many options in the navigation bar:

- Participants take too long to complete tasks or fail (although this could be caused by any number of issues).

- You ask a direct question about it (although the participants' negative opinion doesn't actually mean there is something wrong).

- Participants mention it spontaneously in their feedback (although if they don't mention it, it doesn't mean it's all fine).

In this specific navigation bar example, you should craft tasks that would force participants to use it multiple times and ask direct questions about it.

Creating tasks for participants to complete during online usability testing requires attention to details and feedback from others on the team. There are the primary tasks to do, which can be open- or close-ended, but start with easy ones, if possible. This way, participants feel they are helpful from the first moment. Ending with an easy task will make them finish the session with a similar feeling. For example, "Show us the last thing you searched for on Google.com." Primary tasks may be easy or hard for the participants, but they are the tasks for which the development team is the most unsure.

When you phrase your task, get your participants into the situation by describing a short scenario that explains the motivation for completing the task. Don't just fire instructions at them. This situation of a usability test is not natural for participants, and you can make it a little bit more smooth and realistic if you provide some background and motivation to task scenarios rather than just strictly asking them to do things. For example, instead of saying, "Using Kayak.com, find the cheapest flight from JFK airport to the Caribbean for two people for next week," phrase your task this way: "Imagine your spouse's boss surprisingly gave him or her next week off. You both decided you want to go on a short-notice vacation in the Caribbean, although you are on a tight budget these days. Using Kayak.com, find the cheapest flight for your vacation assuming that you depart from JFK airport." Sometimes, a primary task might be long and complex. In this case, consider splitting it into several smaller tasks. Participants don't always need to know the full scenario at one time, and sometimes tasks can be extended with additional goals. This can also help track which parts of a task are successes or failures.

Another thing to consider when coming up with tasks is how structured they might be.

- **Close-ended tasks:** A close-ended task asks participants to reach a specific, well-defined end result. You will always know what that end result is in advance. For example, "Imagine you just discovered that United Airlines has overcharged your credit card during your recent flight booking. Using United.com, find the phone number for Customer Care."

- **Open-ended tasks:** An open-ended task allows participants to reach one of multiple end-results based on given instructions. For example, "Imagine your family travels to a new city every holiday, and it's your turn to plan the vacation. Find a destination and airline tickets."

Plan on asking participants to complete tasks for no more than 15–20 minutes. This is a reasonable time that participants can stay focused during online usability testing. Longer sessions will result in higher drop-off rates (i.e., participants who abandon the test prior to completion) or more breaks taken without you knowing it (i.e., participants take a break in the middle of a task and mess up your data).

Questions you ask after each task and in the end of the session will help you better understand participants' attitudes about their experience.

At the minimum, ask these questions after each task:

1. This task was easy.

   - Strongly disagree
   - Moderately disagree
   - Somewhat disagree

- Neither agree nor disagree

- Somewhat agree

- Moderately agree

- Strongly agree

2. Comments (optional):

3. I am confident I successfully completed the task.

   - Strongly disagree

   - Moderately disagree

   - Somewhat disagree

   - Neither agree nor disagree

   - Somewhat agree

   - Moderately agree

   - Strongly agree

Ask these questions at the end of the session after all of the tasks:

1. Were there any aspects of the product that you found particularly challenging or frustrating? If so, please describe.

2. Were there any aspects of the product that you thought were particularly effective or intuitive? If so, please describe.

3. For each of the following statements, select the response that best describes your overall reactions to the product you used today. Please only refer to the tasks you have just worked on.

   - I think that I would like to use this frequently.

   - I found this unnecessarily complex.

   - I thought this was easy to use.

   - I think I would need assistance to be able to use this.

   - I found the various functions in this were well integrated.

   - I thought there was too much inconsistency in this.

   - I would imagine that most people would learn to use this very quickly.

   - I found this very cumbersome/awkward to use.

- I felt very confident using this.

- I would need to learn a lot more about this before I could effectively use it.

While the last question might look somewhat strange to you and might cause you to think to yourself, "all these questions kind of look the same, maybe I'll just ask one of them," it is based on a very widely used and standard measure of how users feel about the ease of use of products called *SUS* (system usability scale). Use these two links to better understand how it should look:

- SUS example and template:
  bit.ly/validating/chapter-6-sus-example

- SUS form (this is what participants answer):
  bit.ly/validating/chapter-6-sus-form

You can learn interesting things about your product if after you show participants each task but before they try to complete it, you ask participants how easy they *think* it is going to be. When you compare their answers to the question about ease-of-use you ask *after* they complete each task, you get an interesting perspective (and data to support it) about how easy or difficult it is to use your product compared to people's expectations. This question would look like this:

This task will be easy.

- Strongly disagree

- Moderately disagree

- Somewhat disagree

- Neither agree nor disagree

- Somewhat agree

- Moderately agree

- Strongly agree

If you get tempted to skip this step and just put the product in front of people and see what happens, just be aware that it is going to be somewhat challenging for you to come up with clear conclusions and answers to your questions. The reason for having tasks and questions (some very structured and scientific) is to give you the opportunity to be able to compare data across participants. If participants complete the same tasks and answer the same questions using the same set of possible answers, it gives validity and reliability to your findings. When you keep things very open ended so that participants decide which tasks they perform and you ask them whatever you want whenever you want, it is going to be much harder for you to come up with conclusive results.

STEP 4: **Pilot-test!**

Before you launch your online usability test for 5 or 500 participants, test it first. Testing the test means that you launch the study to only one participant with one goal in mind: making sure that your instructions, tasks, and questions are clear and serve their purpose. For qualitative tests using services such as UserTesting, pilot-test by launching the study with one participant first. For studies that are quantitative in nature, such as ones conducted using services such as UserZoom and Loop11, have a person sit next to you and complete the test as you watch what happens.

Issues you will find in a pilot-test include:

- Jargon that participants don't understand or misinterpret.
- Broken or wrong links to websites, prototypes, and apps.
- Tasks with partial information.
- Missing questions.
- Badly phrased tasks or questions. This one can completely mess up the results of the test. Spot these by how pilot-test participants understand them, how they respond to them, and pilot-test again. Once it goes out to hundreds of participants, it will be too late, so it's worth the extra diligence at this stage.
- Bugs that prevent a certain feature from functioning well (or at all) due to the use of an online usability testing service.
- And more unknown issues. (Otherwise, you wouldn't need to run a pilot-test.)

Keep in mind that an online usability test does not give you an opportunity to clarify a task or question. It's very easy to end up with ambiguous or contaminated results when it's too late to go back and redo the test. Here are some examples of questions that could be understood in multiple ways by test participants and that a pilot-test could help uncover:

- How easy was it to complete that task?' The participant may *think* they completed it correctly and quickly and give a positive score, but actually they completely messed it up!

- Was there anything missing from the options in the menu?' We mean the main navigation menu, but the participant remembers there was a drop-down with many options as part of the task and in his mind this is a menu because of course he doesn't know the correct technical labels for each interactive element within a design.

Practice: Watch this pilot test session conducted through UserTesting and note what needs to change and how the test (not the evaluated product) can be improved.

Pilot-test—bit.ly/validating-chapter-6-pilot-test

After watching the video of the pilot session, make the necessary changes to your test plan, instructions, tasks, questions or anything else that came up during the pilot. Consider running another pilot if changes were significant.

You will *never* regret a decision to run a pilot-test. You will *always* regret skipping this step. Please don't.

STEP 5: **Prepare a rainbow analysis spreadsheet.**

The analysis spreadsheet you prepare depends on the type of study you run. Qualitative test data (using services such as UserTesting or Validately) will be best analyzed with a rainbow spreadsheet, while quantitative data (using services such as UserZoom or Loop11) is usually well-organized by each of these tools (see Figures 6.5 and 6.6).

The rainbow spreadsheet is a helpful tool for making online usability testing a team sport. Taking its name from the different colors used in it to represent the participants, it is a spreadsheet with which all of the data collected during a qualitative online usability test is centrally and simultaneously documented by a team of people. It serves as the centerpiece for lessons learned from a study and later turns into the final report. Team members watch each video of the study together and collaborate on taking notes and figuring out insights.

As you prepare to run the study, your goal is to have a spreadsheet ready to be used, with all of the known information about participants and tasks entered. You also want your team to be well informed on how to use it to document its observations.

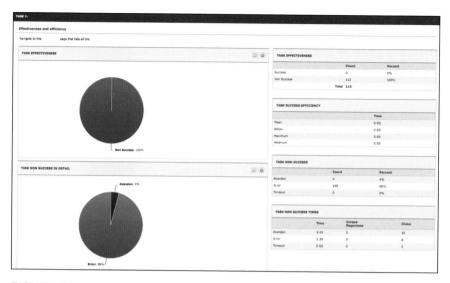

FIGURE 6.5
Task performance data presented in UserZoom.

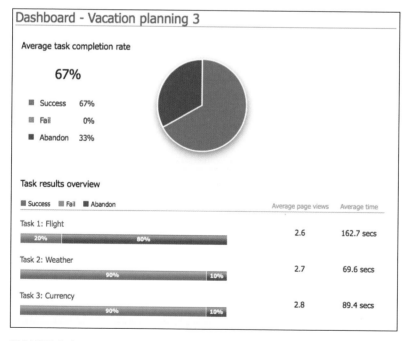

FIGURE 6.6
Usability testing dashboard by Loop11.

A rainbow spreadsheet has the following sheets:

- **Observations:** The primary place where the team notes study participants' behavior or important things they say (see Figure 6.7).

- **Metrics:** If relevant, this sheet includes basic quantitative data collected during this qualitative test. Primarily, time to complete tasks, task success, and satisfaction.

- **Participants:** Basic background information collected from participant profiles or their answers to the screening questionnaire.

- **Raw data:** A place for team members who want to add any type of notes about the study.

- **Summary:** Created after the team watches all the participant videos, it includes answers to research questions, action items, and other findings.

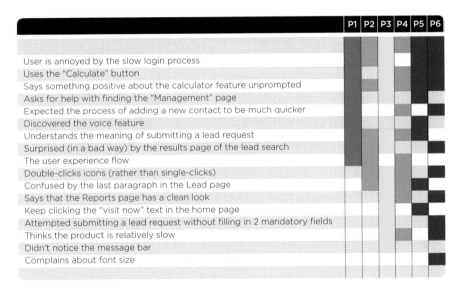

FIGURE 6.7

The observation sheet: repeated observations are highlighted in different colors.

To get the spreadsheet ready for your team's observations, follow these steps:

1. Finalize your study's protocol or discussion guide. Have a very good idea of what you will ask participants to do and what questions you will ask them to answer, in what order.

2. Use this template to create a rainbow spreadsheet for your study: bit.ly/validating/chapter-6-master-rainbow.

3. Enter predetermined observations in the observations sheet. These might be behaviors that you and your team expect participants to demonstrate. For example, "Noticed the green Calculate button." Do not enter double-barreled observations, such as "Noticed and used the green Calculate button" because determining what to indicate in case a participant demonstrates only one of the behaviors is sometimes hard (in this case, either noticing or using the button).

4. Customize the columns for participants to match the number of study participants. The master spreadsheet contains 10 columns, each in a different color. If you have five participants, remove (or hide) columns P6 to P10 (see Figure 6.8). If you have 12 participants, add two more colored columns (Figure 6.9).

	P1	P2	P3	P4	P5	Possible solution
Observation 1						
Observation 2						
Observation 3						
Observation 4						
Observation 5						
Observation 6						
Observation 7						
Observation 8						
Observation 9						
Observation 10						
Observation 11						
Observation 12						
Observation 13						
Observation 14						
Observation 15						
Observation 16						
Observation 17						
Observation 18						
Observation 19						
Observation 20						

FIGURE 6.8

The observation sheet, with five columns for participants.

	P1	P2	P3	P4	P5	P6	P7	P8	P9	P10	P11	P12	Possible solution
Observation 1													
Observation 2													
Observation 3													
Observation 4													
Observation 5													
Observation 6													
Observation 7													
Observation 8													
Observation 9													
Observation 10													
Observation 11													
Observation 12													
Observation 13													
Observation 14													
Observation 15													
Observation 16													
Observation 17													
Observation 18													
Observation 19													
Observation 20													

FIGURE 6.9

The observation sheet, with 12 columns for participants.

5. Share the spreadsheet with your team in an email or meeting. Explain what it is, how it will serve as a summary for the study, and that there will not be another report. Encourage them to attend as many study sessions as possible.

Here is a sample rainbow spreadsheet filled in with data. Use this to understand how to use it better: bit.ly/validating/chapter-6 -sample-rainbow.

STEP 6: Launch the test.

Launch the test to all participants and track their progress. With services such as UserTesting, closely monitor participant videos as they come in. Watch them immediately to make sure they are helpful. A helpful video is where the participant is completing (or attempting to complete) all the tasks and answering all the questions. With services such as UserZoom or Loop11, there's not much you can track other than the number of sessions already completed with some data about the process of collecting data.

For qualitative tests, this time between the launch and completion of the test is also great for the following:

- Enter participant information into the participants sheet in the rainbow spreadsheet. Copy and paste their profile details as well as their answers to the screening questionnaire.

- Summon a team meeting called *research workshop* and explain that you'll be watching study videos and come to conclusions together.

- Ask team members to read the participants sheet prior to watching videos to better understand who the participants are.

When data collection has finished, meaning you have reached the full quota you had hoped for, move on to analysis and crafting results.

STEP 7: Collaboratively analyze results.

To analyze data from qualitative tests (conducted with services such as UserTesting) using a rainbow spreadsheet, follow these steps:

1. Gather team members in a meeting room. Explain you will analyze results together by first watching study videos. Ask them to access the rainbow spreadsheet on their laptops.

2. Ask team members to use the observations sheet during study sessions to note the behaviors of participants.

3. Instruct them to color a participant's cell when a certain behavior occurs. If a particular behavior repeats in sessions with other participants, color the relevant participants' cells, rather than adding one more line for a behavior that's already been noted. To clarify: there is only one spreadsheet, which everyone accesses and works on at the same time.

4. Ask team members to add notes to the raw sheet. Tell them it is there for anyone to add anything that doesn't belong on the other sheets. This sheet usually remains empty, but some people feel more comfortable taking notes there.

5. Add sheets as you see fit. For example, if your team is interested in what questions participants ask when they use a certain product, add a questions sheet and assign a chief questions officer (i.e., someone on the team) to log that data. There are no rules. Feel free to customize this spreadsheet to your team's needs.

6. As the meeting progresses, you'll notice that your team is getting comfortable with the mechanics of using the spreadsheet and is doing an even better job of inputting observations.

7. Facilitating quick debriefings after each video will increase the quality and tightness of the data entered. After the first video is over and after each subsequent video, break for a few minutes. Discuss team observations. Help people understand observations that are not clear to them (rephrasing, if needed). Tighten the list of observations by agreeing with team members on what should be removed. Candidates for removal from this sheet would be duplicate entries and any entry that cannot be considered an observation (such as a conclusion, thought, inference, solution to a problem or action item). Clarify to the team that, at this point, everyone should be entering only things that participants do, don't do, or say, and that you'll discuss everything else in the end.

8. Don't worry about overriding each other's data. People usually self-manage their entries to prevent this from happening. Let it be.

9. Fill in the metrics sheet with data. You can definitely delegate this part to one of the observers. Another option is to assign metric-collecting responsibilities. So, for example, one team member would collect and log the success rates of tasks, another would take care of the time to complete tasks, and so on.

10. Enter data into any other sheets you've created. Don't feel bad if something doesn't work out. This is a learning opportunity for you and your team. Maybe you should do something differently the next time around. Decide together.

11. After you have watched the last video, have a summary discussion. This is the time for deeper analysis to try to find out why things happened the way they did. Figuring out the "why" is the bit that will usually help you select the right "fix" to solve the problem. Agree on the answers to the research questions that you defined in your study plan, identify the primary findings of the study, and decide on the next steps.

12. Add a summary sheet as the first in the spreadsheet. This sheet will have four areas (see Figure 6.10): answers to research questions, answers, action items, and primary findings.

Research Questions	Answers	Action Items
Question 1	Answer 1	AI 1
Question 2	Answer 2	AI 2
Question 3	Answer 3	AI 3
Question 4	Answer 4	AI 4
Question 5	Answer 5	AI 5

Primary Findings

Finding 1
Finding 2
Finding 3
Finding 4
Finding 5

FIGURE 6.10

The summary sheet, with research questions, answers, action items, and primary findings.

13. Facilitate the discussion until you reach the point that the team feels it has captured the essence of what happened during the study and is ready to take action. Don't overanalyze. Avoid "analysis paralysis." If you have 10 important action items, you are in a pretty good shape. There's no need to exhaust every tiny detail of the study's results.

14. Add links to video recordings of the sessions to the participants sheet.

15. Declare the study done and publish the spreadsheet. When you share the spreadsheet outside of your immediate team, don't call it the *rainbow spreadsheet*. Instead, call it *the report*.

In case of a quantitative study, review the data collected by the tool you chose to use and figure out problematic areas, comparison results, and areas to explore in future research.

STEP 8: Make changes.

An online usability test's primary goal is making changes. After you complete your research activity, whether qualitative or quantitative, make the necessary changes and plan your next research to figure out if they improved the user experience. If you don't make any changes, your online usability test has failed. Research never lives in a vacuum. It is always connected and embedded in design. Make sure that your research affects your design.

When you decide what to change, keep the following in mind:

- **Impact:** Focus on changes with a maximum positive effect on the user. Don't waste time on changes that are right and just of secondary importance.

- **Persistence:** Prioritize changes of things that are likely to reoccur and give lower priority to issues that users can learn to overcome on their own.

- **Frequency:** Consider how many users appear to experience the same issue and give higher priority to issues where that number is larger.

- **Politics:** This advice is as important as it is hard to follow. Develop changes as if you live in a bubble. Don't exclude the right changes because someone else might not like them. First, think: What's the right thing to do, rather than considering what can be done?

- **Short and long term:** Separate changes into short- and long-term ones. This will help with priorities and buy-in.

- **More research:** Not all problems have clear solutions. Maybe more research can help. Is there a need to make changes and conduct another usability test? Do you need to go back to your user profiles? Do you need to reconsider the information architecture?

Other Methods to Answer the Question

Online usability testing is hard to replace with other methods. If you choose the qualitative approach to online usability testing, an in-person format of usability testing is helpful in answering the question, although it might require a much longer lead time for finding participants. If you choose the quantitative approach to online usability testing, methods such as Amazon Mechanical Turk combined with a questionnaire might serve as a suitable way to answer the question. Amazon Mechanical Turk is a crowdsourcing Internet marketplace that enables you to ask users (aka *Turkers*) to perform various tasks. To clarify, a survey is never a good replacement for online usability testing since it has no component of tracking behavior and only allows you to capture self-reported, attitudinal data.

> **NOTE** ONLINE USABILITY TESTING RESOURCES
>
> Access the online resource page for Online Usability Testing on the book's companion website at leanresearch.co. You'll find templates, checklists, videos, slide decks, articles, and book recommendations.

Online Usability Testing Checklist

- ☐ Write a one-page plan.
- ☐ Find 5 or 500 participants.
- ☐ Phrase instructions, tasks, and questions.
- ☐ Pilot-test!
- ☐ Prepare a rainbow analysis spreadsheet.
- ☐ Launch the test.
- ☐ Collaboratively analyze results.
- ☐ Make changes.

"I can't believe we're going in this direction," muttered Will.

"I think it's a good focus to try," said Dana. "The new app will support list sharing, updating the list with new items, list update notification..."

"For a situation where the husband is already at the store," Jennifer cut in.

"Right, and sending item photos from husband to wife to make sure the right item is purchased. Also, some cool emoticons sent from the wife to the husband, to indicate if the photo is for the right item to buy."

"I just don't see why that'd be necessary," said Will.

Dana rolled her eyes. "Remember that time I asked you to pick up some laser toner, and you got the wrong one—twice? First, the wrong brand, then for the wrong printer?"

Will shrugged, but she had a point. "I'm just not thrilled that the focus is on such a small niche of households. You know, where the wife is making lists for the husband. But you're right: we've got to pivot. The original idea wasn't working. Also, I'm glad we're doing something a little more technologically challenging."

"I'm glad you're more on board," said Dana.

A few weeks later, they were back to the drawing board—or in their case, the conference room.

"The pivot was a disaster!" said Dana, crumpling a sheet of paper. "Husbands felt like they were doing just fine without the app. And wives felt like we were saying they were control freaks, or that husbands couldn't do anything right. Nobody needed or wanted this app!"

She put her head in her hands. This was a total fiasco. Was this thing ever going to work?

"Well, look on the bright side," said Will. "At least we got the user testing right and figured it out before it got too far."

"Don't give up yet, guys," Jennifer said. "I know it looks bad. But hang in there. We're still zeroing in on the needs. Keep digging."

CHAPTER 7

Which Design Generates Better Results?

The best ideas look initially like bad ideas.

—Paul Graham

Product developers need a fast, effective way for validating learning. They want to know if one design works significantly better for some users than for others, if the product is getting better over time, and if they are winning (or at least leading) the race against their competition. Some consider their MVP (minimum viable product) as an experiment and want to launch and iterate it quickly. This chapter walks you through a simple, straightforward experimentation technique for comparing features, design elements, pages, tasks, or even whole products by answering the question "Which design generates better results?"

Why Is This Question Important?

"Which design generates better results?" is a question that bothers many product owners and entrepreneurs. Answering this question with a valid and reliable experiment saves product development teams time they waste arguing for or against different design options and elements. Answering the question will also help when evaluating whether a product is improving or not. Many practitioners think that they can improve their product only by developing more versions. Rather than assuming this is the case, product owners can prove (or disprove) it.

Lastly, product leaders tend to evaluate their competition by comparing lists of features. In their minds, the product with the longer and more meaningful list of features wins. In reality, the contrary is proven to be right in many cases. For example, when the iPhone first came out, it did not include many features its competitors offered. However, the features it did include were done very well, and the iPhone turned out to be a huge success for Apple.

Here's another example: A startup I interviewed was working on a compact digital camera for travelers. When the founders identified their competition, they compared their list of camera features with their competitors' features: megapixels, zoom capabilities, HD capabilities. The product with the longer list and better numbers was considered to be superior. When the founders discovered that their list of features was shorter, they concluded their product wasn't better than their competition's. Comparing products by the length and quality of feature lists is not going to give you an answer to your question. Answering the question "Which design generates better results?" with live experimentation techniques is key to getting to the truth.

When You Should Ask the Question

The following situations are most suitable for asking yourself the question, "Which design generates better results?":

- **Choose between design options:** When you want to compare multiple design options and decide which one is better than the others. For example, when you want to know which one out of three home page designs performs better in terms of meeting both users' and your business's goals.

- **Better understand customer tastes:** For example, when you are planning a redesign and want to learn what triggers your customers' likings. Learning what people like will help you with future design decisions.

- **Compare to production:** When you want to test changes to a page against the current design and determine which ones produce positive results. For example, when you want to know if a certain call to action button label results in a higher conversion rate than the label you currently use.

- **Compare to itself over time:** When you want to compare different versions of your product over time. For example, when you want to know if version 3 of your product is better than version 2.

- **Benchmark:** When you want to compare your product to the competition's. For example, when you realize you have a competitor, and you want to know if your product works better for users.

Getting an answer to the question "Which design generates better results?" can only be answered when you have design alternatives to show people. You need real live code and finalized designs to do it. That might be easy for small changes here and there, but could be quite a big investment for a completely new design. That said, you can answer the question even when strategizing if you ask it about designs, products, and elements done by others. For example, you can ask yourself which of two competitor's onboarding designs is better. The answer you get, as well as other factors, will help you come up with a great onboarding design. Yet the best times to answer the question are during execution and assessment, when you actually have design options to compare and test (see Figure 7.1).

A common time to ask yourself this question is when you want to experiment and learn what it takes to improve conversion rates in a certain conversion funnel. Conversion rate is the ratio between the number of people who completed a certain task in a certain page and the number of visitors to that page. For example, if 25,000 visited a landing page and 2,500 of them clicked its call-to-action button to download an app, the conversion rate is 10% (2,500 divided by 25,000). A conversion funnel is continuing that route further down to an ultimate goal of your choice. For example, to convert from a landing page visitor to a paying customer, the user needs to go through an app download and an onboarding process, as demonstrated in Figure 7.2.

Which design generates better results?

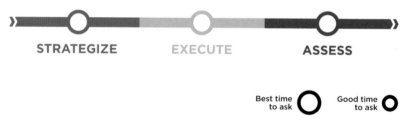

FIGURE 7.1

The big circles represent the best times for asking the question "Which design generates better results?"

A Conversion Funnel

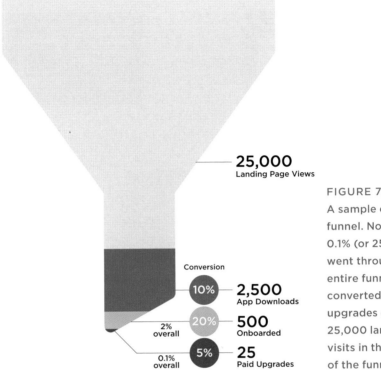

25,000
Landing Page Views

Conversion

10% — **2,500**
App Downloads

2%
overall
20% — **500**
Onboarded

0.1%
overall
5% — **25**
Paid Upgrades

FIGURE 7.2
A sample conversion funnel. Notice that 0.1% (or 25 people) went through the entire funnel and converted to paid upgrades out of the 25,000 landing page visits in the beginning of the funnel.

Answering the Question with A/B Testing

A/B testing is the practice of comparing two (or more) variations of the same page, feature, or products to see which one performs better (see Figure 7.3). Showing each variation to a different set of users and tracking key metrics, such as conversion rates, allows you to find out which one generates better results. A/B testing is also known as *split* or *bucket testing*. A related technique is called *multivariate testing* where you determine which combination of variations performs the best out of all of the possible combinations. We'll discuss this technique later in the chapter.

Measure Clicks on the "Subscribe" Button

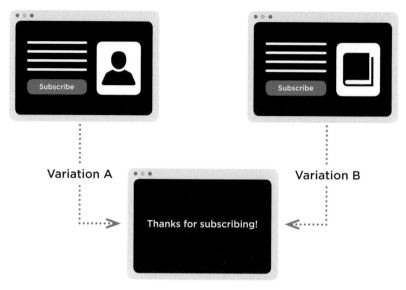

FIGURE 7.3

A/B testing of how a photo variation affects subscription conversion rates.

Is A/B Testing Relevant for Offline or Non-digital Products?

Of course! Although A/B testing can be easily implemented for products such as websites, web applications, and apps, it also applies to desktop applications, such as a Windows-based healthcare management software package, and even hardware, such as drones.

In the case of drones, you can access the data it collects on flight duration, frequency of use, altitude, crashes, malfunctions, etc. and compare it among different drone variations. Or you can ask people to use two versions of a drone and compare conversion to further actions, such as buying accessories, becoming a paid member of maintenance services, or a member of a drone community, etc. Similarly, in physical stores, you can look at the layout of a store against sales of different products, average basket value, and so on. Software packages collect all kind of metrics about their usage in the background. You can tap into that data and compare different versions using it.

Creatively crafting things to track and compare them allows you to apply A/B testing to non-digital products, features, and designs.

Although there are other methods for answering the question "Which design generates better results?" A/B testing is the most practical and effective method. Other methods, such as observing people complete different tasks with evaluated designs while measuring time-on-task, task success rates, and satisfaction, are valid, reliable, and carry many clear benefits. However, they require you to invest a lot of effort in finding research participants and to acquire great moderation skills. If research with people is not your primary job, you might find that it is hard to invest these efforts and acquire these skills in a short amount of time.

Why A/B Testing Works

A/B testing is an effective research technique that carries the following benefits:

- **Understanding users:** Leaving intuition and guesswork aside is hard. However, the immediate benefit of experimentation is learning from real human behavior. A/B testing is a form of evidence-based design that allows you not only to pick a winning design option, but also to understand your audience better, what makes them tick, what they prefer, and what they avoid.

- **Maintaining product development momentum:** Improving through proving—better conversion rates, more sign-ups, higher revenues, better communication, and supreme design. A/B testing is at its best when your goal is to learn what works practically for your customers. It is based on directly monitoring human behavior and results in clear numbers that indicate which design is delivering better results.

- **Consensus building:** Although some people are convinced this is true, not all of us are the second incarnation of Steve Jobs. You never know which design or product decision is the right one to make. You have an assumption, a hypothesis. A/B testing is a decision-making and validation tool. It works best when a team is deliberating about which decision to make. A/B testing helps in getting a team behind a certain design direction or when it tries to validate or invalidate a decision that is already made.

Two things to be aware of when planning, running, and analyzing results of A/B testing:

- **Reaching a local maxima:** A/B testing (especially a series of tests) is excellent for improving a specific design and maximizing its potential. It will bring a design to a better state of what it was before you started A/B testing. That said, A/B testing will never ever tell you or help you uncover what would be a better design, a different feature, or ways to meet your audience needs better. Therefore, it will always help you reach a local maximum, not *the* maximum. For that to happen, other techniques are at your disposal, specifically ones this book guides you through in Chapters 1, 2, 3, and 4.

- **Learning general lessons:** A/B testing is great with identifying what works in a certain design. It is not in any way a technique for crafting a style guide. The fact that a certain photo or label or page layout worked in a certain A/B test does not mean it will work in any other case. It (just) means it worked for what you are testing. Not more, not less. Don't jump to conclusions such as, "Green call-to-action buttons with Helvetica fonts size 24 points will always work in a landing page." They worked for the landing page you tested next to other very specific elements on that page that you compared against other alternatives.

Other Questions A/B Testing Helps Answer

Other than the "Which design generates better results?" question, A/B testing is a great method for answering the following questions as well. In other words, if you ask yourself any one of these questions, A/B testing is a technique that can help you get an answer:

- Which product/feature change results in usage growth?
- What is most effective about the product/feature?
- Which landing page generates higher conversion rates?
- Which version of a new feature results in a larger revenue?
- Which call-to-action results in higher click-through rates?

- Which layout generates more sales?
- Which email campaign performs better?
- Which design results in most sign-ups?

How to Answer the Question

The following is a how-to guide that takes you step-by-step through the process of using A/B testing to answer the question "Which design generates better results?"

STEP 1: Decide what to compare.

Simply put, you can compare almost anything. While A/B testing can work very well for landing pages (see Figure 7.4) and measuring conversion rates, it is also great for evaluating and experimenting with design elements, features, and even comparing complete product features. In other words, it is perfectly okay to A/B test something as small as two different designs of a button label, as well as a whole feature in two competing products. Just be aware that if you test too small of a difference, your test may take too long. The more different the variations, the quicker you will have significant results.

FIGURE 7.4

A landing page.

As a first step, decide what to test, what to compare, and which metrics you are going to monitor to understand which button, label, page, or feature works best for users. For example, imagine that you are interested in learning which online grocery shopping onboarding process works better: one that includes a four-page questionnaire about one's habits and preferences, or one that only asks for a full name and email address. The metric you are looking to affect would be conversion into a registered, "onboarded" user. In other words, you would monitor the ratio between the number of people who started the onboarding process and the number of people who completed it and went on to purchasing items. During the test, you will direct 50% of the traffic to each form. If 10,000[1] people start each evaluated process and 100 of them purchase items after completing the four-page form, and 500 purchase items after completing the shorter form, then conversion rates are as shown on Table 7.1. In this example, these results mean that the shorter process generates higher conversion rates.

TABLE 7.1 CALCULATING CONVERSION RATES

Onboarding	Accessed	Purchased	Conversion Rate
Long	10,000	100	100/10,000 = 1%
Short	10,000	500	500/10,000 = 5%

Another consideration for prioritizing what to compare is a combination of the risk of making a wrong decision without accurate data and how much you know about what you are about to experiment with. Don't waste your time on issues with low risk (for example choosing between 41 shades of light blue for a call-to-action button) or ones you discussed and analyzed in the last ten team meetings. Simply put, prioritize high-risk unknowns (see Figure 7.5). If you struggle with what to test, as a rule of thumb, if there's something you've been 100% certain of from day one and never questioned, then you should definitely put it at the top of your list of things to test!

---

1 You will not always need so many people for A/B testing. Keep reading, explanations coming up.

Prioritize Experiments

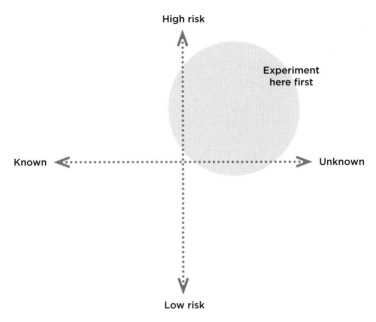

FIGURE 7.5

Prioritize high-risk unknowns for experiments (with permission from Giff Constable).

What *Not* to A/B Test

- **Too many changes at once:** If you make 10 changes in a page and want to experiment to see which changes work best, don't change everything at once. If you do, you have no idea which change affected the good or bad result. Instead, test changes linearly (test change 1, then 2, then 3 until you get to the last change) or run a multivariate test where you test all the possible combinations of changes (more on that coming in Step 2).

- **Prices:** A/B testing is very bad for testing different conditions for a sale or product prices. The reason is that pricing is a sensitive subject in general, and no one wants to feel cheated or ripped off. People might see the different prices and complain to and about you. If you want to experiment with prices, do it in a much less public way than A/B testing.

Compare pages, tasks, features, or elements with an A/B test.

A typical A/B test involves creating two alternative pages, tasks, or features (A and B), showing each of them to a certain percentage of visitors, all the while monitoring a certain result (or metric) to learn which alternative is most effective. To run an A/B test, first create the experiment's variations. Variations are the different options that will be evaluated:

- **Pages:** Compare how different page designs affect a certain measured goal. For example, compare how two different designs for a checkout page affect the rate of orders placed.

- **Tasks:** Compare how the same task is completed with different designs or products. For example, in the onboarding task described previously (see Table 7.1), the metric you might monitor is the conversion rate of completing the onboarding process and becoming a paying customer.

- **Features:** Compare users using two variations of a feature. For example, compare how users add a new contact with two completely different versions of the same feature. For example, variation A is adding a new contact by typing text into a form, and variation B is adding a new contact by voice interaction.

An A/B test is great for evaluating two (or more) variations of a page, task, or feature. If you want to compare different variations of multiple elements within a page, implement a similar technique called a *multivariate test* (see sidebar).

Carefully consider the differences in the variations you choose to test. If the variations are too similar, you are probably going to have a statistical tie unless you are a monster like the YouTube or Amazon home page. Make your variations as different as possible. You'll then have a winner quickly.

Multivariate Tests

When you want to experiment with different elements on a specific page, a multivariate test might come in handy. Multivariate tests are excellent for figuring out which design elements work best together with other elements on a specific page. First, you define elements inside a page (for example, a picture, a text, and a button) and come up with different alternatives to each element. Then, during the test, each element is shown combined with all the other elements to visitors. The resulting combinations are derived from the number of elements multiplied by the number of element variations. In a multivariate test, you put each and every combination to a live test. Results will give you a winning option (or options) and a much better understanding of your visitors. Keep in mind that the number of elements you want to test and the number of variations per element would significantly increase the total number of variations to test (see Figure 7.6).

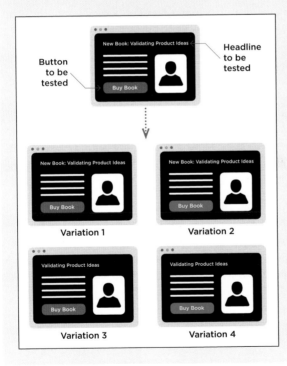

FIGURE 7.6

Two elements (button color and headline) with two variations per element create four variations for testing.

Find research participants.

The good news is that you don't need to recruit participants for an A/B test because some of your traffic will be redirected to the experimental variation (or variations) without being aware of it. The bad news is that to get a decisive answer to your question ("Which design generates better results?"), and to avoid a statistical tie, you need a good combination of several factors, one being the number of visitors (another is how small of a difference you are testing). This calculator will help you with that— bit.ly/validating-chapter-7-ab-testing-calculator.

Keep in mind the importance of matching samples as much as possible. For example, running the two designs at the same time and ensuring that both visitor samples are equally spread across the days and times of day, possibly also referrals (for example, coming from a search results page vs. affiliate link vs. entering URL). Try to avoid situations where you end up running one variation two months after the other variation and getting a confounding seasonal effect.

STEP 4: **Evaluate if it's a good time to test.**

The best time to run an A/B test is when all the variations are on equal footing. In other words, make sure that you are comparing apples to apples. This is not to say that both variations need to be perfected, but make a decision to A/B test when you have two great design solutions that you want input about which will provide better results for people.

For example, comparing a call-to-action screen on the same app over Android and iPhone smartphones is good because it means you are comparing two functioning versions of the same screen. If, for example, the iPhone app didn't have that call-to-action screen feature, it would have been a bad idea to compare the fully functional Android feature with an iPhone prototype or a paper sketch of the same screen. Although it can be done technically and logistically, it is not recommended. Comparing a functioning, released feature with a prototype would bias the results. Think of latency, for example. The time it takes a real product to respond to user actions is very different than that of a prototype that has no database behind it. Make sure that both variations are in a condition that allows for a pure comparison.

STEP 5: Determine what would be an actionable result.

Every experiment and research activity generates results. There are two types of results: the first type comprises an interesting result, which is, well, interesting and nice to know. For example, it's interesting to know a statistic that 40% of your audience uses an iPhone and 45% uses an Android smartphone. If you have no intention of doing anything about it, then this is an interesting, non-actionable result. The second type is an actionable result. These are results you can actually do something about. They help you not only learn more about your audience but also make short- and long-term design and product decisions. For example, imagine that an A/B test resulted in significantly higher conversion rates for a product page that had high-quality photos of people using the product compared to ones that only had high-quality product photos. You now know your audience much better than before. Not only that, you now have a clear, actionable design element you know to be working well for your users and the business.

When you plan an A/B test, think about the end result. Imagine what would you do with them when you get them. If it's not clear or if you are not sure, then you probably sought *interesting* rather than *actionable* results. For example, say to yourself, beforehand, "If design A proves to drive at least 20% more conversions than design B (with statistically significant results), I am going to choose to implement design A, no matter what I personally prefer in design B."

STEP 6: Choose the tool, configure the test, and launch it.

There are dozens of tools to choose from for your A/B test. Some offer very basic and simple configuration for the novice, more clueless explorer. Others require you to know your way around sophisticated code. Some offer support for testing your website and basic landing pages, while other tools support experiments run for native iOS and Android apps. Some even offer all of the above. Two tools that seem to provide decent functionality for most use cases are Google Analytics' experiments and Optimizely.

Beware of Vanity Metrics

The number of users, visitors, and downloads, as well as likes, followers, and number of people you learned from are all examples of vanity metrics. The thing with vanity metrics is that no matter what happens, they will always grow. And come to think of it, they don't mean much. What you'll find to be much more beneficial than metrics are ratios. For example, rather than monitoring the number of site visitors, it is much more meaningful to monitor the conversion rate (the ratio between visitors who completed a task and total visitors). Or you might even come up with a conversion score and track it over time. Figure 7.7 demonstrates how data *for the same time period* is much more valuable and meaningful when you examine a ratio rather than a vanity metric, such as number of visitors.

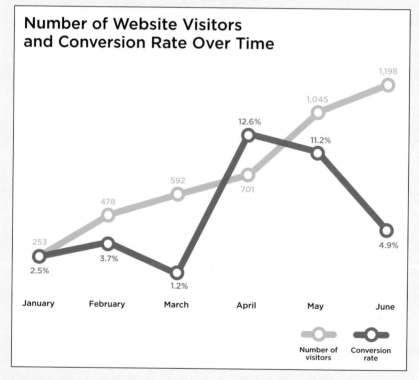

FIGURE 7.7

Notice how for the same time period, data is so much more meaningful when you monitor conversion rates rather than number of visitors. The number of visitors tells you nothing about the increased conversions in April and drop in June.

No matter which tool you pick to run your A/B test, these are roughly the steps you need to go through when you configure your experiment:[2]

1. **Set the metric you will look at.** Configure the result you want to compare. This might be a conversion rate, success rate, click-through rate, revenue, etc.

2. **Set the percentage of traffic to experiment.** If you don't have a lot of traffic, it makes sense to divert an equal amount of traffic to each variation. However, if you have a well-established website or product with many visitors or users, you might want to direct a small percentage (1–5%) of traffic to the evaluated variations.

3. **Point the tool to the evaluated variations.** Tell the tool what the starting points are for each of the variations. For comparing landing pages, these would be their URLs. If you compare conversion rates of two variations of a product page, these would be the URLs of the evaluated product changes. If you compare native apps, these would be containers defined with Google Tag Manager (if you use Google Analytics' Experiments) or through simple configurations in Optimizely's Visual Editor.

4. **Set a confidence level.** The confidence level sets how certain you want to be with the results of the experiment. The conventional level is 95%. This means you can be sure this data will be true 95% of the time when you repeat this experiment. It's up to you to change the confidence level so you are more (e.g., set to 99%) or less certain (e.g., set to 80%). Keep in mind that higher confidence levels require more traffic to reach statistically significant results.

5. **Set the experiment duration or quota.** Calculate how long the test is going to last. As for the timing of the test, make sure that you avoid any known seasonal effects. Each business has different peaks. Be aware of yours and try testing as much as possible at the most typical, average time for your business that represents what happens most of the year.

Advanced tools provide more options for tweaks and configurations, yet the previous list contains the basic configuration required to launch an A/B test.

---

2 Waisberg, 2013.

Whichever tool or service you choose to use, click its launch button and immediately begin monitoring results. Test to see if traffic does indeed get redirected to all variations. Depending on the volume of traffic, it might take between a few seconds and a couple of hours until you get the picture and begin to see data flowing.

STEP 7: Stop the test.

You will be tempted to stop the test as soon as results show a statistically significant winner. However, don't be tempted to stop it prematurely because results seem clear and decisive. This might not always be the case. Stop the test after at least seven days, preferably after 30 days. The reason is that there is a very significant seasonal effect when it comes to weekdays, weekends, and the beginning and ending of a month. These effects highly depend on the type of business you're in, so be sure to take that into account when you are about to stop the test.

STEP 8: Understand the results.

Different A/B testing tools give you various analysis tools for the results of your experiment. Some will drop raw data on your head, with which you need to deal by using statistics software packages such as R, or SPSS, or Excel in some cases. Others, such as Optimizely and Google's Experiments,[3] provide you with clear results dashboards (see Figure 7.8).

These results dashboards will indicate if there's a winner based on your initial configuration for the experiment. The experiment insights dashboard shown in Figure 7.8 indicates a clear winner ("New Design + FB Box") while the one in Figure 7.9 indicates there's not enough data to declare a winner. Notice that in Figure 7.8 only a few dozen visitors were enough to declare a winner while in Figure 7.9 even thousands of visitors did not provide enough data. The reason is that individual results in each experiment had different variance scores. The experiment shown in Figure 7.8 probably had a relatively high variance score, while the one shown in Figure 7.9 had close to zero variance.

---

3 Full disclosure: I work at Google.

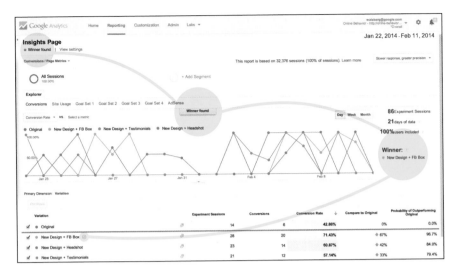

FIGURE 7.8

The Google Analytics Experiments page—a clear winner (contributed by Daniel Waisberg, Analytics Advocate, Google).

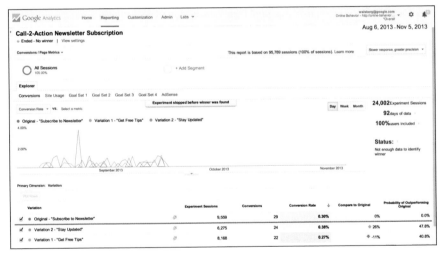

FIGURE 7.9

The Google Analytics Experiments page—no clear winner (contributed by Daniel Waisberg, Analytics Advocate, Google).

The Confidence Interval

A confidence interval indicates the uncertainty of an estimate. You are probably most familiar with its use in election polls. For example, when poll results show that one candidate gained 54% of the votes and the other candidate received 43%, the report usually also says something about the "sampling error." In our example, the sampling error might have been ±5%. This sampling error is a way to describe variability, or how much individual data points differ from each other outside of the poll, in the general population. The sampling error creates the confidence interval (see Figure 7.10). In our example, candidate 1's result can be described this way: Candidate 1 got 54% of the poll votes, and we expect she will get between 49% and 59% in the upcoming election. Candidate 2 got 43% of the poll votes, and we expect he will get between 38% and 48% among the general population. Confidence intervals are 10% wide (±5% from the average).

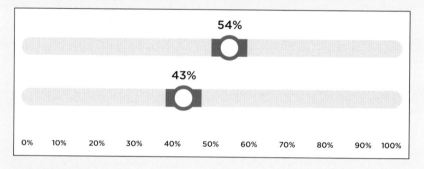

FIGURE 7.10
Candidate 1 with 54% and candidate 2 with 43% ±5% sampling error.
The error bars show the confidence interval.

A statistical tie happens when results are not statistically significant. In other words, when confidence intervals around the averages overlap, you cannot confidently determine which variation is better.

As an example, let's take an A/B test done for two variations of an onboarding process for a certain service. The compared result is the conversion rate of registered users of the service. With a 95% confidence level (meaning we can be sure this data is true 95% of the times we repeat this experiment), the entire user population that uses variation A (not just those who visited the website during the experiment) will have a conversion rate of between 53% and 61% with an average of 57%. As for variation B, the conversion will be between 55% and 65% with an average of 60% (see Figure 7.11). The width of both confidence intervals is overlapping enough that there is no clear winner. These results are not statistically significant. They would have been significant if there were no overlap of confidence intervals. If we were to run this test again, there is a reasonable chance that variation A would get a higher average than variation B. You should try to avoid a no-winner situation since you will obviously not get an answer to the question you started with, "Which design generates better results?" Note that most A/B testing tools will calculate if there's a winner or a statistical tie for you automatically.

The cost of avoiding a statistical tie is having a large number of visitors participate in the experiment. If you can only drive small numbers of visitors to your evaluated variations, you take a risk of reaching a statistical tie. Use the A/B testing calculator to reduce the risk of reaching a statistical tie situation—bit.ly/validating-chapter-7 -ab-testing-calculator.

Onboarding Conversion

Error bars represent 95% confidence interval

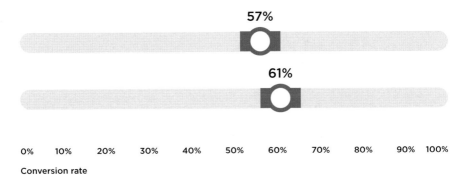

FIGURE 7.11
A statistical tie happens when confidence intervals of the two evaluated variations overlap. In other words, although the average indicates a winning variation, there is no statistical significance, so you cannot conclude that any of the variations is a winner.

Use the Term "Statistical Significance" Correctly

Some people are confused by the term *statistical significance*. I hear people say that, "a usability test with five participants is not statistically significant," or that, "you need at least 500 participants for results to be statistically significant." These are misuses of the term. Statistical significance is determined by *comparing two (or more) sets of data*. If this is not what you are doing, then you are using the term incorrectly. Statistical significance is achieved when there is no overlap between the confidence intervals around the averages of the evaluated datasets and, if you love your stats, when the p in a one- or two-tailed p-test is smaller than 0.05.

Therefore, results of a usability test cannot be statistically significant, no matter how many people participate. And if you compare results in a usability test, then you can definitely reach significance even with five participants (which is a lot less than 500).

STEP 9: Understand "why," not just "what."

A huge downside, disadvantage, and limitation of A/B testing is that results never tell you why things are the way they are. An A/B test gives you accurate, pinpointed data about *what* happened and zero information about *why* it happened. You don't really know what visitors wanted to do or why they did what they did.

Here is an example. Let's say you got a result that, in one variation of your home page, the bounce rate was 99%. In other words, for 99% of the site visitors, the home page was the first and last page they visited. Is that a good or bad result? While high bounce rates are usually a bad thing, it is not necessarily the case here. It all depends on *why* people visited your website. If they wanted to buy a book, it's probably a very bad result. However, if they wanted to see how your company's new logo looks, it might be a great result. A/B testing results will never tell you what people wanted to do. They'll only give you a number—99%. It's great to know that number yet it's only half of the answer to your question: "Which design generates better results?"

To understand the *why*, you can speculate and make an assumption. To test that assumption, have a few people visit the site (including its different variations) while thinking aloud as you watch what they do and listen to what they say. (More on this technique in Chapter 6.)

STEP 10: **Make a decision.**

If you identified a clear, decisive winner, especially if it's not what you currently offer, make a decision to change things and follow through with your decision. Monitor analytics after you make the change to be sure that real-world results align with the findings of the test. For example, if one variation of your product page resulted in a 68% conversion rate (±7%) compared to your current, live product page that resulted in a 43% (±4%) conversion rate, you have a winner. Make a decision to change your product page to what you tested in its variation.

Or you might get results that indicate a tie. A statistical tie is affected by a combination of three variables, two of which you can control:

1. **Sample size:** The smaller the sample size (i.e., fewer visitors to your experiment), the wider the confidence interval. To break a statistical tie, allow for more visitors to participate in your A/B test. For example, if only 30 people accessed each of the A/B test variations, it is more likely that you break the tie and reach statistical significance with 300 visitors per variation.

2. **Confidence level:** The higher the confidence level, the wider the confidence interval. To break a statistical tie, lower the confidence level. For example, if you are not risking a lot with the decision you are about to take after A/B testing, lower the confidence level from the conventional 95% to 90%. Be aware, though, that in a way, by doing that, you are "forcing" a winner. Consider this option carefully, as well as continuing the test for more time or leaving it as is and moving on to the next test. However, if it is a high-risk decision you are about to make, increase your confidence level to 99%, to be very sure of the results.

3. **Variability of results:** Variability is the only variable you cannot control. As the variability of the population you are sampling from increases, the confidence interval of your sample gets wider, increasing the chances of getting results that are not statistically significant. To break a statistical tie, you can only play with the two previously mentioned variables (sample size and confidence level) and hope variability is not too high.

In case results indicated a statistical tie, your decision might be to continue the experiment until a winner is declared or end the test and proceed to a more meaningful one.

Decide what to test next.

A/B testing's most known goal is to determine which alternative page, design element, task, feature, or product is better. However, a much more important goal of A/B testing is to understand customers better, to uncover what makes them tick, and to identify their problems. That said, after you have collected data in an A/B test, understood the results, and made a decision, it is now time to decide what to test next. A/B testing is almost always a starting point, not a final destination. If you tested one element, maybe your next test involves combining it with another element. Or if you perfected a set of elements, test layout changes. If you have two variations of the same page, test which one works better and then test elements within that variation. What would be your next experiment? There's (almost) always something to learn from an A/B test.

Other Methods to Answer the Question

The following methods can also be used to answer the same question instead of A/B testing:

- **Online usability testing,** where you ask dozens or hundreds of representative users to complete tasks with the evaluated variations while measuring their efficiency, effectiveness, and satisfaction (see Chapter 6).

- **In-person usability testing,** where you ask a number of representative users to complete tasks with the evaluated variations in front of your eyes while measuring their efficiency, effectiveness, and satisfaction. Read all about it in *Rocket Surgery Made Easy* by Steve Krug.

NOTE A/B TESTING RESOURCES

Access the online resource page for A/B testing on the book's companion website at leanresearch.co. You'll find templates, checklists, videos, slide decks, articles, and book recommendations.

A/B Testing Checklist

- ☐ Decide what to compare.
- ☐ Compare pages, tasks, features, or elements with an A/B test.
- ☐ Find research participants.
- ☐ Evaluate if it's a good time to test.
- ☐ Determine what would be an actionable result.
- ☐ Choose a tool, configure the test, and launch it.
- ☐ Stop and test.
- ☐ Understand the results.
- ☐ Understand "why," not just "what."
- ☐ Make a decision.
- ☐ Decide what to test next.

"What are we doing here?" Will whispered to Dana.

"First-hand observation," she whispered back. Dana felt sure that, even if the shopping list angle wasn't the right one, there was still something with shopping that note.io might help out with. So they were spending a few hours with Lisa, a research participant, and her two kids as they went grocery shopping.

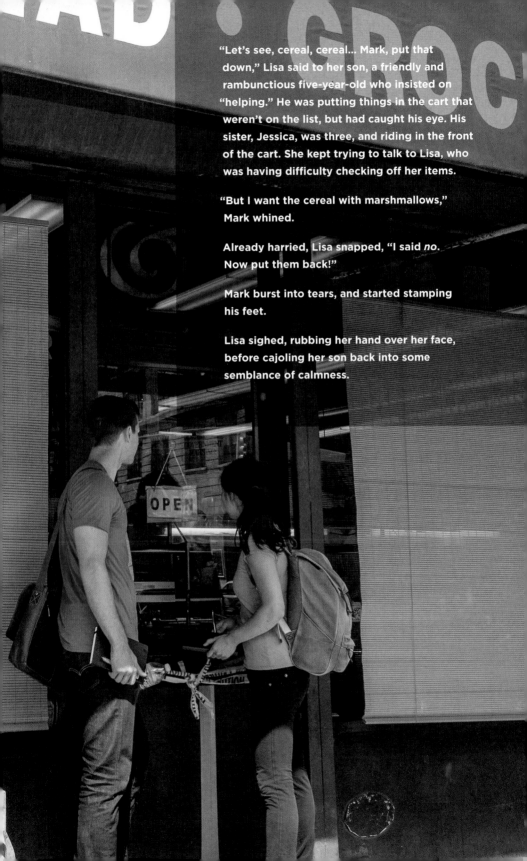

"Let's see, cereal, cereal... Mark, put that down," Lisa said to her son, a friendly and rambunctious five-year-old who insisted on "helping." He was putting things in the cart that weren't on the list, but had caught his eye. His sister, Jessica, was three, and riding in the front of the cart. She kept trying to talk to Lisa, who was having difficulty checking off her items.

"But I want the cereal with marshmallows," Mark whined.

Already harried, Lisa snapped, "I said *no*. Now put them back!"

Mark burst into tears, and started stamping his feet.

Lisa sighed, rubbing her hand over her face, before cajoling her son back into some semblance of calmness.

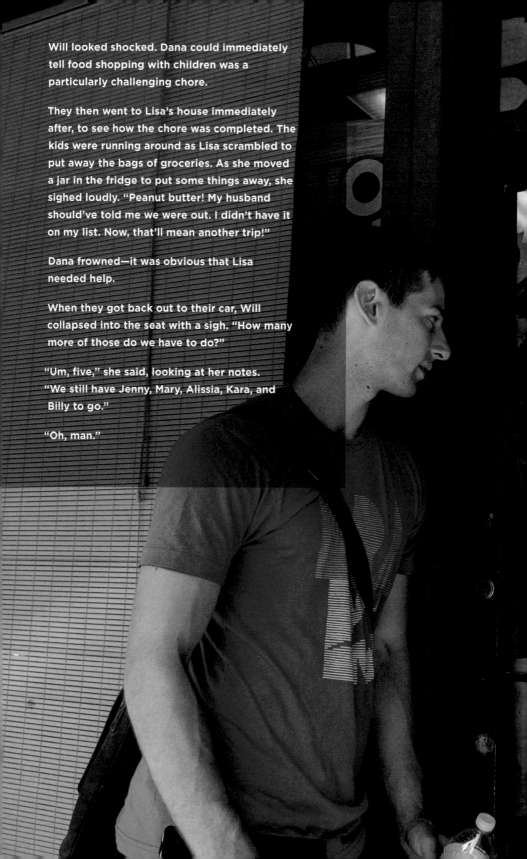

Will looked shocked. Dana could immediately tell food shopping with children was a particularly challenging chore.

They then went to Lisa's house immediately after, to see how the chore was completed. The kids were running around as Lisa scrambled to put away the bags of groceries. As she moved a jar in the fridge to put some things away, she sighed loudly. "Peanut butter! My husband should've told me we were out. I didn't have it on my list. Now, that'll mean another trip!"

Dana frowned—it was obvious that Lisa needed help.

When they got back out to their car, Will collapsed into the seat with a sigh. "How many more of those do we have to do?"

"Um, five," she said, looking at her notes. "We still have Jenny, Mary, Alissia, Kara, and Billy to go."

"Oh, man."

When _____, I
so I can _____

"Okay, Jennifer said we should work with Clay
Christensen's Jobs framework for product
design," Dana said, after they'd done all
the research.

Will was grateful to be back in the office. The
trips with the families had been grueling, to say
the least. Still, some of what they'd seen had
been eye opening. It had made a difference
to get the real world study and see what the
needs really were.

"We'll want to look at it from a motivation, goal,
and intended outcome viewpoint," said Will.

"We can design each problem in a job,"
Dana added. She walked over to the
whiteboard, writing:

When _____, I want to _____,
so I can _____.

"I noticed that for Lisa, she was upset when
she got home to find the peanut butter nearly
empty," Dana said, picking up a marker. "So, at
home, when *a grocery item is out*," she wrote
underneath, "I want to be *notified*, so I can *buy
a new one at the store*."

1. At home, when a
is out, I want to
I can buy a new

2 "I saw that the kids often had meltdowns when they were being ignored or told no," Dana said, writing another line. "A lot of the parents were impatient, then felt badly about it, or said that they were really trying to keep it together. Maybe we can work with that. So at the store, when *my child has a tantrum*, I want to *control myself better*, so I can *be a better role model*."

"And when they got back, they were trying to keep track of their kids *and* get all the groceries put away," added Will, getting into the spirit of it. "When *I'm back from the store*, I want *the kids to help*, so I can.... What?"

"So you can *do it quickly*," Dana wrote in, "and *so they can learn a life lesson*."

They surveyed the board.

"We may be onto something here," Will mused.

CHAPTER 8

How Do People Find Stuff?

You can't use what you can't find.[1]

—Peter Morville

Many people tend to think they don't have enough time. Not enough time to read, not enough time to sleep, not enough time to eat properly, and not enough time to run necessary errands. People spend good chunks of their lives looking for stuff. They look for car keys, Worcestershire sauce in the grocery store, baggage information in an airline website because they can't find their suitcases, and where their bank decided to hide the check deposit function on its mobile app. Not being able to find stuff in products such as websites and apps is a cause for delayed task completion, failure to complete those tasks, and feelings of frustration and dissatisfaction.

This chapter will guide you through an evidence-based process for learning how people find stuff and what you can do about it in your product to support user behavior to make finding stuff in your product easy, fast, and smooth.

Why Is This Question Important?

One of the most frustrating things for people who use digital products such as websites, Web applications, or mobile apps is the time they waste on finding where in the product they can accomplish their tasks and meet their goals. They struggle with unclear navigation hierarchies, have trouble figuring out what to click first, and in many cases, they are just lost.

The question "How do people find stuff?" is important for understanding and learning about *findability*, or the ease with which information can be found. Findability is one of the key aspects that impacts what people think about the quality of your product.[2] Since the inability to find stuff is one of the biggest reasons that prevents task completion,[3] answering this question is key for your (and your product's) success.

---

1 Morville, Peter. *Ambient Findability: What We Find Changes Who We Become.* Sebastopol, CA: O'Reilly Media. 2005.

2 The Impact of Findability on Student Perceptions of Online Course Quality and Experience: bit.ly/validating-chapter-8-findability-affect-1

3 IA Task Failures Remain Costly: bit.ly/validating-chapter-8-findability-affect-2

When Should You Ask It?

"How do people find stuff?" is a question far too few product development practitioners answer on time. There are three great times to ask the question: toward the end of strategizing your product, during development (prior to launch), and just after launch (see Figure 8.1). When you strategize, you figure out a lot of things about the need for your product, your target audience, and what it wants. Toward the end of strategizing, you begin planning how to organize information and content in your product and how to structure it in a logical way so that people who use it can find what they want. During development, findability comes up when you craft your first product design mockups or prototypes. This is a great time to evaluate the design to learn if people understand the navigation hierarchy, labeling, and the structure of information in the product. Lastly, after the product has launched and people start using it, it is yet another opportunity to learn if they get lost, what they click on first, and how they find stuff in it.

How do people find stuff?

STRATEGIZE　　　EXECUTE　　　ASSESS

Best time to ask ◯　　Good time to ask ◯

FIGURE 8.1

When is a good time to ask "How do people find stuff?" The larger circle represents the best time, while the smaller ones indicate other times recommended for asking the question.

Answering the Question with Tree Testing, First-Click Testing, and Lostness Metric

Three effective ways for answering the question "How do people find stuff?" are tree testing, first-click test, and using the lostness metric. These research techniques can all be applied as part of a usability test (online, as described in Chapter 6, or in-person) or as a stand-alone study targeted solely on findability. These are all extremely easy to implement and provide a high ROI (return on investment) since you learn critical lessons about findability in your product while investing very little effort.

Tree testing is a research method in which participants are asked to find stuff by using the product's information structure, represented by a tree (see Figure 8.2). Services such as Treejack by Optimal Workshop and UserZoom's tree testing study provide the functionality required to launch such a study quickly and get clear, immediate results. Figure 8.3 shows how tree testing looks in UserZoom.

FIGURE 8.2
Navigation hypothesis for A-Z Airways in a Treejack test.

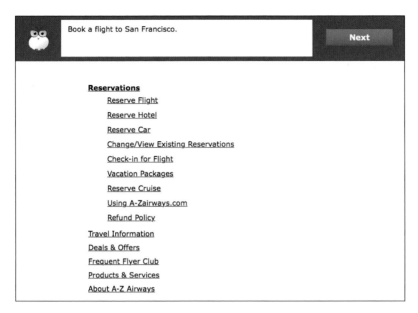

Book a flight to San Francisco.

Next

Reservations
Reserve Flight
Reserve Hotel
Reserve Car
Change/View Existing Reservations
Check-in for Flight
Vacation Packages
Reserve Cruise
Using A-Zairways.com
Refund Policy
Travel Information
Deals & Offers
Frequent Flyer Club
Products & Services
About A-Z Airways

FIGURE 8.3
Navigation tree testing for A-Z Airways in a UserZoom test.

Taking a wrong turn, particularly when it's the first turn, has a
critical effect on task completion. Think about driving from your
home to an unfamiliar destination four hours away. How big would
your mistake be if you took a wrong turn in the beginning of your
journey? You might end up driving eight instead of four hours. When
it comes to digital products, the situation is not so different. Users
who click down the right path on the first click complete their task
successfully 87% of the time, while those who click down the wrong
path on the first click tend to only complete their task successfully
46% of the time.[4] A first-click test, where you learn specifically about
the first step people take on their way to accomplish a certain goal
or specific task, can inform your design in ways that will significantly improve your product. First-click tests can be completed with
mockups, screenshots, prototypes of any fidelity level, wireframes,
or existing websites, apps, or other digital products. Figure 8.4
demonstrates what a first-click test looks like in Chalkmark, a tool by
Optimal Workshop for running online first-click tests with remote or
in-person participants.

---

4 bit.ly/validating-chapter-8-first-click

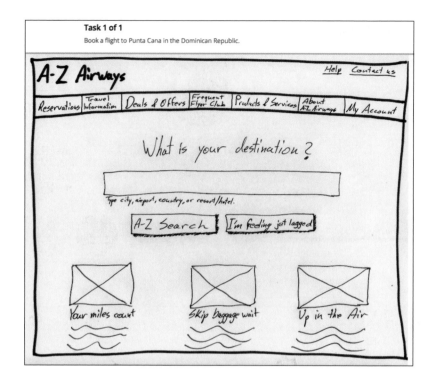

FIGURE 8.4
Navigation hypothesis for A-Z Airways in Chalkmark.

The lostness metric is a measure of efficiency using a digital product or service. It tells you how lost people are when they use the product (see Figure 8.5). Lostness scores range from zero to one.

A high score (closer to 1) means that people are very lost and having trouble finding what they need. A low score (closer to 0) means that people find what they want relatively easy. At lostness scores of about 0.4 and up, it is very clear a person is lost even if you sit next to him and watch what he does. The lostness metric can only be measured in a meaningful way if you know what users want to do. This means that measuring it by looking at analytics data or logs is useless because you have no idea what people wanted to do, or which task they wanted to complete. The best way to measure lostness is in a usability test where participants are asked to complete a task. This way, you know exactly what they are trying to do, what the optimal path to do it is, and how lost they are.

Low Lostness

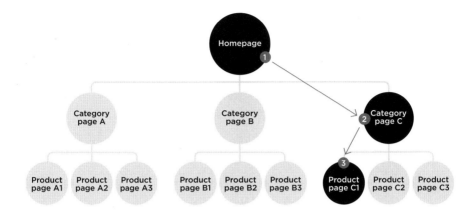

High Lostness

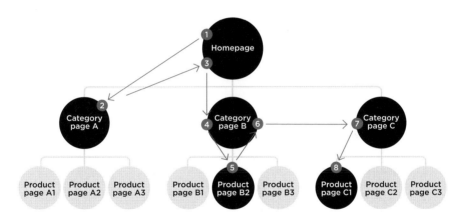

FIGURE 8.5

Lostness example: reaching the same website location with different lostness levels. (with permission from Bill Albert)

Why Tree Testing, First-Click Testing, and Lostness Metric Work

Tree testing, first-click testing, and lostness metric are excellent ways of learning about product findability for the following reasons:

- Fast turnaround time for results

- Very early validation before one line of code is written, as well as with advanced prototypes or released products

- Powerful comparison data to indicate if design is improving (or better than another design)

- Eye-candy deliverables to attract attention and help get buy-in for making changes

Other Questions Tree Testing, First-Click Testing, and Lostness Metric Help Answer

Other than the "How do people find stuff?" question, tree testing, first-click testing, and lostness metric are great methods for answering the following questions as well. If you ask yourself any one of these questions, tree testing, first-click testing, and lostness metric can help you get an answer:

- Can people use the product/feature?

- What is the overall experience of people with the product/feature?

- How lost are people when they use the product/feature?

- Does the product/feature load users' minds?

- How do people organize information in the product/feature?

- What are the product/feature's design strengths?

- What are the things that should be improved in the product/feature?

- How easy or hard is it to learn how to use the product/feature?

- Why does a product/feature work well?

- Why does a product/feature fail?

- Do people notice a certain screen element?

- What signals the product/feature's success or failure?

- What pain points do people have related to the product/feature?

- Where are people getting stuck on the product/feature?

How to Answer the Question

The following is a how-to guide that takes you step-by-step through the process of using tree testing, first-click testing, and lostness metric to answer the question "How do people find stuff?"

STEP 1: Write a one-page plan.

Discuss the following information with your team, come to an agreement, have a shared understanding of what's going to happen during the test, and write a one-page plan (similar to the plans in Chapters 2 and 6). See the following sidebar for a one-page plan of a comparative tree test.

1. **Background:** What led us here to learn about findability?

2. **Goals:** What is the reason for this study? What is the end result of this research activity? (For example, it might be to improve the product's information structure.)

3. **Research questions:** What do we specifically want to learn? For example, are there too many options in the navigation bar? Do people find out how to sign up for the service quickly enough? What are the elements that attract the most attention?

4. **Methodology:** Which research technique will be used, how long will it take, and where?

5. **Participants:** What are the characteristics of the people we want to participate in this study?

6. **Schedule:** When do we need results? When can people in the team be available to come together about their conclusions?

A-Z Airways Flight Booking—Tree Testing

(Sample One-Page Plan)

by Jane Kay-Smith, co-founder, Jane@azairways.com

Background

Since January 2009, when A-Z Airways was introduced to the world, it was known for its high-quality flight experience. That said, there were repeated complaints about the company's online flight booking experience. The vast majority of complaints (68%) were about not being able to find existing functionality and content. We also saw a 12% increase of calls to our call center about help with finding where to complete different tasks in the booking system. A new information architecture was designed, and the team wanted to compare it to the current design.

Goals

Validate that the new information architecture for A-Z Airways' online flight booking system improves the user experience.

Research Questions

1. How does findability compare between the old and new information architecture for the A-Z Airways online flight booking system?

2. What are the primary findability challenges people have when completing the top five tasks with the new navigation scheme for A-Z Airways' online flight booking system?

Methodology

Compare findability metrics between the old and new information architecture for the A-Z Airways online flight booking system by running a tree test for both designs. There are 250 people who will complete a tree testing activity per design (a total of 500 participants) by using an online tool. Study results will include the following metrics:

- Success
- Task difficulty
- Speed
- Directness
- Confidence

Participants

500 participants who meet the following criteria:

- Business or leisure travelers
- Ages 22 to 75 (an even mix)
- 50% booked online with A-Z Airways before, 50% who didn't
- Two-thirds complained about the A-Z Airways booking system in the past year, one-third did not

Schedule

Study dates: September 25–26

Results available: September 28

STEP 2: **Find 500 research participants.**

Findability research requires a relatively large number of study participants. A ballpark number to work with is 500 participants. Table 8.1 shows the sample size you will need to achieve 95% confidence with the findability rates. For example, at a sample size of 93, if 50% of the users locate an item, you'll be 95% confident that between 40% and 60% of all users would find the item given the same tree test. You will need to quadruple your sample size (381) to cut your margin of error in half (5%).[5]

TABLE 8.1 SAMPLE SIZE FOR PROPORTIONS USED TO ASSESS FINDABILITY (with permission from Jeff Sauro)

Sample Size	Margin of Error (+/-)
10	27%
21	20%
30	17%
39	15%
53	13%
93	10%
115	9%
147	8%
193	7%
263	6%
381	5%
597	4%
1064	3%

To find the right participants for your findability test that both qualify to participate and are willing and available to do so, craft a screening questionnaire that will screen people into or out of your study:[6]

1. List your assumptions about participant criteria (e.g., business traveler).

---

5 bit.ly/validating-chapter-8-tree-testing

6 The same list is in Chapters 1, 3, 6, and 8.

2. Transform participant criteria into measurable benchmarks (e.g., travels for business at least three times a year).

3. Transform the benchmark into a screening question or questions (e.g., How often do you go on an airplane?). If a person chooses the "right" answer, she's in. If not, she's out.

4. Craft a screening questionnaire (also called a *screener*) you can send people. (Here is a sample screener— bit.ly/validating-chapter-8-screener.)

5. Pilot-test the screener with a couple of people and make improvements.

6. Utilize social media to find research participants quickly and effectively. Chapter 9 guides you through social media usage for finding research participants, as well as detailed steps and examples for creating a great screener.

STEP 3: **State product navigation assumptions.**

In tree testing, you ask research participants to complete findability tasks by using an information structure (the "tree") presented to them. As they navigate the tree, participants are asked to determine where in it they think they'd be able to complete the task presented to them. Tree testing is extremely useful in two situations:

- When you want to evaluate an information structure, identify its weaknesses, and set a baseline for future comparisons.

- When you want to compare two different information structures to learn which one has better findability (by running the same tasks on the two trees and comparing findability metrics).

In any case, start by stating a navigation hypothesis, which is the tree (or trees) you will eventually test. If you already have a product, use either the navigation tree you currently have (if you want to validate/ invalidate it) or a new one you want to put to a test. If you're trying to make a decision between two (or more) information structures, construct them in detail. A complete navigation assumption for A-Z Airways is demonstrated in Figure 8.6.

In the next few steps, you'll craft a tree test in order to test the navigation assumption you have just created.

FIGURE 8.6
A full navigation
assumption for
A-Z Airways.

STEP 4: **Phrase instructions, tasks, and questions.**

When it comes to what study participants get from you and what
you need to prepare for them, there are three things you must craft:
instructions, tasks, and questions.

Instructions are what participants see first when they click the link
to participate in the tree testing study. The role of the instructions is
to briefly explain to participants what is going to happen, why, and
what is expected of them. Instructions must take into account that
there are two types of participants—ones that are new to using an
online tree testing tool and those that have gained experience with it.
Figure 8.7 provides instructions for participants in a treejack study.

Instructions

Here's how it works:

You will be asked to find a certain item and presented with a list of links.

Click through the list until you arrive at one that you think helps you complete the task.

If you take a wrong turn, you can go back by clicking one of the links above.

Please don't use the back button on your browser.
This is not a test of your ability, there are no right or wrong answers.

That's it, let's get started!

Continue

FIGURE 8.7
Instructions in treejack.

Creating tasks for participants to complete during tree testing requires attention to detail and feedback from others in the team. Craft tree testing tasks that focus on two areas that might overlap:

- Core tasks for which you want to validate or invalidate that people walk in the right, most optimal path.

- Tasks designed to test a specific area where you assume the information architecture is challenging. These assumption might be derived from past observations, usability tests, analytics data, or a gut feeling that something was designed in an incorrect way.

In any case, both types of tasks look the same. For example, "Imagine you are planning a trip to Bora Bora with your spouse in the first week of April of next year. You have already booked your air travel and hotel and all you have left is to book a rental car for your trip. You have received an email from A-Z Airways that said something about significant car rental discounts offered through their website. Use the tree below to indicate where you can find car rental discounts."

Another way to craft tasks takes into account the reality that participants can't really complete tasks in a tree test, so they do not need tasks with tons of details. For example, "Book a flight to San Francisco."

Tasks can either focus on core areas of the website or on areas already known to be challenging for users.

Plan on asking participants to complete tasks for no more than 15–20 minutes. This is a reasonable timeframe that people can remain focused during online tree testing. Longer sessions will result in higher drop-off rates (i.e., participants who abandon the test prior to completion) or in invalid and unreliable data due to participant fatigue. If you don't have a good feel for how long each tree testing task lasts, try it out first with a few people in person while measuring time to complete the tasks.

Questions you ask after each task and in the end of the session will help you better understand participant attitudes about their experience. Good questions to ask in a tree testing study are the following:

- Overall, how confident are you that you've completed the task successfully? (See Figure 8.8.)

- Overall, how difficult or easy was the task to complete? (See Figure 8.9.)

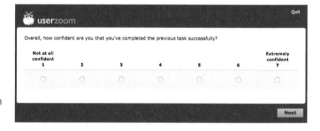

FIGURE 8.8
Confidence question in
UserZoom.

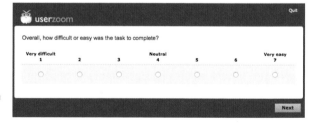

FIGURE 8.9
Task difficulty question
in UserZoom.

Launch a tree testing study.

Configure your tree testing study with a tool of your choice by adding the tree, instructions, tasks, and questions you've crafted. The tool will generate a URL you can send to people who qualified to participate in your study (based on your screener questions).

Before you launch your tree test to 500 participants, run a pilot-test. Testing the test means that you launch the study to only one participant with one goal in mind: making sure that your instructions, tasks, and questions are clear and serve their purpose. Have a person sit next to you and complete the test as you watch what happens. Don't say a word, just watch. Issues you will find in a pilot-test might include:

- Badly phrased tasks or questions
- Jargon that participants don't understand or misinterpret
- Broken or incorrect links to websites, prototypes, and apps
- Tasks with partial information
- Missing questions
- And more unknown issues (otherwise you wouldn't need to run a pilot-test)

Keep this in mind: after your test is launched to hundreds of people, it is too late to fix problems with it. The time you spend testing and perfecting it prior to launch is well worth the investment. You'll never regret running a pilot-test.

After you launch the study, track responses as they go in, and if possible, increase your recruiting efforts to make sure the study is completed as soon as possible. Figure 8.10 shows how UserZoom allows you to monitor test participation.

Project Content	All Participants	%		Previews
Project Monitor [Refresh]				
Intercepted	73 (56.2%)			0
Welcome Page	41	100%		2
Instruction Page	41	100%	⏏ 4	1
Questionnaire	37	👤 1 90%	⏏ 6	2
Complete	**30/100**	👤 1 **73%**	⏏ 10	1

FIGURE 8.10
Monitoring study participation in UserZoom.

STEP 6: **Analyze results and make a decision.**

Data collected in a tree test might have different shapes, colors, bells, and whistles. Figures 8.11–8.13 demonstrate what it might look like in Treejack and UserZoom.

FIGURE 8.11

Task results in Treejack.

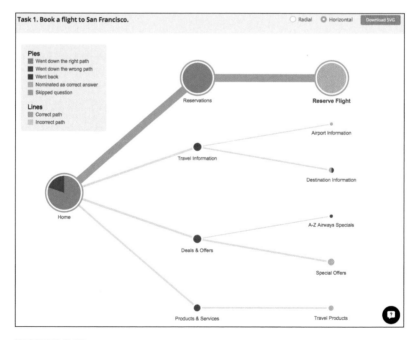

FIGURE 8.12

Pie tree results in Treejack.

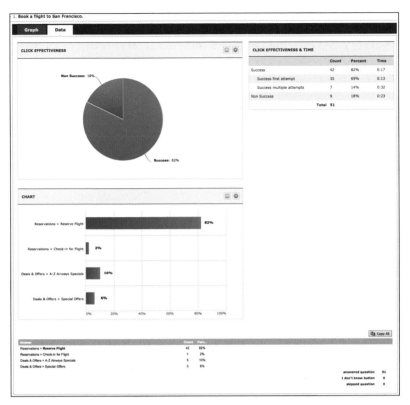

FIGURE 8.13
Tree testing results in UserZoom.

Tree testing tools use different terms and jargon for data they track. The following are the primary metrics collected during tree testing. These will help you understand results better and will be even more helpful when compared between two information structures.

- **Success:** The percentage of people who selected a correct item to complete the task.

- **Success in first attempt or direct success:** The percentage of people who clicked through an optimal path (or paths) toward a correct item to complete the task.

- **Success in multiple attempts or indirect success:** The percentage of people who clicked through an imperfect, ineffective path (or paths) toward a correct item to complete the task. These people selected the correct answer, but went back up the tree at least once.

- **Failure:** The percentage of people who clicked through a path (or paths) toward an incorrect item to complete the task, whether directly or indirectly.

Figures 8.14 and 8.15 demonstrate how success results are visualized in UserZoom and Treejack. When you compare results of two navigation structures, it is best to either present the data side by side (see example in Figure 8.16) or craft comparison charts manually (example in Figure 8.17).

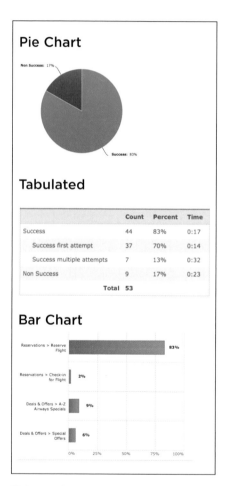

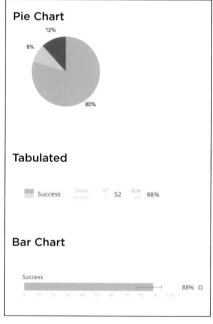

FIGURE 8.14
Tree testing success results in UserZoom.

FIGURE 8.15
Tree testing success results in Treejack.

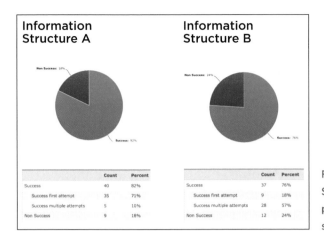

FIGURE 8.16
Side-by-side comparison of tree testing success results.

Comparison of Tree Testing Success

Error bars represent 95% confidence interval

Information Structure A

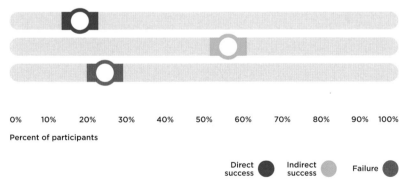

Information Structure B

0%   10%   20%   30%   40%   50%   60%   70%   80%   90%   100%

Percent of participants

Direct success   Indirect success   Failure

FIGURE 8.17

A manually created chart for comparing success results. In this example, it is easy to conclude that information structure A is better than B. Direct success is much higher, and indirect success and failure are lower. All indications point in favor of information structure A.

- **Directness:** Directness represents the percentage of participants who didn't backtrack up the tree at any point during a task. The higher this score is, the more confident you can be that participants were sure of their answers. When results show a low success score but a high directness score, it is probably because participants thought the answer was somewhere you didn't. Figure 8.18 shows how directness is presented for two tree testing tasks in Treejack.

- **Speed or time taken:** The time taken for participants to complete a task. Figure 8.19 demonstrates how Treejack presents time to complete tree testing results.

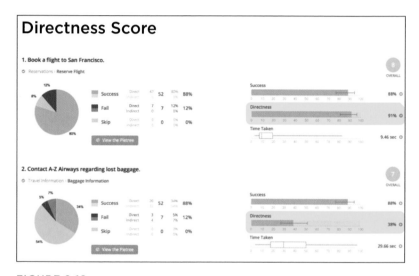

FIGURE 8.18
Tree testing success results in Treejack.

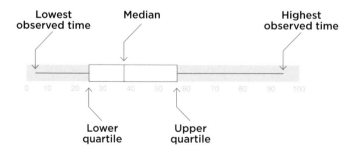

FIGURE 8.19
Tree testing time-to-complete-task results in Treejack explained.

- **Task difficulty:** A self-reported measure that provides an indication of participants' perception about how easy or hard it was to find an item. Figure 8.20 demonstrates how UserZoom presents task difficulty data.

- **Task confidence:** A self-reported measure that provides an indication of participants' perception about how sure or unsure they are that they found the correct item. Figure 8.21 demonstrates how UserZoom presents task confidence data.

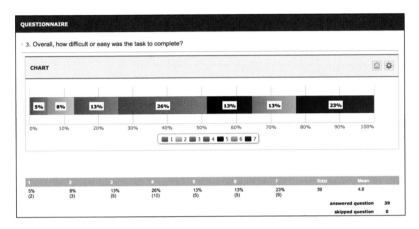

FIGURE 8.20
Task difficulty results in UserZoom. 1 (blue) means "Very difficult" and 7 (burgundy) means "Very easy."

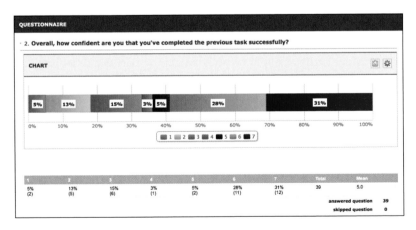

FIGURE 8.21
Confidence results in UserZoom. 1 (blue) means "Not at all confident" and 7 (burgundy) means "Extremely confident."

After you review tree testing results, make a decision about what to change in the product's information structure. Changes you make might include:

- Changing a label
- Changing a tree location
- Removing an item on the tree
- Adding or removing duplicated item locations
- Splitting items
- Merging items
- Rethinking item grouping

After you craft a revised information structure, run another tree test to validate (or invalidate) that it is better than the previous one. Findability metrics will help you come to this conclusion, especially if you ask participants to complete the same tasks.

STEP 7: Launch a first-click test.

A first-click test will help you evaluate either an information structure (as described in previous steps) or an existing screen design, sketch, mock-up, prototype, or fully baked and launched product. First-click tests are great for digital products, websites, and mobile apps. Yet, principles, practices, and research of finding out what your users' first action is are similar in effectiveness for non-digital products as well.

First clicks are best measured by asking participants to complete a task without letting them know they are taking part in a first-click test. As in tree testing, craft instructions (see example in Figure 8.22), tasks, and questions (see Step 4). Next, decide how you are going to track first clicks. You can do it manually by simply sitting down next to or watching videos of participants who attempt to complete tasks. A better alternative would be using an online tool with first-click testing capabilities, such as UserZoom or Chalkmark by Optimal Workshop.

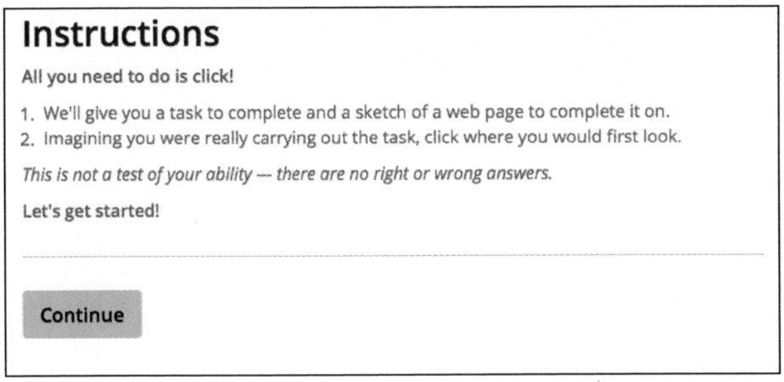

FIGURE 8.22

Instructions for a first-click test in Chalkmark.

Decide what to evaluate in the first-click test. Ideally, you'll test some design of a screen so that participants are "confused" in a good way in that they are presented not only with information structure or navigation elements but also with other screen elements that represent the final layout of the page better. That said, you can evaluate any of the following in a first-click test:

- Information structure (a "tree")

- Paper sketch

- Mockup

- Wireframe

- Low- to hi-fidelity prototype

- A half-baked to almost released product

- A released product at any stage

During the first-click test, track where participants click first and measure the time to that first click. Questions you ask after each first-click task will help you understand participants' attitudes about their experience better. Good questions to ask in a first-click test are similar to those you use in tree testing (see Figure 8.23):

- Overall, how confident are you that you found the right location?

- Overall, how difficult or easy was the task to complete?

- If you selected five or less in the previous question, please elaborate on why you chose that answer.

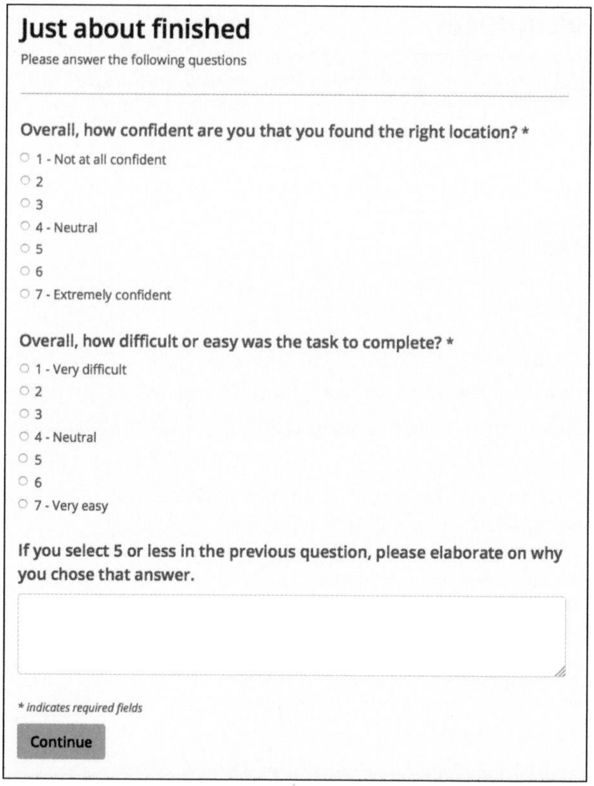

Just about finished

Please answer the following questions

Overall, how confident are you that you found the right location? *

○ 1 - Not at all confident
○ 2
○ 3
○ 4 - Neutral
○ 5
○ 6
○ 7 - Extremely confident

Overall, how difficult or easy was the task to complete? *

○ 1 - Very difficult
○ 2
○ 3
○ 4 - Neutral
○ 5
○ 6
○ 7 - Very easy

If you select 5 or less in the previous question, please elaborate on why you chose that answer.

* indicates required fields

Continue

FIGURE 8.23
Post-task questions in Chalkmark.

STEP 8: Analyze first-click results.

Identify, in advance, before you look at any result, what the best first click is to complete the task. List other first-click options that will be second-best choices, but would still lead users to complete the task successfully.

After data collection is completed, review the results:

- **Clickmap:** A typical clickmap shows you "hot" and "cold" areas of where participants clicked first. Figure 8.24 shows a sketch of a home page of an imaginary airline called A-Z Airways. Figure 8.25 is a clickmap of that page following a first-click test with 101 participants. While a heatmap of the page is providing some insight, a much better way to review data is by using areas of interest (see Figure 8.26). This way, you can select areas you are interested in and get specific first-click data about them.

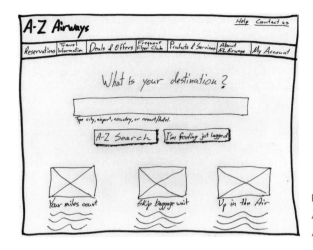

FIGURE 8.24
An imaginary A-Z
Airways home page.

Task 1. Book a flight to Punta Cana in the Dominican Republic.

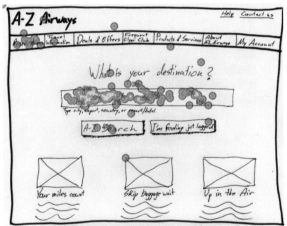

FIGURE 8.25
A clickmap of the A-Z
Airways home page.
Participants thought the
large search box is where
they could complete
the task, "Book a flight
to Punta Cana in the
Dominican Republic."

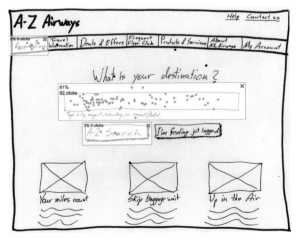

FIGURE 8.26
A clickmap of the A-Z
Airways home page
where areas of inter-
est are selected. 81%
of participants clicked
the search box first, 9%
clicked on Reservations,
and an interesting 3%
clicked the A-Z Search
button first.

- **Time to first click:** Calculate the time to first click, the range, and margin of error. In the study for which results are presented in Figures 8.25 and 8.26, the average time to first click was 9.4 seconds. This result in itself does not mean much unless it is either extremely unusual (what if it were 127.3 seconds?) or compared to time to first click in another design option.

- **Confidence:** If more people tend to be sure about their first click, that's a good sign. Figure 8.27 shows sample confidence results.

- **Task difficulty:** Similar to confidence, when more people tended to perceive their first click choice as an easy one, that's also a good sign. Figure 8.28 shows sample task difficulty results.

FIGURE 8.27
Results of a confidence question in a first-click test.

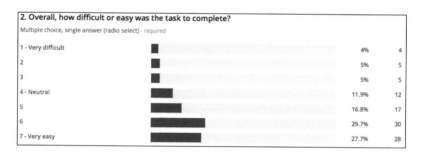

FIGURE 8.28
Results of a task difficulty question in a first-click test.

- **Open-ended difficulty feedback:** If you ask participants who thought the task was difficult to explain why, you can get some qualitative data to shed some light on the first-click numbers. Here are some examples based on participant responses to the study shown in Figures 8.25 and 8.26:

  - "I'm trusting that search will return the location I'm looking for."

  - "I expected to see 'book a flight' in the main nav, as this seems to be standard in the airline sites I use."

  - "I kept getting distracted by the three ads at the bottom, thinking they were the most important things on the page and, therefore, where I should click."

  - "It felt like a Google search, which was a different way to find a flight than similar websites."

  - "I didn't spend a lot of time looking about. Saw a form field and simply clicked it."

  - "I don't know if the search engine will find the right destination."

  - "Heading didn't associate with an action very well."

- **Some participants will contribute responses that will not help you understand task difficulty.** They'll complain about different things irrelevant to what you're looking for. Some will give you tips for future, similar tests. Here are some (real) examples:

  - "Lo-fi mockups are a shitty way of testing."

  - "To start with the intention of the sketch that was shown was not clear. So the whole testing failed before it even started."

  - "Handwriting was kinda hard to read."

  - "Difficult to locate and identify small interface elements on my cell phone."

  - "Who? What? I did not understand what happened here."

- **Compare:** First-click test results become much more meaningful when you compare between two or more designs. In most cases, all it takes is a short glance at comparison results to get a crystal-clear understanding of which design has better findability. The following are results of a comparison of two first-click studies conducted with Chalkmark in which 200 participants evaluated two design options for the (imaginary) A-Z Airways home page.

One hundred participants on Design A and 100 on Design B were asked to complete the same task ("Book a flight to Punta Cana in the Dominican Republic") without knowing this was a first-click test. They were then asked to answer three questions about their experience. Here are the results of the comparison (see Figures 8.29 and 8.30).

Task 1. Book a flight to Punta Cana in the Dominican Republic.

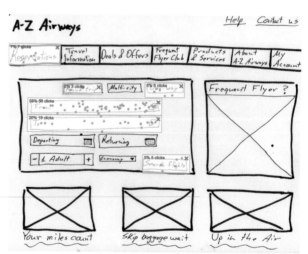

FIGURE 8.29

Side-by-side clickmap results of a Chalkmark study in which the same task was completed by 200 people on two different designs for the same page. 100 participants evaluated Design A and 100 evaluated Design B.

FIGURE 8.30
A clickmap of a second
A-Z Airways home
page where areas of
interest are selected.
55% clicked the From
field first, 20% clicked
the To field, 7% clicked
Reservations, and 5%
mistakenly clicked
the Search flights
button first.

- Clickmaps
- Time to first click was 9.2 seconds on Design A and 13.9 on Design B (see Figure 8.31).
- Confidence was 6.3 on Design A and 5.3 on Design B.
- Task difficulty was 6.3 on Design A and 5.3 on Design B.

These results mean that Design A is better than Design B in measured aspects of findability and should be further experimented with as a part of an iterative design and research process.

TABLE 8.2 FIRST-CLICK AREAS OF INTEREST IN DESIGNS A AND B HOME PAGE

Design A (Figure 8.29)	Design B (Figure 8.29)
81% clicked the search box	55% clicked the From field
9% clicked Reservations	20% clicked the To field
3% clicked the A-Z Search button	7% clicked Reservations
	5% clicked the Search flights button

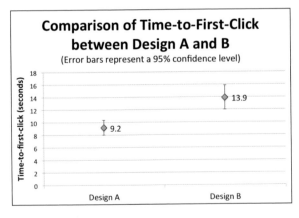

FIGURE 8.31

A comparison of time to first click between Design A and B of A-Z Airways. Results show a significant result where time to first click in Design A was faster.

STEP 9: Track lostness.

The lostness metric is a measure of efficiency using a product or service. It tells you how lost people are when they use it.[7] Lostness scores range from zero to one and are calculated based on a formula shown in Figure 8.32 where:

- L is lostness.

- N is the number of different pages visited while performing a task.

- S is the total number of pages visited while performing the task, counting revisits to the same page.

- R is the minimum (optimum) number of pages that must be visited to complete a task.

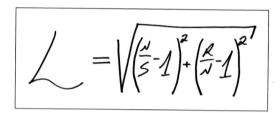

FIGURE 8.32

The lostness formula.

$$L = \sqrt{\left(\frac{N}{S}-1\right)^2 + \left(\frac{R}{N}-1\right)^2}$$

If the previous formula scares you, have no fear. Let's go over an example to explain the N, S, and R parameters in it. Later, all you need to do is track them and then enter them into a spreadsheet, which will *automagically* give you the lostness score.

Our example involves finding product page C1 in the website shown in Figure 8.33. The shortest, most effective path to get to this page from the home page is through category page C. This is the R parameter in the lostness formula. In this case, since the minimum number of pages required to complete the task is three, R equals 3 (see top chart in Figure 8.33).

---

7 Smith, P. A. (1996). Towards a practical measure of hypertext usability. *Interacting with Computers, 8* (4): 365–381.

Low Lostness

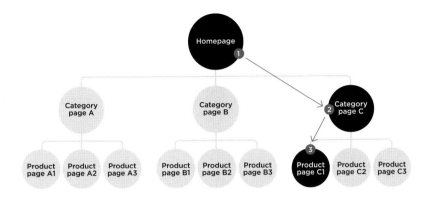

High Lostness

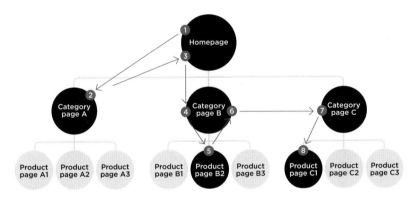

FIGURE 8.33

Lostness example: reaching the same website location with different lostness levels (with permission from Bill Albert).

Let's assume you are looking at what one participant did while completing the task (see bottom chart in Figure 8.33). That participant took eight steps to get to product page C1:

1. Home page

2. Category page A

3. Back to home page

4. Category page B

5. Product page B2

6. Back to category page B

7. Category page C

8. Product page C1

This is also S in the lostness formula, which is the total number of pages visited while performing the task, counting revisits to the same page, so S equals 8.

Our participant visited these pages while completing the task:

1. Home page

2. Category page A

3. Category page B

4. Product page B2

5. Category page C

6. Product page C1

In the lostness formula, this is N, which is the number of different pages visited while performing a task. So N equals 6.

This allows you to calculate the lostness score for this participant in this task (see Figure 8.34), which is 0.56. A high score (closer to one) means that people are very lost and having trouble finding what they need. A low score (closer to zero) means that people find what they want relatively easy. At lostness scores of about 0.40 and up, it is very clear a person is lost when you sit next to him or her and watch what happens.

FIGURE 8.34
Calculating a lostness score where N=6, R=3, and S=8. Lostness score is 0.56. Isn't math fun?

$$L = \sqrt{\left(\frac{6}{8}-1\right)^2 + \left(\frac{3}{6}-1\right)^2} = \sqrt{\left(-\frac{2}{8}\right)^2 + \left(-\frac{1}{2}\right)^2} =$$

$$= \sqrt{\frac{1}{16} + \frac{1}{4}} = \sqrt{\frac{5}{16}} = 0.56$$

To track and calculate lostness, use these two sheets:

1. **Lostness matrix** (Figure 8.35): Use this sheet when you observe a usability test or when you look at the path that each study participant took to complete a task: bit.ly/validating-chapter-8 -lostness-matrix.

Lostness Matrix | Study:_____ | Date: __/__/____

S: # of pages visited while performing tasks, counting revisits to the same page
N: # of different pages visited while performing tasks
R: minimum # of pages that must be visited to accomplish tasks

	Task 1			Task 2			Task 3			Task 4			Task 5		
	R	N	S	R	N	S	R	N	S	R	N	S	R	N	S
P1															
P2															
P3															
P4															
P5															
P6															
P7															
P8															
P9															
P10															

FIGURE 8.35
Lostness matrix sheet.

2. **Lostness spreadsheet** (Figure 8.36): Use this spreadsheet (after duplicating it) to add the lostness parameter data you collected during a study: bit.ly/validating-chapter-8-lostness-data. The spreadsheet is set for 5 participants who complete 5 tasks. Feel free to add or remove participants and tasks to match your study setup. As you enter the N, R, and S parameters into the spreadsheet, lostness scores are immediately calculated per participant and task.

Task 1 / Task 2 / Task 3 / Task 4

	Task 1			Task 2			Task 3			Task 4	
	N	S	R	N	S	R	N	S	R	N	
P1	8	13	28	2	4	6	2	3	3	1	2
P2	8	14	38	2	4	8	2	2	2	1	2
P3	8	13	27	2	6	7	2	2	4	1	3
P4	8	17	34	2	3	4	2	5	6	1	2
P5	8	22	63	2	4	4	2	2	3	1	3

Participant Lostness Scores

	Average N	Average S	Average R	N/S	N/S-1	R/N	R/N-1	Power 1	Power 2	Lostness	
P1	6	14	3.4	0.43	-0.57	0.57	-0.43	0.33	0.19	0.72	P1
P2	5.8	12.6	3.4	0.46	-0.54	0.59	-0.41	0.29	0.17	0.68	P2
P3	5.6	9.6	3.4	0.58	-0.42	0.61	-0.39	0.17	0.15	0.57	P3
P4	6.2	10.4	3.4	0.60	-0.40	0.55	-0.45	0.16	0.20	0.61	P4
P5	7	15.6	3.4	0.45	-0.55	0.49	-0.51	0.30	0.26	0.75	P5

Task Lostness Scores

	Average N	Average S	R	N/S	N/S-1	R/N	R/N-1	Power 1	Power 2	Lostness	
Task 1	15.80	38.00	8	0.42	-0.58	0.51	-0.49	0.34	0.24	0.76	Task 1
Task 2	4.20	5.80	2	0.72	-0.28	0.48	-0.52	0.08	0.27	0.59	Task 2
Task 3	2.80	3.60	2	0.78	-0.22	0.71	-0.29	0.05	0.08	0.36	Task 3
Task 4	2.40	2.40	1	1.00	0.00	0.42	-0.58	0.00	0.34	0.58	Task 4
Task 5	5.40	12.40	4	0.44	-0.56	0.74	-0.26	0.32	0.07	0.62	Task 5

FIGURE 8.36

Lostness spreadsheet.

STEP 10: Make changes and re-evaluate.

Did tree testing prove that your participants have trouble finding what they want? Are first clicks not improving or not making you proud? Is your product's lostness score too high? These are all evidence that should make you take action. Make changes to your information structure, navigation, hierarchy, labels, element size, shape and location, as well as layout. After you do, re-evaluate with tree testing, first-click testing, and/or lostness metric tracking to validate (or invalidate) that changes are working well for users. That's evidence-based design at its best.

Practice Tracking Lostness

1. Watch this video of a participant attempting to complete a task:
   bit.ly/validating-chapter-8-lostness-video.

2. Track lostness as the participant completes the task and calculate the lostness score for it:
   bit.ly/validating-chapter-8-lostness-data.

3. Watch the annotated video to verify that you calculated the right lostness score:
   bit.ly/validating-chapter-8-lostness-annotated-video.

Other Methods to Answer the Question

While a tree testing, first-click testing, and lostness metric are fast, effective ways for answering "How do people find stuff?" a research technique called *card sorting* is also great for answering the same question. In card sorting, research participants are asked to group cards that represent leaves in a hierarchy tree of a product or website into logical groups and give each group a name. This exercise uncovers how people think about finding stuff in the product and is helpful in structuring a navigation paradigm, organizing information, and labeling areas in a product. Donna Spencer's book, *Card Sorting*, is a wonderful, highly recommended resource for going deeper into this method.

> **NOTE** TREE TESTING, FIRST-CLICK TESTING, AND LOSTNESS METRIC RESOURCES
>
> Access the online resource page for tree testing, first-click testing, and lostness metric on the book's companion website at leanresearch.co. You'll find templates, checklists, videos, slide decks, articles, and book recommendations.

Tree Testing, First-Click Testing, and Lostness Metric Checklist

☐ Write a one-page plan.

☐ Find 500 research participants.

☐ State product navigation assumptions.

☐ Phrase instructions, tasks, and questions.

☐ Launch a tree-testing study.

☐ Analyze results and make a decision.

☐ Launch a first-click test.

☐ Analyze first-click results.

☐ Track lostness.

☐ Make changes and re-evaluate.

"I came up with the idea after going with my friend Joanne and her son Zack, to a local grocery store," said Dana, excitement in her voice, as she and Will spoke with Clark. "That was a nightmare—even after our other six test subjects. Zack kept screaming, crying, and generally preventing Joanne from finding what she wanted to buy at the store."

"We decided to take everything we'd learned from our research and build an MVP for a shopping cart app for kids," said Will, showing the app to Clark. "The idea was to give kids responsibility over parts of grocery shopping, like managing home inventory, getting groceries at the store, and unpacking them at home."

"There are pictures and a clickable list for them to use—big icons, really easy to understand," Dana continued. "I had Joanne try it. Zack was so eager to help, and it was so easy to use, she was able to make it fun for him, like a game. And she was able to get all her shopping done much more easily and quickly. She's even got him helping at home with putting away, using the app!"

Clark grinned broadly. "Sounds like you've got a winner," he said.

"Well, we'll know soon enough," said Dana, feeling pride warm her chest.

"User research is certainly pointing that way," Will said, to Dana's surprise. He'd gone from a scowling doubter to a full-blown convert. And the product seemed to be showing the benefit of his change in attitude.

Grocer.io is a huge success!" Dana crowed.

Will beamed. Their app's launch had gone very, very well. Acceptance was overwhelming, and the ratings were fantastic. Reviews were great, too. Now, investors were starting to show interest. Most importantly, users were coming back highly engaged and satisfied.

Facebook of note-taking," he said ruefully, and Dana laughed. "What were we thinking?"

Doesn't matter," said Dana. "We're on an elevator to meet with Jeff Clavier, founder and managing partner of SoftTech VC."

Will grinned. SoftTech was one of the most established seed VC firms in Silicon Valley.

Big dreams, huh?"

She smiled back.

Huge."

How to Find Participants for Research?

One of the biggest bottlenecks of research and a topic of unjust misconceptions is finding people who will participate in research. It's a bottleneck because without participants there is no research. A common misconception is that finding participants for research is hard, costly, and time consuming, almost an unachievable goal, especially from the perspective of those who never conducted research with humans.

Where to Find Participants for Research

Table 9.1 shows a list of several dozen options of ways to find participants for studies. As you can quickly see, some ways are relevant for consumer-facing products, some for business-to-business ones, some are easy, others hard, some are free, and others will cost a lot. In any case, you have multiple ways of finding participants.[1]

It is critical that you identify and recruit the right people for your customer research. Who are these right people? These are the people whom you currently envision as your target audience. For example, if you live in Europe and your target audience is in North America, you are not collecting good data if you go to the nearest mall and interview people. Recruiting the right participants will ensure that you collect the right data, learn the best lessons, and truly validate or invalidate your assumptions.

This chapter focuses on the last item on the list of ways to find participants for research—social media. Social media can help get you to the target audience you are looking for. In this chapter, you will utilize social media to recruit research participants quickly and effectively. That said, the following Steps 1, 2, 3, and 9 are universal for any technique you choose for finding research participants.

---

1 I'd like to thank the following people who responded to my Facebook post on this topic, which made the list grow twice as much: Chauncey Wilson, Cindy Alvarez, Amy Kidd, Diego Mendes, Chris LaRoche, Elizabeth Rosenzweig, Whitney Hess, Jen McGinn, Danielle Gobert Cooley, Michael Ryan, Susan Mercer, Stavros Garzonis, and Steve Denning.

TABLE 9.1   WHERE TO FIND PARTICIPANTS FOR STUDIES

Technique for Finding Participants	Required Effort	B2C or B2B	Cost
Ask people who work in the organization that develops the product (ask employees who are not part of the product/design team).	Almost no effort	Both	$
Ask family and friends of people who work in the organization that develops the product.	Very light	Both	$
Ask to recruit from a friend's large pool of potential participants as a favor.	Light	Both	$
Partner with another company (ask them to volunteer their employees for your research).	Moderate	B2C	$
Partner with another company who purchases, resells, and supports your products.	Light	Both	$
Snowball: let everyone you know who you are looking for.	Light	Both	$
Source on LinkedIn by searching for people with specific criteria and using inMail or second-degree intros to contact.	Light	Both	$$
Ask passersby on the street, malls, or stores, e.g., at Starbucks.	Moderate	B2C	$
Ask students.	Moderate	B2C	$
Recruit from a client customer list (be aware of company regulations that might prevent you from spamming customers).	Moderate	Both	$
Recruit past research participants (ask them in advance if it's okay and keep their details, especially good for specific audiences).	Almost no effort	Both	$
Ask people in large, tech-savvy areas (e.g., Silicon Valley, New York City, etc.).	Light	Both	$
Go to where your audience physically lingers (e.g., college campuses for students).	Light	Both	$
Ask conference attendees.	Very hard	B2B	$$$
Recruit to a pool of people who generally want to participate in research (aka, a user group), then when specific needs arise, recruit from this pool for a specific research study.	Moderate	Both	$$
Ask participants you find to refer friends or colleagues.	Almost no effort	Both	$
Tap into regular feedback surveys you or your clients send to their customers.	Almost no effort	Both	$
Search your customer database for users who have commented on the product.	Almost no effort	Both	$

continues on next page

TABLE 9.1   WHERE TO FIND PARTICIPANTS FOR STUDIES (continued)

Technique for Finding Participants	Required Effort	B2C or B2B	Cost
Have a sign-up form and rotating calls to action to link to a form strategically placed on your own website.	Light	Both	$
Ask new hires.	Almost no effort	Both	$
If you want say, physical chemists, you might check out research databases and look for chemists locally and remotely. Many research articles provide email contacts.	Hard	B2B	$$
Hang print ads on street corners or (physical) message boards.	Moderate	Both	$$
Call through a newsletter.	Almost no effort	Both	$
Intercept visitors on your app or website (through services such as Ethn.io).	Moderate	Both	$$
Intercept people coming off trials of your product.	Light	Both	$
Publish a blog post or article.	Light	Both	$
Post signs in libraries.	Light	Both	$
Cold call people.	Hard	B2C	$
Publish an ad on Craigslist or an equivalent service.	Almost no effort	B2C	$
Publish an ad on Google Adwords or Facebook.	Moderate	Both	$$
Publish an ad on a relevant website.	Moderate	Both	$$
Publish an ad in a print newspaper or magazines.	Moderate	Both	$$$
Publish an ad on radio or TV.	Hard	B2C	$$$
Amazon's Mechanical Turk.	Hard	B2C	$$
Hire a panel company (usually, for large samples).	Moderate	Both	$$$
Hire a participant-recruiting agency.	Moderate	Both	$$$
Post on social media (Facebook, Google Plus, Twitter).	Light	Both	$

How to Answer the Question

The following is a how-to guide that takes you step-by-step through the process of using social media to answer the question "How to find participants for research?"

STEP 1: Identify participant criteria.

> **NOTE** WORKSHEET FOR THIS CHAPTER
>
> In this chapter, you are guided through a process of gathering information from different websites and Web services. To better organize that information, here is a Google Doc worksheet. Make a copy of this worksheet and use your own copy of it: bit.ly/validating-chapter-9-worksheet.

Gather your team, pull out the chapter worksheet (bit.ly/validating -chapter-9-worksheet) or a piece of paper, set a timer for 10 minutes, and together, with your teammates, list a minimum of five attributes of your target audience. Don't limit yourself to just five attributes. If you have 10 or 20, that's perfectly fine as a starting point.

Here's a sample list of research participant criteria for an imaginary dancing app.

- Resides in the U.S.
- Has a smartphone.
- Wants to learn how to dance.
- Uses Facebook.
- 20% of participants are male, 80% female.

STEP 2: Transform criteria into screening questions.

Pull out the list you created in Step 1. If you are on a team, keep working together.

The funny thing about people is that if you ask if they want to participate in research, most of them will say yes. Some will even twist reality a little bit to participate. "Yes, of course I have a smartphone," they'll tell you, even if they only plan to buy one next year. Contrary to what you might expect, generally speaking, people are happy to help, especially when you pay them to participate. But you don't need people who just *want* to participate; you want to find people who *qualify* to participate.

To find out if people qualify to participate in your research, transform the criteria you identified in Step 1 into measurable benchmarks. For example, a criteria such as "Uses Facebook" becomes measurable when you turn it into the benchmark, "Posts on Facebook at least once a week."

The way from a benchmark to phrasing a screening question is short and easy. To avoid leading people or revealing the answer you are looking for, phrase the question in a neutral way. Rather than asking "Do you post on Facebook at least once a week?" or even "How often do you post on Facebook?" ask "How often do you post something on the following websites?" and then list a few options (see Figure 9.1). If a person chooses the right answer, they're in. If not, they're out.

How often do you post something on the following websites? *					
	Never	Once a month or less	Less than once a week	Several times per week	At least once a day
Facebook	○	○	○	○	○
Twitter	○	○	○	○	○
Google Plus	○	○	○	○	○
Pinterest	○	○	○	○	○
LinkedIn	○	○	○	○	○

FIGURE 9.1
Mask your screening criteria by asking broader questions and adding answers irrelevant to what you are looking for.

Next, gather your team, pull out the chapter worksheet (bit.ly/ validating-chapter-9-worksheet) or grab a piece of paper, and create a three-column table. On the first column, list the criteria you identified in Step 1. On the second column, try to transform each criterion into a measurable benchmark. Then, on the last column, translate the benchmark into a screening question (see Table 9.2). Set your timer to 10 minutes and go.

TABLE 9.2 FROM PARTICIPANT CRITERIA TO SCREENING QUESTIONS

Criterion	Measurable Benchmark	Screening Question
Uses Facebook.	Posts on Facebook at least once a week.	How often do you post something on the following websites?

STEP 3: Create a screening questionnaire.

Now that you have a good understanding of who you want and don't want to learn from, it's time to compile a screening questionnaire (also, called a *screener*) that you can send people. In addition to screening people in and out of your research activity, a good screener also collects information about people's availability to participate, as well as their contact information. Asking about availability in the screener saves you from endless back-and-forth email/phone coordination.

Google Forms (as well as other tools) is a great tool you can use for free to create a screener quickly. Here is a sample screener— bit.ly/validating-chapter-9-screener. Have a look at it and try to match your questions with these different screener goals.

- Screen people in.

- Screen people out.

- Collect contact information.

- Understand availability.

Use Google Forms to create a screener based on the questions you already phrased. Try to keep it simple. Create a one-page, straightforward form without branching and unnecessary complications.

STEP 4: Identify keywords for your audience.

Switching gears. Now that you have a solid screener, it's time to start thinking about finding people who will take it. These are the screener respondents, because they respond to the screener, but do not yet become study participants. A respondent becomes a study participant when he or she qualifies and is available to participate.

To find respondents over social media, it is critical to address your message to the right people. For example, to find people who meet the criteria for the imaginary dancing app mentioned earlier, it would make sense to look for them where they linger. In the real world, they can be found at dance schools, clubs, shows, contests, etc. Online, you'll find them in various social media groups and communities, following public figures known for their dance knowledge, showmanship, or great advice.

To find these online hubs of interest, you need to learn the language and jargon of your audience (see Figure 9.2) and identify keywords that will help you find social media groups, communities, and pages.

FIGURE 9.2
Your target audience uses a unique language and jargon. To find study participants, learn that language.

There are three ways to identify relevant keywords:

- Brainstorm keywords with your team.

- Use a thesaurus for finding relevant synonyms.

- Use Google's Keyword Planner.

While #1 and #2 are relatively trivial, we'll focus here on #3. Using Google's Keyword Planner may require that you register for a Google Adwords account (only if you do not yet have a Google account), but that doesn't cost money, and you won't need to run any ads. All you will use it for is to discover the right keywords.

Follow the instructions below and complete them one by one. The imaginary dancing app serves as an example. Use your topic instead.

1. Access Google Adwords at adwords.google.com.

2. Open an account if you don't have one already. (To reiterate, opening a Google Adwords account is free, and you don't have to run any paid advertising campaign.)

3. Click the Tools tab and select Keyword Planner (Figure 9.3).

FIGURE 9.3
Keyword Planner is under Tools.

4. Click the first option "Search for new keywords" (Figure 9.4). You now see some options for filtering and configurations.

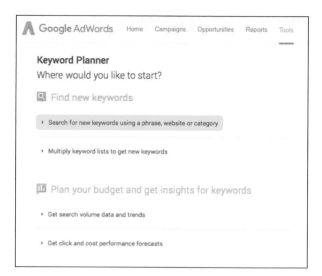

FIGURE 9.4
Search for keyword
and ad group ideas.

5. Start typing a word that represents your domain under "Your product category" (Figure 9.5). As soon as you start typing, a drop-down menu shows you matching product categories (Figure 9.6). Select the one closest to your domain. Not all words will match an existing product category in Keyword Planner easily. Try things out and find a category that best fits your word.

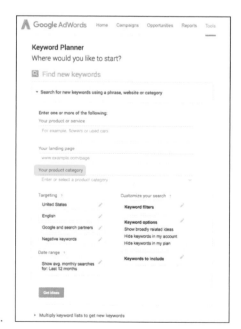

FIGURE 9.5
Type your product
category into this field.

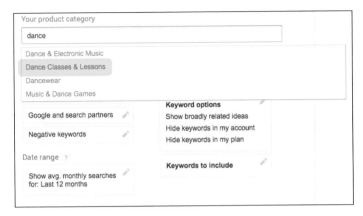

FIGURE 9.6
Select a product category closest to your domain.

6. If you want, or feel it is needed, go ahead and also configure more granular (or different) targeting criteria (Figure 9.7). You can configure a country, state, county, district, town or city, and you can also configure a language for keywords. Don't change any other fields, though.

7. Click Get Ideas (Figure 9.8).

FIGURE 9.7
Target by location or language if you need to.

FIGURE 9.8
Isn't that a wonderful label for a button?

8. Before you even begin to figure out what is going on, click the Ave. Monthly Searches column header (Figure 9.9) to sort ad group ideas in order, from most popular to least popular (Figure 9.10).

FIGURE 9.9

Sort by clicking the Ave. Monthly Searches column header.

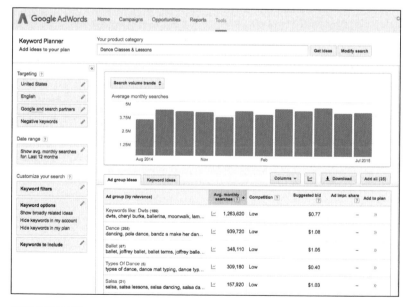

FIGURE 9.10

Ad group ideas are sorted in order of popularity.

9. Take five minutes to scan the "Ad group ideas" (Figure 9.11) and "Keyword ideas" tabs and list 10 keywords that relate strongly to your topic. Without going into too much detail about what an Ad Group is on Adwords, also click on a relevant one and scan keywords in that group (Figure 9.12). The keywords you are selecting here are ones that are most popular among people who use Google Search to find websites in the product category you selected. That's a lot more than using a thesaurus for finding synonyms in your domain. When you are picking keywords, consider social media groups, communities, and pages and the names they'll choose for themselves. Keep in mind that you should not automatically select the 10 most popular keywords. The reason is that some product categories would have several domains of keywords. For example, the category "Boston" includes keywords for both Boston the city and Boston the music band. Keep that in mind when you select keywords.

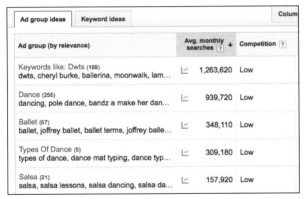

FIGURE 9.11
Scan the list of ad group ideas and select ones that seem relevant to your domain.

FIGURE 9.12
Drill down into ad groups (Dance, in this case) to scan for more relevant keywords.

Find target groups and pages on Facebook.

Work with the list of keywords you created in step 4 to identify Facebook groups and pages where your audience is likely to belong or follow. Many Facebook groups and pages are extremely popular and generate a lot of engagement. Audiences on various niches are attracted to these hubs and either read, respond, or actively create the conversation. For you, it is a gold mine you cannot miss. It's a great opportunity to learn from and engage with your audience.

As in the previous step, follow the instructions and complete them one by one. The examples introduce keywords related to the imaginary dancing app discussed earlier. You'll use your topic instead.

1. Log in to Facebook and place your cursor in the social graph search box (Figure 9.13).

2. Type your first keyword (Figure 9.14) and press Search.

FIGURE 9.13

Invoke a social graph search on Facebook.

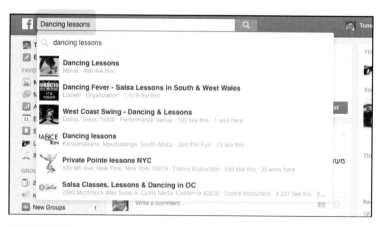

FIGURE 9.14

Type your first keyword into the search box.

3. Select the Pages tab (Figure 9.15).

4. Scan the results and select pages with a title that seem relevant to your domain and ones with a relatively large number of Likes. Copy the URL of each page you selected to your worksheet. Figure 9.16 demonstrates page selection for the dancing app.

5. After you have selected 10 pages, go to the top of the page and select Groups (Figure 9.17).

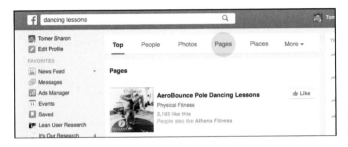

FIGURE 9.15
Select Pages.

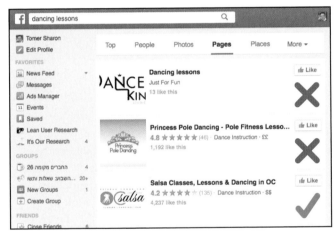

FIGURE 9.16
The first page does not have enough Likes. The second's title indicates it is not a good fit for the domain. The last one has both a relevant title and a good number of Likes.

FIGURE 9.17
Select Groups.

6. Scan the results and select groups that seem relevant to you, that have a relatively large number of members, and that are Open groups. Copy the URL of each group you select to your worksheet. Figure 9.18 demonstrates group selection for the dancing app.

7. You are done with this step when you have identified 10 pages and 10 groups.

FIGURE 9.18

The first group has a relevant title, a good number of members, and it's open. The second seems relevant and with a good number of members, but it is closed. The last one's title indicates it is not a good fit for the domain.

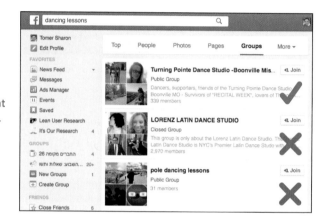

STEP 6: Find target hashtags on Twitter.

In this step, you'll identify Twitter hashtags that will point you to your audience. Twitter is a powerful social medium. It is where many people interested in numerous topics linger and where they get the most updated information and thoughts of thought leaders, businesses, and other like-minded individuals. Twitter has a sea of information you need. You just need to know where to look.

A Twitter hashtag is a way for people to search for tweets that have a common topic. For example, if you search for #dancing, you'll get a list of tweets where people used that hashtag (see Figure 9.19). What you won't get are tweets that say "I was dancing yesterday when I lost my wallet" because "dancing" isn't preceded by the hashtag symbol. See an example of a "good" tweet in Figure 9.19.

FIGURE 9.19

A tweet with the hashtag #dancing.

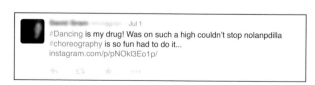

Take the list of keywords you identified in Step 4 and turn them into hashtags. For example, the keyword "Belly Dance" would become the hashtag #bellydance, and "Hip Hop Dancing" becomes #hiphop or #hiphopdancing. You will use these hashtags in Step 8 when you post your screener. Don't think this through too much now. Just create the list of hashtags. A keyword can become two or three hashtags. That's perfectly fine. Add those hashtags to the chapter worksheet.

Before we move on to Step 7, use Twitter to search for the hashtags you created to see if they're of high quality. Go to the Twitter search box and type a hashtag, for example, #dancing (see Figure 9.20).

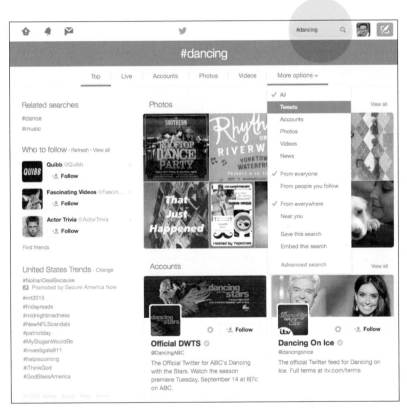

FIGURE 9.20

Search the hashtags you created on Twitter.

Scan the results and see if there's a lot of action going on for this hashtag. If you see very old or too few tweets, remove this hashtag from your list. Identify ones that are being used a lot by many people. Not all of the tweets will be relevant, as you'll see very quickly. Take five minutes to evaluate the quality of your hashtags.

STEP 7: Find target communities and pages on Google Plus.

During this step, you will identify Google Plus communities and pages that your audience is likely to belong to or follow. It is extremely similar to what you did with Facebook in Step 5.

Google Plus is Google's social media service. Google Plus is extremely successful among a growing number of niche domains, interests, and topics. Many people consider Google Plus as the social network where quality audiences meet and exchange ideas.

Again, follow the instructions. The examples introduce keywords related to the imaginary dancing app. Use your topic instead.

1. Log in to Google Plus and place your cursor in the search box (Figure 9.21).

2. Type your first keyword and press the search button.

3. Ignore the results you see on the page and select People and Pages (Figure 9.22).

FIGURE 9.21
Start at the Google Plus search box.

FIGURE 9.22
Select People and Pages.

4. Notice that the results include both pages and people (Figure 9.23), while you are only interested in pages, so try to focus on these for now.

5. Select pages that seem relevant to you based on their title, and that have a relatively large number of followers. Click the page to see the number of followers there (see Figure 9.24).

6. Copy the URL of each page you selected to the chapter worksheet.

7. After you have selected 10 pages, go to the top of the page and select Communities (Figure 9.25).

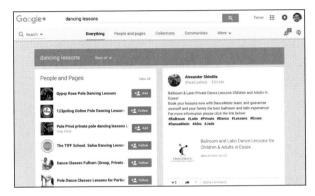

FIGURE 9.23
People and Pages.

FIGURE 9.24
Check the number of followers of a Google Plus page.

FIGURE 9.25
Select Communities.

8. Scan the results and select Communities that seem relevant to you, that have a relatively large number of members, and that are *Open* communities. These are differentiated by "Join" for open and "Ask to join" for closed communities (Figure 9.26). Copy the URL of each Community you select to your worksheet.

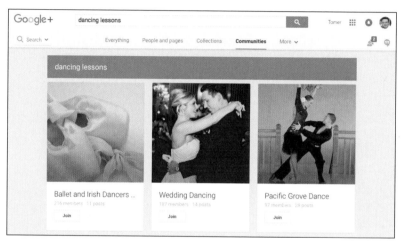

FIGURE 9.26
Open and closed communities.

9. You are done with this step when you have identified 10 pages and 10 communities.

Next, you'll see how to use all of the precious information you collected to recruit participants for your research.

STEP 8: Post screener to Facebook, Twitter, and Google Plus.

Use the screener you created and post it to the social media targets you identified on Facebook, Twitter, and Google Plus. So far, you have identified a meaningful number of pages, groups, communities, and hashtags on Facebook, Twitter, and Google Plus. It is now time to post. Access each and every one of the pages, groups, and communities you identified and post a call to participate in your research. Some of them might prevent you from doing so, yet many don't, and some even encourage it. Give it a try. Figures 9.27 and 9.28 demonstrate a page that allows you to post and one that doesn't.

FIGURE 9.27

This page allows posting.

FIGURE 9.28

This page does not allow posting.

Make sure that you include an interesting, attractive picture with your post. This will increase your chances of people actually paying attention to what you say (Figure 9.29).

Another approach is to write a post on your wall while tagging Facebook or Google Plus pages (Figure 9.30). When you do that, and if the owners of these pages didn't block this option, your post will appear on their walls, so their audience will see it, too.

FIGURE 9.29
A Google Plus screener post with an attention-grabbing photo.

FIGURE 9.30
A Facebook screener post with a tag for the "Dancing with the Stars Vote" page.

A good post provides a succinct description of your request and a URL to take your screener. Don't forget to provide a clear call to action (Figure 9.31).

Try to find a way to include a hashtag in the sentence and ask people to re-tweet. Most people won't, but those who will, will extend your reach. All you need to do is ask (see Figure 9.32).

FIGURE 9.31
A Twitter screener tweet with a clear call to action.

FIGURE 9.32
Ask people to retweet and use hashtags.

STEP 9: Track responses and select participants.

In this step, you'll identify respondents who meet your criteria and decide whom you want to invite to participate in your user research activity.

From the moment you start posting on social media, it can take minutes up to several hours until you begin seeing responses to your screener (see Figure 9.33). As soon as you get responses, it's time to start deciding who's in and who's out.

F	G	H	I	J	K	L	M	N	O	P
Gender:	Age:	If you're currently working, what's your occupation?	Where do you live?	What is the make and model of your phone?	How often do you use the following social media? [Facebook]	How often do you use the following social media? [Twitter]	How often do you use the following social media? [Google Plus]	How often do you use the following social media? [Pinterest]	How often do you use the following social media? [LinkedIn]	In the past month, what did you want to learn?
Male	31-40	Architect	Boston, MA	iPhone 5	At least once a day	Several times per week	Less than once a week	Never	Less than once a week	Dancing, Writing
Female	24-30	Dancer	New York, NY	HTC	Less than once a week	Several times per week	Less than once a week	Less than once a week	Once a month or less	Singing, Dancing
Female	Under 18	High school	Dublin, CA	iPhone 5S	At least once a day	Never	Never	At least once a day	Never	Dancing, Texting
Male	31-40	Architect	Worcester, MA	iPhone 5	At least once a day	Several times per week	Less than once a week	Never	Less than once a week	Dancing
Female	24-30	Dancer	New York, NY	HTC	Less than once a week	Several times per week	Less than once a week	Less than once a week	Once a month or less	Singing, Dancing
Female	31-40	Engineer	Philadelphia, PA	iPhone 5S	At least once a day	Never	Never	At least once a day	Never	Dancing

FIGURE 9.33
Responses to a sample screener.

Scan the responses page of your screening questionnaire and see who meets your criteria and who doesn't. Easiest decisions first, highlight rows with respondents who do not qualify with a red background (see Figure 9.34).

Next, scan responses to see who meets the criteria and highlight them in green (see Figure 9.35).

	F	G	H	I	J	K	L	M	N	O	P
	Gender:	Age:	If you're currently working, what's your occupation?	Where do you live?	What is the make and model of your phone?	How often do you use the following social media? [Facebook]	How often do you use the following social media? [Twitter]	How often do you use the following social media? [Google Plus]	How often do you use the following social media? [Pinterest]	How often do you use the following social media? [LinkedIn]	In the past month, what did you want to learn?
	Male	31-40	Architect	Boston, MA	iPhone 5	At least once a day	Several times per week	Less than once a week	Never	Less than once a week	Dancing, Writing
	Female	24-30	Dancer	New York, NY	HTC	Less than once a week	Several times per week	Less than once a week	Less than once a week	Once a month or less	Singing, Dancing
	Female	Under 18	High school	Dublin, CA	iPhone 5S	At least once a day	Never	Never	At least once a day	Never	Dancing, Texting
	Male	31-40	Architect	Worcester, MA	iPhone 5	At least once a day	Several times per week	Less than once a week	Never	Less than once a week	
	Female	24-30	Dancer	New York, NY	HTC	Less than once a week	Several times per week	Less than once a week	Less than once a week	Once a month or less	Singing, Dancing
	Female	31-40	Engineer	Philadelphia, PA	iPhone 5S	At least once a day	Never	Never	At least once a day	Never	Dancing

FIGURE 9.34

The first respondent does not qualify because she is under 18. The second because he is not interested in learning how to dance. The third does not qualify because she posts on Facebook less than once a week.

	F	G	H	I	J	K	L	M	N	O	P
	Gender:	Age:	If you're currently working, what's your occupation?	Where do you live?	What is the make and model of your phone?	How often do you use the following social media? [Facebook]	How often do you use the following social media? [Twitter]	How often do you use the following social media? [Google Plus]	How often do you use the following social media? [Pinterest]	How often do you use the following social media? [LinkedIn]	In the past month, what did you want to learn?
	Male	31-40	Architect	Boston, MA	iPhone 5	At least once a day	Several times per week	Less than once a week	Never	Less than once a week	Dancing, Writing
	Female	24-30	Dancer	New York, NY	HTC	Less than once a week	Several times per week	Less than once a week	Less than once a week	Once a month or less	Singing, Dancing
	Female	Under 18	High school	Dublin, CA	iPhone 5S	At least once a day	Never	Never	At least once a day	Never	Dancing, Texting
	Male	31-40	Architect	Worcester, MA	iPhone 5	At least once a day	Several times per week	Less than once a week	Never	Less than once a week	
	Female	24-30	Dancer	New York, NY	HTC	Less than once a week	Several times per week	Less than once a week	Less than once a week	Once a month or less	Singing, Dancing
	Female	31-40	Engineer	Philadelphia, PA	iPhone 5S	At least once a day	Never	Never	At least once a day	Never	Dancing

FIGURE 9.35

Responses highlighted to indicate respondents who qualify or do not qualify to participate in research.

You might have a situation when you have too many reds and too few greens. In this case, you have two options: either go back to Facebook, Twitter, and Google Plus and find more groups, pages, and communities to post your message, or relax your criteria. For example, consider recruiting 40% instead of 20% males or accept people who use Facebook a little less than once a week.

As soon as you have enough participants who qualify with your criteria, it's time to start scheduling study sessions.

> **NOTE** RESOURCES FOR FINDING RESEARCH PARTICIPANTS
>
> Access the online resource page for finding participants for research on the book's companion website at leanresearch.co. You'll find templates, checklists, videos, slide decks, articles, and book recommendations.

Checklist for Finding Research Participants on Social Media

- ☐ Identify participant criteria.
- ☐ Transform criteria into screening questions.
- ☐ Create a screening questionnaire.
- ☐ Identify keywords for your audience.
- ☐ Find target groups and pages on Facebook.
- ☐ Find target hashtags on Twitter.
- ☐ Find target communities and pages on Google Plus.
- ☐ Post screener to Facebook, Twitter, and Google Plus.
- ☐ Track responses and select participants.

SHAKE, RATTLE, AND ROLL

Research with users is scary. It forces you to recognize the things you know to be true as assumptions, and in many cases, research results invalidate those "truths." Yes, research is great when you have questions to which you don't have answers. It's even better when you're really confident you already know the answers. That's when you learn the most. I hope this book and its accompanying website and social media resources helped (and will continue to help) you get answers to your most burning questions about people and your users and potential users. All you need to do is take the first step, shake, rattle, and roll. You won't regret it.

If you ever have a quick, research-related question, feel free to run it by me. I'm listening on Twitter @tsharon. I also love drones, snowmobiles, and WWE, so we can have quick Twitter exchanges about those as well.

INDEX

close-ended tasks, 185
color matching experiment, 151
comparison charts, tree
    testing, 258–259
Concierge MVP
    basic description of, 145–146
    benefits of, 146–147
    board, 150
    checklist, 161
    data analysis, evaluating data and
        moving on, 159
    designing a, 149–150
    experiment examples, 151–152
    experiment type, selecting, 147–149
    participants, finding, 152–153
    resources, 160
    serving to customers, 154–155
    strengths, 149
    template, 150
    tracking customer behavior, 154–156
confidence analysis, first-click testing, 266
confidence level, A/B testing
    configuration, 221, 224–225
consensus building, benefits of A/B
    testing, 211
context
    observing study participants, 96
Contract MVP, 148
conversion funnel, 208–209
conversion rates, 214
crowdfunding, designing Fake Door
    experiments, 157
cultural differences, 63
customers
    serving Concierge MVP to, 154–155
    tracking behaviors of, 154–156

D

data analysis
    A/B testing, 222–225, 227
    Concierge MVP, 159
    diary study, 125–127
    experience sampling, 19–20
    Fake Doors experiment, 159
    first-click testing, 264–269
    interview question, 64–65
    with KJ Technique, 56–57, 64–65
    observation, 101

online usability testing, 194–196
    tree testing, 256–260, 262
data collection
    diary study, 117–119
    for experience sampling question, 16
    for interview questions, 56–57
    observation, 101
data points, determining for sampling
    answer questions, 13–15
debriefs, observation, 98–101
delights, observing study
    participants, 96–97
demographic labels *versus* human
    behaviors, 35–36
design questions. *See also* A/B testing
    design variations, evaluating, 216
    importance of, 206
    what and when to ask, 207–208
design thinking, 159
desktop application, A/B testing for, 210
diary studies
    as alternative to experience sampling
        questions, 25
    as alternative to interview
        questions, 66
    as alternative to observation, 103
    apps, 118
    basic description of, 114
    benefits of, 114–115
    checklist, 129
    choosing dairy type, 116–117
    data analysis, 125–127
    data collection tool, setting up, 117–119
    entries, tagging in Reframer, 126
    interviews as alternative to, 129
    observation as alternative to, 129
    participants
        briefing, 120–121
        finding, 119–120
        interviews with, 125
        prompting for data, 124–125
    pilot-test, 124
    preparing instructions for, 120–121
    resources, 129
    sample workflow constructed with, 127
    screening questionnaire, 120
    structuring, 116–117
    themes, uncovering with Reframer, 126
    unstructured, 117

and user workflow, 112
  video game instruction example, 122–123
directness score, tree testing, 260
drones, 210

E

empathy, interview benefits, 39
equipment, observation, 90–92
events, structuring diary study by, 116
evidence-based feature generation, 4
exhaustive list questions, 50
experience sampling questions
  about behaviors, 8
  answering question with, 4
  asking specific, 7
  bar charts, 21–22
  basic explanation of, 4
  benefits of, 4–6
  checklist, 26
  choosing medium for sending and
    collecting data, 16
  classifying answers to, 16–17
  data analysis, 19–20
  deciding on data points needed
    for, 13–14
  defining scope and phrasing the, 6–9
  determining amount of time
    participants will answer, 13
  diary studies as alternative to, 25
  eyeballing the data, 22–23
  finding research participants, 12–13
  frequency of asking, 15
  imaginary scenario, 10
  interviewing as alternative to, 25
  observations as alternative to, 25
  participant expectations, setting, 17
  pilot-test, 18
  questions to avoid, 8–10
  resources, 25
  samples of, 11
  spreadsheet, 20
  tabulated data, 21–22
  thanking participants, 18
  themes, identifying, 22–24
  useful and unuseful questions, 14
experiment duration, A/B testing
  configuration, 221

experiments. *See* MVP (minimum viable
  product)
expert users, deciding who to
  interview, 44
extreme users, deciding who to
  interview, 43

F

Facebook, 296–298, 302–304
facial expressions, during interviews, 63
Fake Doors experiment
  basic description of, 146
  benefits of, 146–147
  checklist, 161
  data analysis, evaluating data and
    moving, 159
  designing a, 156–158
  determining threshold of, 158–159
  experiment type, selecting, 147–149
  resources, 160
field guide, observation, 82–83
fill in the blank questions, 53
findability, 240. *See also* first-click
  testing; lostness metric; tree testing
finding research participants
  checklist for, 307
  on Facebook, 296–298, 302–304
  on Google Plus, 300–304
  identifying keywords of
    audience, 290–295
  identifying participant criteria, 287
  resources for, 307
  screening questions for, 287–289
  techniques for, 285–286
  through social media, 284
  tracking responses, 305–307
  on Twitter, 298–300, 302–304
first-click testing
  basic description of, 243
  benefits of, 246–247
  card sorting as alternative to, 275
  checklist, 275
  confidence analysis, 266
  data analysis, 264–269
  design comparison analysis, 267–268
  launching, 262–263
  open-ended difficulty feedback, 267
  participants, finding, 250–251

T

tabulated charts, 258
task confidence measurement, tree testing, 261
tasks
  close-ended, 185
  difficulty results
    first-click testing, 266
    tree testing, 261
  online usability testing participants, 184–187
  open-ended, 185
  tree testing participants, 253
team, observation, 86
technology, advancement and effectiveness of, 147
template, Concierge MVP, 150
testing. *See* online usability testing; pilot-test
thanking
  experience sampling participants, 18
  interview participants, 60
  observation participants, 93
themes
  diary data, uncovering with Reframer, 126
  identifying in experience sampling questions, 22–24
three wishes questions, 53
time interval, structuring diary study by, 116
time to first click analysis, first-click testing, 266, 269
transitions, observing study participants, 97
tree testing
  A-Z Airways flight booking example, 248–249
  benefits of, 246–247, 251
  card sorting as alternative to, 275
  changes to, 262
  checklist, 275
  comparison charts, 258–259
  data analysis, 256–260, 262
  directness score, 260

navigation hypothesis, 242, 251–252
participants, finding, 250–251
phrasing instructions for, 252
pilot-test, 255
plan, 247
planning tasks for, 253
questions to ask, 254
resources, 275
task confidence measurement, 261
task difficulty results, 261
Treejack tree testing, 242, 256, 258, 260
Twitter, 298–300, 302

U

usability testing. *See* online usability testing
user needs questions. *See also* experience sampling questions
  answering with experience sampling, 4–6
  importance of, 2
  when to question, 3
user workflow, 113. *See* diary studies
users, deciding who to interview, 43
UserTesting, 183, 188
UserZoom, 189–190, 242–243, 255, 257–258, 261
UX terminology, 159

V

vanity metrics, 219
video game, diary study instruction example, 122–123
viewpoint comparison questions, 51

W

workflow, 127. *See also* diary studies

Y

yes/no questions, avoiding in experience sampling, 9

ACKNOWLEDGMENTS

Writing a book is the hardest job I have ever completed. It has caused me both physical and mental pain—hopefully, nothing permanent. At some point, I even considered quitting my career as a user researcher, moving to Punta Cana in the Dominican Republic, and starting my own Shakshuka restaurant. (Use your favorite search engine to see what Shakshuka looks like— it's really good, and mine is awesome.) My wife hopes I'm over that phase by now.

I thought about the idea for this book two years before I actually started writing it, which took an additional two years. Five people were key to making it happen. To them I am grateful, appreciative, and forever thankful:

- **Iris**, the love of my life, who gave me the time, support, and patience that I needed so much.

- **Lou Rosenfeld**, my dearest publisher and friend, who was interested in the topic and helped turn the book into the great thing you can now hold, read, enjoy, and use. His wisdom and openness was (and still is!) inspiring.

- **Marta Justak**, my fearless editor, butt-kicker, and therapist. Not that I'm going to, but if I ever write another book, I wouldn't want anyone but Marta to be my editor.

- **Filip Healy**, one of my reviewers, who took precious time off his schedule and for about a year made sure that I was going to have a great book. I loved the opportunity to exchange ideas and thoughts with such a smart person.

- **Benjamin Gadbaw**, an IDEO designer and one of the sharpest pencils around. Benjamin not only kindly wrote a beautiful foreword for the book, but also kicked my butt for a year with his feedback, comments, and questions that forced me to make this book much better than what I started with.